THEOLOGY OF RELIGIONS

A Sourcebook for Interreligious Study

Eugene F. Gorski, CSC

Paulist Press
New York/Mahwah, NJ

IMPRIMI POTEST: Very Reverend David T. Tyson, CSC, Provincial Superior of the Indiana Province of the Congregation of Holy Cross

August 22, 2007
Notre Dame, Indiana

The scripture quotations contained herein are from the *New Revised Standard Version: Catholic Edition*, Copyright © 1989 and 1993, by the Division of Christian Education of the National Council of the Churches of Christ in the United States of America. Used by permission. All rights reserved.

Extracts from the documents of the Second Vatican Council are the author's translation and from Walter Abbot's edition of *The Documents of Vatican II* © 1966 by America Press used by kind permission of America Press. Visit: www.americamagazine.org.

Cover design by Sharyn Banks
Book design by Lynn Else

Library of Congress Cataloging-in-Publication Data
Gorski, Eugene F.
    Theology of religions : a sourcebook for interreligious study / Eugene F. Gorski.
        p. cm.
    Includes bibliographical references.
    ISBN-13: 978-0-8091-4533-1 (alk. paper)
    1. Theology of religions (Christian theology) 2. Christianity and other religions. 3. Catholic Church—Relations. I. Title.
    BT83.85.G67 2008
    261.2—dc22

                                                        2008003370

Published by Paulist Press
997 Macarthur Boulevard
Mahwah, New Jersey 07430

www.paulistpress.com

Printed and bound in the
United States of America

CONTENTS

Introduction: Theology of Religions in Historical and
Phenomenological Perspective   v

PART ONE
The Axial Age and the World Religions   I
       1. Pre-Axial Religion   5
       2. Post-Axial Religion   23

PART TWO
Historical Development and the Defining Characteristic
of the Post-Axial Religions   41
       3. Zoroastrianism   45
       4. Hinduism   63
       5. Buddhism and Jainism   105
       6. Confucianism and Daoism   131
       7. Shinto and Mahayana Buddhism   165
       8. Judaism, Christianity, and Islam   198
       9. Eschatological Dimension   231
       Conclusion to Part Two   238

PART THREE
The Theological Status of the Non-Christian Religions   243
       10. A Common Human Existence   245
       11. True Religion   256
       12. The Uniqueness of Christianity   281
       13. Interreligious Dialogue   302

Conclusion: The Mystery of the World Religions   315

Selected Bibliography   319

* In memory of my mother, father, and sister
* In gratitude to the Congregation of Holy Cross
* In gratitude to my Howard Hall family

Introduction

THEOLOGY OF RELIGIONS IN HISTORICAL AND PHENOMENOLOGICAL PERSPECTIVE

What should Catholics, and indeed all followers of Jesus, think about the other great religions of the world? Hinduism, Buddhism, Judaism, Islam, Zoroastrianism, Jainism, Daoism, Sikhism, and Shinto[1]—will their adherents be saved? Might it be that the one true God—the Father, Jesus in the Spirit—is active in these religions, working out the divine plan of salvation? Or are they hindrances to God's plan? In short, are the great non-Christian religions true religions? That is, is the one true God operative in them, and do they lead to salvation? What does it mean for Christians to live with men and women of other faiths? What is the relationship of Christianity to the other religions? These are some of the questions we explore in the present work. They pertain to the academic discipline known as the theology of religions, a field of study that considers what scriptures, tradition, and the teaching of the church have to say about the ultimate meaning and value of the non-Christian world religions.[2]

Currently, the theology of religions has become a subject of widespread interest and importance. It is one of the fastest growing areas of theological inquiry.[3] Recent world events, as well as the frequent encouragements of our late pontiff, Pope John Paul II, have placed it among the main concerns for committed Catholic thinkers and leaders. This position of prominence is also due to the growing presence, within the church in general and in certain theological circles, of confused ideas and opinions, especially regarding the salvific event of Jesus Christ, the necessity of the church for salvation, and a relativism that regards all religious positions as equally authentic and valuable. To address these problems, the Vatican's Congregation for the Doctrine of the Faith, in 2000, issued a "declaration" entitled *Dominus Iesus.*[4] It is said that this document—proclaimed by the congregation with Pope John Paul's ratification *certa scientia et auctoritate sua apostolica*—that is to say, "with his certain knowledge and apostolic authority," which makes it for Catholics a weighty document—was written as a response to the work of Asian bishops struggling with issues of pluralism and fidelity in widely non-Christian contexts.[5] After the issuing of the declaration, the increased Vatican concern for these matters can be seen in the excommunication of the Sri Lankan priest-theologian Tissa Balasuriya (subsequently reinstated) and the investigation of the works of Jacques Dupuis, the Belgian theologian who worked for thirty-six years in India.

While *Dominus Iesus* was meant to resolve problems, its publication reinforced the controversy among Christian theologians who are strongly interested in our new sense of religious diversity. Criticism came especially from within those sectors of Catholic theology most involved with ecumenical theology, Jewish-Christian relations, and interreligious dialogue.[6] The declaration also had an impact on many Catholics around the world for whom the theological status of the non-Christian religious paths has become a vital and controversial question. The various answers given to this question carry wide and concrete implications as to how they will live their lives as believers.

In the lively debate underway concerning religious pluralism, what is at issue is nothing less than what Christian believers should think about the non-Christian religions and their adherents, who are more and more not simply inhabitants of distant lands but their friends and neighbors. "Other religions which used to be distant, exotic topics for enjoyable conversation, if not a vague reality that could be totally ignored, have come much closer to us whether we live in the West or elsewhere."[7] Also in question here is how Christians will come to comprehend and appreciate their own religion and their own personal self-identity in new ways as a consequence of their encounter with their non-Christian neighbors. Finally, the most important issue is how Christians will come to understand more deeply the reality of Jesus, Father, and the Spirit as a result of their dialogue with religious pluralism.

To address the issues that were prominent before the appearance of *Dominus Iesus* and that persist in the continuing debate since its publication, Catholics must be able to assess the truth-value, or the theological status, of the non-Christian religions. What is needed to facilitate this appraisal is a theology of religions. The purpose of this work is to set forth reflections intended to lead to the development of such a theology.

To make these reflections, the following method is used. We look into the sources of Christian revelation and faith—in the Bible, tradition, and the teaching of the church—to find out what is said there about the meaning and value of the non-Christian world religions. We also ponder those findings in light of the current controversy and debate among theologians concerning religious pluralism and interreligious dialogue. One of the goals of this theological investigation is to determine whether or not the non-Christian religions are true religions, whether or not the one true God is operative in them, leading their adherents to eternal salvation. In this study it is also important for us to attempt "to think theologically about what it means for Christians to live with people of other faiths and about the relationship of Christianity to the other religions."[8]

As an introduction to this strictly theological investigation, and as an integral part of our overall theological methodology, we make an historical and phenomenological study of the principle religions of the world, one that brackets the question of truth in order to study other important and strictly factual matters. This exploration prepares us for our strictly theological study in several ways: first, it locates the origins of the world religions in the broad scope of world history and seeks to discover whether they have undergone a significant historical development; second, it describes what appears to be the essential characteristics of these religions as well as the basic experiences of the their founders; third, it searches to see if the world religions may share certain attributes and a common, defining spiritual structure; fourth, it specifies what appears to be the relationship of Christianity to the other religions; finally, it raises questions that pertain to the ultimate truth of the world religions, questions that point beyond history and phenomenology and find their resolution only within the transcendent sources of Christian theology.

The overall methodology used in this book is distinguished from the approach taken by those who assume that the question concerning the salvation of non-Christians is really the only question for the Christian who is thinking theologically about the fact of the multiplicity of religions in the world. That approach also supposes that the distinction between one religion and another is ultimately irrelevant. These two assumptions have been determinative for the modern debate about religious pluralism. As former prefect of the Congregation for the Doctrine of the Faith, Joseph Cardinal Ratzinger, stated:

> Even the three basic lines of response in the present discussions about Christendom and world religions—exclusivism, inclusivisim, pluralism—are all determined by this way of putting the question: the other religions are always treated as being ultimately of more or less equal value, always looked at from the point of view of their value for salvation.[9]

The approach taken in this book is based on the conviction that an historical and phenomenological investigation, which does not straightaway concern itself with the truth-value of the world religions for eternity, needs to precede such theological judgments about other religions. The author of this work is of the opinion that we ought, first of all, to seek an overall view of the great religions of the world and try to discern whether that panorama may be characterized by certain types of religion, by an inner development, and by a spiritual structure. It is appropriate not just to discuss "religion" *en masse*, as an undefined entity we did not examine closely in practice. Rather, we should make efforts to discover whether there was any kind of continuous historical development here and whether any basic kinds of religion could be recognized. This approach, it is suggested, will facilitate and make accessible to human reason a tenable theological appraisal, derived from religious faith, of the relative truth of the non-Christian religions and the uniqueness and absolute value of Christianity.

Locating the historical origins of the world religions, tracing their historical development, observing the experiential phenomena from which they arise, seeking to identify elements that unify them, as well as pondering the questions that become evident as the result of this introductory study—these procedures of historical and phenomenological analysis deal with issues of great significance and will facilitate our search for, and interpretation of, the strictly theological data that disclose the ultimate significance of the non-Christian religions. Therefore, our introductory or preliminary study of the world religions is integral to our overall theological methodology, and consequently it is pursued at length in the first and second parts of this book.

Notes

1. While Shinto is almost exclusive to Japan, it is regarded as an important major religion of the world by reason of the number of its adherents and according to the definitions used by classical scholars of religions. Therefore, it is included in this study.

2. Recently some authors have proposed the label "theology of religious pluralism," as evident in the monumental work of Roman Catholic Jacques Dupuis, SJ, *Toward a Christian Theology of Religious Pluralism* (Maryknoll, NY: Orbis, 1997). An earlier book by Alan Race, *Christians and Religious Pluralism: Patterns in the Christian Theology of Religions* (Maryknoll, NY: Orbis, 1982) shows the same orientation in the way he defines theology of pluralism: "The Christian theology of religions has come to be the name for the area of Christian studies which aims to give some definition and shape to Christian reflection on the theological implications of living in a religiously plural world" (ix). The focus on pluralism in defining the content of theology of religions is appropriate in that it highlights the most significant challenge to theology of religions. Nevertheless, the phrase "theology of religions" most probably has gained an established status as a general title for this field of study. See Veli-Matti Karkkainen, *An Introduction to the Theology of Religions* (Downers Grove, IL: InterVarsity Press, 2003), 20–21.

3. "As a separate field of study, theology of religions is a rather recent phenomenon. It emerged first in the Catholic circles beginning with the radical reorientation of Catholic Theology as a result of the Second Vatican Council (1962) and soon spread to the Protestant sphere as well. In the wake of these dramatic Catholic changes, the World Council of Churches, under the leadership of Stanley Samartha of India, published the *Living Faiths and Ultimate Goals* in 1974, followed the next year by *Towards World Community: Resources and Responsibilities for Living Together*. Currently, theology of religions is one of the most (if not the most) rapidly growing branches of theological studies. Beginning in the late 1980s, there has been a steady flow of publications that intensified at the turn of the millennium." Karkkainen, *Theology of Religions*, 22.

4. A summary of the principle elements of the declaration is available in *Origins* 30:14 (September 14, 2000), 220–22.

5. It appears that the declaration was also intended as a response to the work of Catholic theologians such as Paul Knitter, Raimondo Panikkar, Hans Küng, Leonardo Boff, and others like them who have been working during the past several years to rethink a Catholic understanding of salvation outside the church as a response to our increasing experiences of pluralism, globalization, multiculturalism, of the constant status of Christianity as a small minority in many sections of the world.

6. What most of the declaration's critics complained about, both inside and outside the Catholic Church, was the condemnatory tone and narrowness of vision more than its central doctrinal affirmations. For an overview of the strong and widespread negative reaction to the document as well as the positive reaction see Richard McBrien, "*Dominus Iesus:* An Ecclesiological Critique," *Bulletin/Centro Pro Unione* 59 (Spring 2001), 15–18.

7. Karkkainen, *Theology of Religions,* 17.

8. Ibid., 20.

9. Joseph Cardinal Ratzinger, *Truth and Tolerance: Christian Belief and World Religions,* trans. Henry Taylor (San Francisco: Ignatius Press, 2004), 17.

PART ONE

THE AXIAL AGE AND THE WORLD RELIGIONS

We begin our factual study of the origins of the world religions by calling upon the scholarly contributions of Karl Jaspers (1881–1969), the celebrated German psychologist, historian, philosopher, and one of the main representatives of the existentialist movement. In his efforts to grasp the meaning of world history, Jaspers looked for a great historical turning point, an empirically evident axis that would be valid for the whole of humankind. He believed he found what he was searching for. "It would seem that this axis of history is to be found in the period around 500 BC, in the spiritual process that occurred between 800 and 200 BC. It is there that we meet the most deepcut dividing line in history. Man, as we know him today, came into being. For short, we may style this the 'Axial Period.'"[1] According to Jaspers, and indeed many other scholars, a historical period identified as the *Axial Age* has become a widely accepted interpretive concept in circles devoted to the study of the history and phenomenology of religion. It is *axial* because it was pivotal to the spiritual development of humanity. It is identified as one of "the massive facts of religious history."[2] John Hick states:

> The phenomenology of religion is a vast jungle of proliferating diversity in which discordant facts have continually attacked and destroyed large-scale theories and in which few generalizations have been able to survive. Nevertheless, two broad interpretive concepts have emerged to very widespread acceptance....The first concept is the virtual universality throughout human life of ideas and practices that are recognizably religious....The second widely accepted large-scale

I

interpretive concept is the distinction between pre-axial religion, centrally (but not solely) concerned with the preservation of cosmic and social order, and post-axial religion, centrally (but not solely) concerned with the quest for salvation or liberation. Recognition of what is often referred to as the axial period or axial age is more widespread than the use of these particular terms.[3]

The Axial Period was a "hinge" era of extraordinary changes in religion. It was a threshold through which the founders of the world religions passed, a watershed that had far-reaching consequences not only on religion but also on all of culture and humankind's self-understanding. In this relatively short period, the world religions—such as Judaism,[4] Zoroastrianism, Hinduism,[5] Buddhism, Jainism, Confucianism, and Daoism—either have their origins or are—like Christianity, Islam, and Sikhism[6]—directly dependent upon those that do. While each of the world religions is, of course, a distinct and unique entity, each shares some common characteristics derived from the forces active in the Axial Age. Consequently, they form a composite phenomenon we identify as *post-Axial religion*.

We explore the essential characteristics of post-Axial religion. But, first, to set the stage, we examine *pre-Axial religion*. This allows us the opportunity to see our main subject in light of the differences and similarities it has with the historical phenomena that preceded it and were the stepping stones to it.

Notes

1. Karl Jaspers, *The Origin and Goal of History*, trans. Michael Bullock (New Haven: Yale University Press, 1953), 1.

2. Robert N. Bellah, *Beyond Belief: Essays on Religion in a Post-Traditional World* (New York and London: Harper & Row, 1970), 22, 32. The concept of the Axial Age is discussed by Jaspers, *Origin and Goal*, 1–21; Ernest von Lasaulx, *Neuer Versuch einer Philosophia der Geshichte* (Munich: J. G. Cotta, 1856); Victor von Strauss, *Lao Tzu Commentary* (Leipzig: F. Fleischer, 1870); A. C. Bouquet, *Comparative Religion* (London: Pelican Books, 1941); G. F. Moore, *History of Religions* (New York: Charles Scribner's Sons, 1948); Eric Voglein, *Order and History* (Baton Rouge: Louisiana State University Press, 1956–78); Lewis Mumford, *The Transformation of Man* (London: George Allen & Unwin, 1957); John B. Cobb Jr., *The Structure of Christian Existence* (Philadelphia: Westminster, 1967, and London: Lutterworth); Benjamin I. Schwartz, "The Age of Transcendence," *Daedalus: Wisdom, Revelation, and Doubt: Perspectives on the First Millennium BC* 104:2 (1975); S. N. Eisenstadt (ed.), *The Origins and Diversity of Axial Age Civilizations* (Albany: State University of New York Press, 1986); Robin Cooper, *The Evolving Mind: Buddhism, Biology and Consciousness* (Birmingham, UK: Windhorse, 1996); Bruce Lerro, *From Earth Spirits to Sky Gods: The Sociological Origins of Monotheism, Individualism, and Hyperabstract Reasoning from the Stone Age to the Axial Iron Age* (New York: Lexington Books, 2000); Lloyd Geering, *Christian Faith at the Crossroads: A Map of Modern Religious History* (Santa Rosa, CA: Polebridge, 2001); Karen Armstrong, *The Great Transformation: The Beginning of Our Religious Traditions* (New York/Toronto: Knopf, 2006). For an interpretation of world history different from Jaspers' and those who follow his lead, see John C. Landon, *World History and the Eonic Effect: Civilization, Darwinism, and Theories of Evolution*, 2nd ed. (New York: Eonix Books, 2005). Landon interprets world history from a different perspective: "Jaspers' concept of an 'Axial Age' is useful, though flawed, for it tends to be a secular version of an 'age of revelation.' We suspect a larger pattern where the terminology suggests a unique period. Nor can we find the origin of the sequence. Its goal is a speculative additional assumption. Jaspers' brilliant insight, with its classical breadth, is still nonetheless theological, and is really experiencing a reality check on his Christian assumptions, the shock of recognition, the particular seen in the general....We will move to replace the term 'axial,' indeed 'eonic,' with a completely abstract terminology of so-called 'eonic sequence,' summarized in the construction of a model to organize this data....The term 'Axial' is useful in a first look at the eonic effect, but we still find problems with its definition, among them the wrong interval chosen, i.e. −800 to −200. We will find this collates two things, that the real seminal interval is a transition and slightly ear-

lier, ca. −900 to −600, with an onset of a new period after that. We will use the term in an introductory fashion and then replace it with a more neutral term as we complete our model" (100–101).

3. John Hick, *An Interpretation of Religion: Human Responses to the Transcendent* (New Haven and London: Yale University Press, 1989), 21–22.

4. The view here is that Judaism began with the work of the great prophets, Amos, Hosea, Jeremiah, the Isaiahs, Ezekiel. However, it may be said that Judaism began not with the prophets but with the exodus some four centuries *before* the beginning of the Axial Age, or indeed with the figure of Abraham. Nevertheless, even though Abraham is the ancient patriarch of Judaism and the exodus is the founding event, still the distinctive understanding of God and the manner in which this understanding became expressed in a tradition were formed very largely by the great prophets and biblical redactors of the Axial Period.

5. In India, the *Vedas* existed before the Axial Age, but while these are foundational scriptures, the transition from the religion of the Vedic Age into the complex of classical Hinduism began during the Axial Period with the *Brahmanas,* compiled between 1000 and 700 BCE.

6. Jesus and the rise of Christianity, as well as Muhammad and the rise of Islam, are seen as major developments within the prophetic stream of Semitic religious life. The growth of Mahayana Buddhism is seen as a development of early Buddhism.

Chapter One

PRE-AXIAL RELIGION

Pre-Axial religion is a term used by historians to identify the common characteristics of the religions practiced by the communities with which history begins. These are the first societies to have developed into *civilizations;* they belong to a period of about two thousand years, sometimes known as the Archaic or Traditional Age. Before studying the chief characteristics of the pre-Axial religions, we examine briefly some of the features of the ancient civilizations from which they emerged. And since the notion of civilization as distinct from tribe is of importance here, we focus first on it.

Civilization

A *civilization* is the coming together of a large group of people to achieve feats or projects impossible at the family or small tribal scale. Such feats include the construction and maintenance of irrigation systems, great cities, and temples. Most of the early civilizations arose in fertile and well-watered river valleys in warm regions. Another essential attribute of a civilization is the long-term unification of the societal group under common, complex forms of culture and religion. These include important tools for the organization of the new projects, such as writing instruments and skills. Also at the origin of the better understood civilizations is the experience of some psychological moment that challenged and moved men and women to cooperate on a large scale to invent written symbols for words and to develop new forms culture and religion.

We go on now to explore the various pre-Axial civilizations, beginning from the fourth millennium to about 1200 BCE. First, we turn to

5

the early societies of Sumeria (in southern Mesopotamia) and of Egypt. In these two areas of the world—namely, the river valleys of the Tigris-Euphrates and the Nile—the first literate civilizations emerged from Neolithic villages, which in turn rested on accomplishments in domesticating plants and animals and improving material culture over the previous eight centuries. The appearance of these two centers was a major turning point in human history. These regions "are the two traditional centers of the earliest civilizations, and if by this we understand the first literate societies, living in cities, and having a complex social and political structure and division of labour among many kinds of specialists, archeology has abundantly confirmed this assumption."[1] The other early civilizations are those in Pakistan-India, Crete, China, and America.

The Pre-Axial Civilizations

Sumer

In Sumeria of southern Mesopotamia, around 4000,* we find a culture that was the culmination of centuries of rapid economic, social, and political elaboration. The Sumerians created an advanced civilization that perhaps more than any other established the foundation for future civilizations. It occupied the jungle swamps around the lower areas of the Tigris and Euphrates river system, which arises in the mountain ranges of eastern Turkey and runs through Iraq, flowing into the Persian Gulf. Because of the nature of the land between these two rivers, civilization was a possibility. The flood plains of the rivers allowed for intensive cultivation of the grains required to sustain cities. So the Sumerians opened up these rivers for an irrigated cultivation that eventually flourished.

> The whole population of the area could easily live on the produce of the land and barter the surplus for what they wanted from abroad. It is important to remember too that this was not subsistence agriculture; it was a well organized

---

*All the dates in the first and second parts of this book refer to BCE.

agriculture with a complex system of irrigation canals. Irrigation and drainage involved complicated and co-operative efforts requiring control, organization and a centralized society.[2]

The whole of Sumer, which was approximately the size of Connecticut, may have attained a population of 500,000 persons. It had at least twenty major cities and a number of lesser towns. Sumerian civilization was born of the increasing interdependence of the city-states in Mesopotamia. An intricate and flexible patchwork of alliances linked city to city and ruler to ruler. The sources seem to indicate that the city-states were theocracies run by a group of powerful families that controlled the religious rituals. Each of them, small in area, constantly competed, fought, and traded with one another in a volatile political environment. Yet the Sumerians considered themselves a single people—they referred to themselves as the "black-haired people"—but at the same time they were loyal to their individual city-states and the divinities associated with the cities.

The Sumerian civilization was highly developed and sophisticated. "It was the genius of the Sumerians that invented the wheel, glass, bronze, writing, the calendar and the city. It may have been something special in their make up...."[3] Samuel Kramer suggests that "the psychological factor responsible to no little extent for both the material and cultural achievements of the Sumerians was an all-pervading and deeply ingrained drive for pre-eminence and prestige, for victory and success."[4] As we shall see, the Sumerians influenced the eventual emergence of the Egyptian and Indus Valley civilizations.[5]

Egypt

The second civilization in human history developed in the Nile river valley of Egypt at about the same time as the Sumerian city-states. The Nile arises from sources in east Africa and, from the First Cataract (a set of falls and rapids), serves to divide Egypt in the north from what is now Sudan in the south. This area differed significantly from Mesopotamia "not only in its outward and material aspect, but in its whole orientation and ethos. In Egypt conditions were more favorable to the enterprises of man."[6] Crops and animals, such as barley and wheat and cattle and sheep, were brought into the Nile Valley from the Near East between 5000 and 4500 BCE. J. D. Evans suggests that the stimulus raising the Egyptians from a primitive society to an organized civilization was the authority of Menes, the first pharaoh of the first dynasty, who was motivated in part by the cultural advances made in Sumer.[7] Glyn Daniel, however, insists on the originality and magnificence of Egyptian achievements, especially in architecture. "Even if the Sumerians were the first civilization, and even if it was their stimulus and example that catalyzed the emergent or nascent synoecism of Egypt, the pyramids of the Nile Valley still pay silent and dramatic witness to the organization and power of the second civilization to develop in human history."[8]

By 3000, the patchwork of a number of kingdoms that had sprung up along the Nile and traded and competed with each other became a unified state. From the earliest days of agriculture, Egypt had comprised two worlds: Upper Egypt, a narrow flood plain that extended from the First Cataract to modern Cairo, and Lower Egypt, which encompassed the broader valley downstream and the flat delta. The first pharaoh to rule over a united Egypt was King Horus-Aha. He and his successors consolidated their small kingdoms into a single political entity.

Consequently, early Egyptian civilization focused on the pharaoh, the god-king, who was viewed as the son of Horus, the falcon god, and was destined to join the gods. It was the pharaohs who were the lynchpins of Egypt's cultural development. The construction as well as the enhancement of the royal centers and shrines was driven by the pharaoh's need to project his sacred power and to gain the favor of the gods. The pharaohs constructed their pyramids both as religious and secular projects. From a religious viewpoint, the pyramids were structures where life and light-darkness met, symbolic sunrays that served as a ladder to enable the king to join the gods in the heavens. Building pyramids was also a means of bonding the villagers who worked on the royal tombs to the service of the pharaoh, the god who ruled the state.

Crete

As the influence of Egyptian and Mesopotamian culture spread into Asia Minor and across the Eastern Mediterranean, there appeared in this area a number of new civilized and semi-civilized powers. One of these was the Minoan Empire of Crete, beginning around 2000 BCE. It was on the island of Crete that civilization emerged in the Aegean world.

After 2500, on the Cyclades Islands of the Aegean, throughout Crete, and on the Ionian Islands of western Greece, many villages and small towns were founded. The beginnings of town life on the islands resulted in considerable cultural diversity throughout the Aegean, a diversity promoted by constant trading activity and by a trend toward greater political and social complexity. The greatest complexity of Aegean society was achieved on Crete, while mainland Greek society lagged for many centuries, with only sporadic connections offshore.

The people of Crete devised a hierarchical society, and by 2100 the kings of the city of Knossos had united the island and established control of the sea. Knossos soon became the major center of the emerging civilization and culture of the island, which was named *Minoan* after King Minos. The basis of its prosperity was not agricultural, as in the Mesopotamian kingdoms, nor did it depend on military conquest, as with the Hittites. It rested rather on something entirely new in the history of the world. It was the first society to work a systematic exploitation of the sea and become a maritime commercial empire. The Minoans were excellent sailors and kept in close contact with surrounding lands. Under the protection of the king, Minoan ships eventually carried commodities from all over the eastern Mediterranean world, from as far as central Europe and North Africa. Most important was the close and continuous contact kept with Egypt. Under the impetus of new intercourse with Egypt in the Early Dynastic Period, the first great advances in Cretan culture were made. From then on, there was a constant flow of trade between the Delta and the Cretan ports.[9]

Minoan religious practices and beliefs were centered on caves and palaces, where people offered sacrifices to individuals who transformed themselves into deities. There were no supreme Minoan rulers, or divine kings, in the sense of an Egyptian pharaoh. The palaces served as the principle centers of religious life. It may be that the Cretan nobility had a strong interest in portraying themselves in divine form, to the extent that the imagery of the gods and rulers fused into one. It should be noted that some Minoan gods and goddesses appear on the palaces' walls.

Minoan worship also took place on hilltops or case, where shrines were visited at certain times of the year or at time of need. From Knossos there is evidence that their religious beliefs may have included occasional human sacrifices connected to the fertility of the soil and rainfall.

Indus Valley

Pakistan's Indus River Valley was the cradle of south Asian civilization. Its vast alluvial flood plain provided soft, easily turned soil for subsistence agriculture, which began before 6000 BCE. During the third millennium, a period of explosive growth took place on the Indus plain. Villages became towns, which then developed into cities. An important shift in trading patterns brought the people of the Indus in direct contact with the Persian Gulf and Mesopotamian civilization. The Indus people had mastered the basic irrigation and flood control challenges of their capricious environment. When Egypt and Sumer were already well established, the Harappan civilization of the Indus Valley was founded in Pakistan and northwestern India by 2500. Named after the city of Harappa, this civilization developed and flourished over an enormous area of just under half a million square miles, a region considerably larger than modern Pakistan. Like the Sumerians, the Harappans adopted the model of the city as way of operating and controlling their society. There were at least five major Harappan cities.

While the accomplishments of the Harappans were due partly to their awareness of the achievements of Sumer and Egypt, Mortimer Wheeler, the archeologist, believes it was not simply the outpost of the earlier civilizations.

> The Indus civilization, with its individual technology and script and its alien personality, was no mere colony of the West. But ideas have wings, and in the third millennium the idea of civilization was in the air in western Asia. A model of civilization, however abstract, was present to the minds of the Indus founders. In their running battle against more spacious problems than had been encountered either in Mesopotamia or in Egypt, they were fortified by the consciousness that it had been done before. And in that consciousness, after one failure and another,—they won through. In some such manner may be reconstructed the ini-

tial phase of the Indus civilization as the ultimate triumph of a village or small-town community, determined, well-led and inspired by a great and mature idea.[10]

The religious beliefs of the Harappans reflected their unpredictable and often violent environments with their extremes of heat and rapidly moving floods. Like the Mesopotamians, they seem to have believed that humans lived to be of service to the gods, who caused the crops to grow and the soil to be fertile. The fundamental roots of their later Indian religion may have lain in the age-old fertility cults that gave the assurance that life would continue and fertility be renewed. Harappan civilization reached its peak after 2000. By 1700, the time of the Middle Kingdom of Egypt and the Minoan civilization, the Harappan cities went into decline and soon were abandoned. Their populations were dispersed into small communities and their volume of trade declined substantially.

China

Before 7000 BCE, the beginning of rice cultivation in southern China was thought to have taken place in the Yellow River Valley. By 3000, agricultural societies that were much more sophisticated flourished throughout China. These Longshanoid cultures were regional societies that were in regular contact with each other. Although their cultures were very different, their farming processes were somewhat similar to those operative along the Nile before the unification of Egypt. In nearly every respect, the institutions and economic practices of the Longshanoid societies foreshadowed the Shang civilization.

In 2100, the Shang civilization was created in the valley of the Yellow River in northern China. Here, as in the civilizations spoken of previously, local people were confronted with the challenge of taming a marshy, thickly vegetated valley prone to flooding. Glyn Daniel asks, Was the Yellow River civilization an outpost or colony of the Sumerians? Was it, like the Indus civilization, a native development that was spurred on and excited by contacts with the more ancient west? To most people, he responds, it would now seem that the Yellow River civilization was the result of individual growth:

Here, as in southern Mesopotamia, we are observing an independent process of synoecism....Chinese civilization was, then, born in the Yellow River and by local growth there: it does not seem to have had the stimulus diffusion from Sumer for which we argued in Egypt and the Indus Valley; but it does seem to have borrowed some cultural features from the west....[11]

Shang cities were considerably larger than Longshanoid enclosures. It is probably more precise to think of them as "urban clusters," because they were much more dispersed than the later compact Chinese cities. The city or cluster of Anyang is renowned for its royal tombs. Their royal owners were buried with magnificent jades, fine bronzes, weapons, and many clay vessels. In death, as in life, the Shang elite were surrounded by the bodies of persons sacrificed in honor of their ancestors. The Shang rulers were themselves specialists of the religious rituals, most likely the sole intermediaries between the people and the ancestors and the gods. The rituals generally occurred in royal precincts and included divinations and ancestor worship, which involved human sacrifice.

Shang was the most important early civilization in China, but it encompassed only a small area of northeastern China, surrounded by other, still unknown small states that came into being at about the same time. In 1027 BCE, the last Shang ruler was overthrown by a rival state to the west, the Zhou.

Central America: The Olmec

Civilizations evolving from primitive societies appeared in Central and South America. The origins of Mesoamerican civilization date to the remote past, to an era when maize and bean farmers flourished over an expansive area of the highlands and lowlands of Central America. By the middle of the second millennium BCE, the egalitarian societies of earlier times were changing into more elaborate cultures in which ritual and social ranking played an increasingly important part. These developments took hold in many areas of the highlands and lowlands, but the most famous of these early societies was the Olmec. The Olmec had a revered place in the legend and lore of later Mesoamerican civilizations.

By about 1250, the Olmec had created a common culture that flourished from 800 to 400 in the sweltering Gulf Coast of Mexico. This was an environment very different from those of Egypt, Sumeria, India, and China. The Olmec was a series of chiefdoms along the Veracruz and Tabasco coasts, in a low-lying, tropical homeland rich in animals and plant foods. They built earth pyramids and carved jade, but they lived without metals or large cities. The birds, fish, and land animals of the forest formed an important part of a very sophisticated art style, which was to put a permanent imprint on Mesoamerican life. Olmec society flourished in an era when art motifs, religious symbols, and ritual beliefs were shared among chiefdoms in many regions due to trading activity and contacts between kin leaders.

Earlier generations of scholars viewed the Olmec as a "mother civilization" for Mesoamerica, the ancestor of all later civilizations in the region. In the legend and lore of later Mesoamerican civilizations, the Olmec people occupied a revered place. Maya priests recognized the deep cultural legacy they owed to these ancestral Mesoamericans. So did the Aztecs of the highlands, whose rain god, Tlaloc, may have originated as one of the principle deities of the Olmecs.[12]

The Chavin

About 750, another civilization, known as the Chavin, emerged in the formative period of Peru. This society has its place at the beginnings in South America of the Andean civilization, which advanced over many centuries along numerous pathways, creating a highly varied mosaic of kingdoms, states, and empires that shared many common religious beliefs. There were two poles of Andean civilization: one was centered along the north coast of modern-day Peru, the other, in the south-central Andes Mountains. The northern pole was located on the virtually rainless coastal desert, where more than forty rivers and streams dissect the arid terrain. This area is an arid, demanding terrain, yet it was here that the first Andean civilization developed.

The Chavin leaders were able to organize large labor forces to build ceremonial centers and to create the irrigation facilities needed to allow cultivation of river valley soils, which in turn provided the impetus for major changes in coastal society. After 1800 BCE, a series of competing kingdoms developed along the north and central coasts where sedentary villages each housed several hundred people and were home to skilled weavers; this was the start of a long Andean tradition. This initial period of Chavin civilization saw an elaboration of religious life, the appearance of new forms of religious architecture, the building of earth and stone or adobe pyramids, and the creation of a fine style of art. The Andean equivalent to the Mesoamerican Olmec is the distinctive Chavin art style, which made an impact on the enormous area of the lowlands and highlands about 900.

The Chavin art style seems to be grounded in a defining ideology, a defining set of religious beliefs, centered on a place called Chavin de Huantar in the Andean foothills. This ceremonial center or shrine was the home of an elaborate, well-developed icononography. Chavin de Huantar itself, a terraced shrine, had a truncated pyramid with passageways and rooms. It appears that the center had been a place of mediation between the heavens and the underworld, between the living and the supernatural. Priests could cause water to thunder through the tunnels and channels in the shrine, replicating the connection between the rain-giving mountains above the temple and the cosmos. As a result of these very impressive performances, with the water flowing rapidly through the channels, Chavin de Huantar, between about 850 and 200, was an important place of pilgrimage with a sizable population. However, it never became a fully fledged state, and eventually, the center of pilgrimage collapsed. But its religious ideas endured, and they were one of the catalysts for the development of civilization both on the lowlands and on the highlands.

Conclusion

Historians regard the Sumerians, Egyptians, Indus Valley people, Minoans, Yellow River people, Olmecs, and Chavin as the seven pioneer, pre-Axial civilizations. With them human history begins, and the attributes that characterize all human civilizations can be traced back to one or more of these.

The Common Characteristics of the Pre-Axial Religions

We go on to explore the common characteristics of the religions that emerged from the pre-Axial civilizations. Since our intention is to treat those religions not in abstract concepts but rather as lived human experience and consciousness, it is appropriate first to make some remarks about the level or stage of human consciousness in the pre-Axial civilizations.

Stage of Human Consciousness

It is very hard to imagine what experience must have been like in the early civilizations. All one has to go on is the evidence of social and economic life unearthed by archaeologists, together with objects of religious art and architecture; writing at first was used only to keep records of collective work, levies, trade, and so on. Later, written records give more insight into the mentality of the time. There are the annals of royal dynasties, royal proclamations, codes of law, texts on gods and their rituals, and heroic and tragic epics.[13]

In light of the research done on the available archeological and written resources, it is reasonable to conclude that, most likely, a level of full self-reflective consciousness was extremely rare in pre-Axial civilizations. In an influential account of its appearance, Julian Jaynes finds no evidence of self-reflective consciousness before the second millennium. In the pre-Axial civilizations, the stage of self-awareness had not yet developed to a strong and stable degree, but appeared only occasionally and weakly, including consciousness of the self as the originator of one's actions. In the Archaic or Traditional Age of the very early civilizations, the level of human consciousness, Jaynes proposes, is reflected in Homer's poem, the *Iliad*.[14]

What is especially characteristic of the consciousness of this age was a strong feeling of *membership*. Ken Wilber, in his survey of the development of consciousness, *Up from Eden*, defines this characteristic as

membership of a coherent group from which each person unquestion-
ingly derived his or her values and worldview. This may be called the
traditional age in which unbending loyalty to cultural traditions best
served the interests of human communities.[15] Undoubtedly this sense
of membership was an aspect of the religious sensibility of pre-Axial
civilizations.

Culture and Religion

Taking into account the available historical evidence as well as the
stage of human consciousness in pre-Axial societies, we do not find a separate, unified entity that was identified as "religion." It is only considerably later that religion became a separate and distinct part of culture.[16]
Pre-Axial men and women were not aware of possessing a religion. What
we choose to describe as religion was an integral part of their culture to
such an extent that it could not be divorced from it and objectified as an
entity in itself. Their religion was but a dimension of the total way of life
they had inherited from their mythical past. But by focusing on the structure of beliefs, rituals, institutions, and ethical norms by which the pre-
Axial peoples responded to ultimate questions of their existence, we are
able to discern what may be identified as their religion. But even here caution is required. For when our pre-Axial ancestors made reference to such
concepts as gods, spirits, and sacred disclosure in order to interpret their
experience of the forces of nature, these constituted the raw material not
only of their religion but also of their science and knowledge. So we may
conclude that "their religion is to be found not so much in the concepts
themselves, as in the feelings of awe and in the attitudes of faith and obedience which they experienced in relation to them."[17]

Common Characteristics

What follows is a treatment of some of the basic, common features of the religions practiced by the pre-Axial communities.[18] Rather
than an exhaustive study of the subject, it is a presentation of those
characteristics in an *ideal type*. This ideal type focuses on the feelings of
awe and the attitudes of faith and obedience of pre-Axial peoples expe-

rienced as a consequence of the impact on them of what they perceived to be sacred. It intends to make these religious phenomena more or less comprehensible.

Sense of the Sacred in the One World

The men and women of pre-Axial civilizations grew in the awareness of the Sacred, which they usually sensed as a numinous presence within the world around them and themselves. They experienced a complex of unseen entities—powers, spirits, gods—superior to human beings, varied in character, both beneficent and hostile, and with distinct advantages over the world of nature and humankind. With awe, wonder, and fear they perceived the world as alive with these mysterious, sacred powers. The gods permeated, actively controlled and dominated, and were revealed in, the human world of nature and civilization, for example, in thunder or in rivers or in ritual sacrifices. Especially important were the high gods of the heavenly regions, whose vision, knowledge, and power were conceived as very extensive. Because it was believed that the high god was more or less inaccessible, he tended to fade from the religious consciousness. Some believed that gods, men, women, animals, insects, and rocks all participated in the same divine life. And all were subject to an overarching cosmic order that sustained everything in being. Even the gods had to be obedient to this order, and they cooperated with human beings in the maintenance of the divine energies of the cosmos. If these were not replenished, the world would lapse into a primal void.

There was a belief in a world somewhat different from the human world, usually higher and stronger. However, even though there was a continuous stress on the difference between the transmundane world and the human world, there was, in the awareness of most pre-Axial persons, a close, intimate connection between them.[19] Indeed, humans felt they did not have a world of their own. The sacred world of the gods was the prototype of human existence, and since it was stronger, superior, and more enduring than anything on Earth, men and women wanted desperately to participate in it. They felt they were dependent on and at the mercy of the gods. The gods and their world, therefore, were sacred entities with which humans must deal in a definite and purposive way.

Disclosure of the Sacred
and the Embrace of Faith

Pre-Axial men and women experienced the gods revealing themselves in and through the natural and human realities of the world in which they lived. They embraced this disclosure of the gods with a faith imbued with feelings of awe. At the core of their faith was the acknowledgment of dependency on the gods for basic realities: maintenance of personal, social, and cosmic harmony; subsistence and propagation; preservation of the unity of the tribe or people; and for attaining specific goods that assure an abundant life in the world, such as rain, harvest, food, and reproduction, success in battle. An afterlife for them was not a major concern, for they believed that death led to a shadowy semi-existence in some vaguely designated place in this world.

Religion

Pre-Axial men and women experienced the revelation of the gods and responded to it in faith. Their religion was what they *did* about their faith. It was their faith expressed in a structured complex of beliefs, myths, and sacrificial rites of worship and supplication, ethical codes and lifestyles, and social organizations. In their religious activity they sought to render obedience to the gods and supplicate them to bestow benefits for an abundant life in this world. For them, there was no second, truly transcendent world or a truly fulfilling and blissful afterlife. The ultimate concern of their religion, therefore, had to do chiefly with life in this world. It was based on the status quo, was little concerned with speculative reflection on the meaning of life, and saw sacred truth not as something sought for but as given, as passively received.[20]

Ritual sacred dramas and animal sacrifice were central to the religious quest of pre-Axial times. In the performance of these rites, the participants encountered the divine and were introduced to another level of existence. Animal sacrifice was a universal tradition in the ancient world. It was a practice that recycled the depleted forces that kept the world in being. There was a strong conviction that life and death, creativity and destruction were inextricably bound together. People realized that they survived in life because the lives of other creatures were laid down for their sake. So the animal victim was honored for its *self-sacrifice*.[21]

When they reenacted the mythical sacred dramas and sacrifices in their ceremonial liturgy, worshipers felt that they had been lifted into sacred time. Often they would initiate a new project by performing a rite that represented the original cosmogony. This was intended to give their fragile mortal activity an infusion of divine strength. Nothing could persist if it were not animated or endowed with a *soul* in this way.[22] Only when they imitated the gods in sacred rites and gave up the lonely, frail individuality of their secular lives did they truly exist. They enhanced and fulfilled their humanity when they ceased to be simply themselves and repeated the gestures of others.

Ethics

Ethical behavior based on codes and laws reflecting what they perceived to be their obligations to the gods and to humans was an important component of their religious activity. Their moral sense did include toleration of failure to live up to their social and moral ideals and the possibility for repentance. It was believed that through sacrificial worship they could atone for particular acts of unfaithfulness. While pre-Axial civilizations valued commitment to ethical standards, an awareness of an autonomous, distinct moral order qualifiedly different from this world developed only to a minimal degree.

Conservative and Noncritical

In pre-Axial times life was variously enjoyed as well as endured, for there was always a realistic awareness of suffering, insecurity, and mortality. But life was never fundamentally criticized. Consequently, pre-Axial religion accepted life as it was and sought to continue it on a stable basis. The ultimate concern that drove it was conservative: a defense against chaos, meaninglessness, the breakdown of social cohesion; keeping fragile human life unchanging and on an even keel. What is not found in pre-Axial religions is the hope for a radically different and better human existence, whether in this life or in a future life to come.

The sacrifices to the gods, the placating of ill-disposed spirits, the rules for using without being injured by *mana*, the new year festivals, the observance of taboos, the methods of disposal of the dead—all were intended to keep the life of the community on an even keel and the fabric of society intact....The religious system functioned to renew or prolong the existing balance of good and evil and to ward off the possible disasters which always threatened.[23]

Pre-Axial religion was focused on conservation, and "it did not have in view any basic transformation of the human situation. There was no sense of a higher reality to which a limitlessly better future is possible."[24]

Ethnic and Regional

The religions of the pre-Axial civilizations had no names and were not universal, but they were always *ethnic*. That is, they were associated with a particular ethnic community and a particular region, and their objects of veneration were a specific group of deities. They expressed the identity of the group rather than that of the individual. Each of the pre-Axial religions was not a self-contained entity, but rather a dimension of the particular group's culture and total way of life inherited from the mythical past. Furthermore, each person was born into the religion and could not opt out of it.

Superseded

None of the religions of the early civilizations survived the advent of the Axial Period. They may be regarded as stepping stones to the religions of the Axial Age and as such were left behind or superseded. While the first civilizations developed remarkable technical skills and achieved a high level of sophistication and may have been magnificent in their own way, "they appear in some manner unawakened.... Measured against the lucid humanity of the Axial Period, a strange veil seems to lie over the most ancient structures preceding it, as though man had not yet really come to himself."[25]

Notes

1. J. D. Evans, "The Neolithic Revolution and the Foundation of Cities," *The Concise Encyclopedia of World History*, ed. John Bowle (New York: Hawthorne Books, 1958), 38. In addition to the sources directly cited in this chapter, the sources for the treatment of the first civilizations also include the following: Kenneth W. Harl, *Origins of the Great Ancient Civilizations* (Chantilly, VA: Teaching Company, 2005); Brian M. Fagan, Human Prehistory and the First Civilization (Chantilly, VA: Teaching Company, 2003), parts 1–3.

2. Glyn Daniel, *The First Civilizations: The Archeology of Their Origins* (New York: Thomas Y. Crowell, 1968), 70.

3. Ibid., 81.

4. Samuel Kramer, cited in Daniel, *First Civilizations*, 82.

5. Daniel, *First Civilizations*, 131.

6. Evans, "Neolithic Revolution,"41.

7. Ibid., 42.

8. Daniel, *First Civilizations*, 92–93.

9. George Forrest, "Mediterranean Culture: Crete, Mycenae, Athens," *Concise Encyclopedia of World History*, 48.

10. Mortimer Wheeler, "The Civilization of Subcontinent," *The Dawn of Civilization*, ed. Stuart Piggott (New York: McGraw Hill, 1961), 248.

11. Daniel, *First Civilizations*, 134.

12. Ibid., 170–73; Robin Cooper, *The Evolving Mind: Buddhism, Biology and Consciousness* (Birmingham, UK: Windhorse, 1996), 117–18.

13. Cooper, *Evolving Mind*, 119. Many of the early texts can be found in English translation in William H. McNeil and Jean W. Sedlar, eds., *The Origins of Civilization* (New York: Oxford University Press, 1968).

14. Julian Jaynes, *The Origin of Consciousness in the Breakdown of the Bicameral Mind* (London: Penguin, 1982), 211; cited in Cooper, *Evolving Mind*, 120.

15. Ken Wilber, *Up from Eden: A Transpersonal View of Human Evolution* (Garden City, NY: Anchor Press/Doubleday, 1981), 102–4.

16. Cooper, *Evolving Mind*, 121.

17. Lloyd Geering, *Christian Faith at the Crossroad: A Map of Modern Religious History* (Santa Rosa, CA: Polebridge, 2001), 17.

18. Mircea Eliade, *Myths, Dreams and Mysteries: The Encounter between Contemporary Faiths and Archaic Realities*, trans. Philip Mairet (New York: Harper Torchbooks, 1979), 59–228; Mircea Eliade, *The Myth of the Eternal Return*, trans. Willard R. Trask (London: Routledge & Kegan Paul, 1955); Walter Burkert, *Homo Necans: The Anthropology of Ancient Greek Sacrificial Ritual and Myth*, trans. Peter Bing (Berkeley, Los Angeles, London: University of California Press, 1983),

1–82; Karen Armstrong, *The Great Transformation: The Beginning of Our Religious Traditions* (New York/Toronto: Knopf, 2006), xv–xviii.

19. The elements that constitute this close connection are the following: relatively similar symbolic terms were used to define both the gods and human beings; the home of the gods was symbolically structured according to principles very similar to those of the lower home of humans, and it was usually equated with a concrete setting not entirely unlike the human world in detail; the mythical and cyclical conception of time of the transmundane world was often only mildly differentiated from the past, present, and future of the human world.

20. Some historians designate the religion of pre-Axial societies as nature religion. They view it as relating men and women of the first civilizations to the unseen forces and powers of the natural world: religious activity warded off those powers found to be evil and destructive and cultivated the support of those that were beneficent. However, what historians call the forces and powers of nature were, in the faith experience of the pre-Axial peoples, the dynamic attributes of sacred beings. In their eyes, the world of nature was alive with the revealing and powerful gods. In their faith experience, their religion was not a response to the powers of nature, but to the revelation of the mighty gods.

21. Burkert, *Homo Necans,* 116–22.

22. Eliade, *Myths, Dreams and Mysteries,* 81–82; Eliade, *Myth of Eternal Return,* 17–21.

23. John Hick, *An Interpretation of Religion: Human Responses to the Transcendent* (New Haven and London: Yale University Press, 1989), 28.

24. Ibid.

25. Cooper, *Evolving Mind,* 121.

Chapter Two

POST-AXIAL RELIGION

After examining pre-Axial religion, we are prepared to explore our main subject of interest, namely, post-Axial religion. This term is used to designate the composite of common traits of the several religions that emerged in and passed through the Axial Period and survive until the present. These are the world religions: Zoroastrianism, Hinduism, Jainism, Buddhism, Daoism, Confucianism, Judaism, Shinto, and those that are directly dependent on them, such as Christianity, Islam, and Sikhism. In our study of post-Axial religion, we focus in this chapter on the nature of the Axial Period, the traits of the Axial sages, the essence of their religious experience, and the common characteristics of the post-Axial religions.

The Axial Period

The Axial Period is the historical age around 500 BCE, and the spiritual process of great importance that occurred between 800 and 200. "Although confined to China, India and the West, and though there was to begin with no contact between these three worlds, the Axial Period nonetheless founded universal history, and, spiritually, drew all men to itself."[1] This was the period of the Buddha, Confucius, and Jeremiah, the mystics of the Upanishads, Mencius, and Laozi. During this age of intense creativity, spiritual and philosophical-theological geniuses—the Axial sages—pioneered an entirely new kind of human experience. This age was a "hinge" or axis on which human history turned. To the achievements of this deep-cut dividing line in history, the preceding efforts of humankind seem to converge; and from that historical demarcation, human culture moved forward into new and advanced forms not only of religion but also of philosophy and science, all tracing their origins back to the innovative departures and revolutions of the Axial sages. "The Axial Age was one of the most seminal periods of intellectual, psychological, philosophical and religious change in recorded history; there would be nothing comparable until the Great Western Transformation which created our own scientific and technological modernity."[2]

The changes in religion were not firmly engraved patterns. What we are dealing with here is "a very large-scale transition, without precise boundaries and complicated by contrary eddies. The axial age was spread over centuries and much more was going on during these centuries than is captured by the axial image."[3] Hick cautions that "the inevitable danger in identifying and naming this immensely significant transition of some two and a half millennia is that it may thereby be made to appear more dramatic and sharply delineated than it must have been at the time."[4] But keeping this caution in mind, we may conclude with Hick that "the axial age was a uniquely significant band of time. With certain qualifications we can say that in this period all the major religious options, constituting the major possible ways of conceiving the ultimate, were identified and established and that nothing of comparably novel significance has happened in the religious life of humanity since."[5] All the religious traditions founded in this period pushed forward the frontiers of human consciousness and discovered a transcendent reality in the core of their being.

The Axial Sages

For centuries and even millennia, the conditions of human existence remained fundamentally unchanged, and generation after generation lived and died within the same familiar mental horizon. But eventually, "in the imperceptibly slow evolution of human life through long periods of time the conditions gradually formed for the emergence of individuality."[6] Creative and innovative persons with a keen sense of their individuality—among them, the founders of the world religions, or the *Axial sages*—came forth. Many of them worked anonymously, but others became visionaries with insights about what a human being should be. They were a cohort of brilliant thinkers whose teachings left profound impressions on the way human beings thought about themselves and the world around them. In modern times, men and women are still living out the ideas and ideals they introduced in separate areas of the Eurasian continent.

In East Asia, in what we now call China, Confucius and his followers provided the religious, philosophical, and political grounds for more than two thousand years of Chinese culture. At the same time, Daoist thinkers who wrote the famous *Daodejing* created a compelling alternative to Confucianism. In South Asia, a countercultural school of ascetics and mystics composed a collection of teachings called the *Upanishads* that endowed an emerging Hinduism its characteristics features. Close to the same time and place, both the Buddha and Mahavira were enlightened with new insights that gave rise to Buddhism and Jainism. In West Asia, in Palestine, the prophets of Judah helped shape the nascent religion of Judaism. Also in West Asia, in Iran, Zarathustra had recently founded Zoroastrianism, which served as the state religion of three powerful empires. Finally, in the northern Mediterranean—in the land of ancient Greece—Thales, Pythagoras, Heraclitus, Socrates, Plato, and Aristotle developed the Western philosophical tradition.

Equally as fascinating as the depth of genius in these Axial centers is the similarity and ways of thinking that the sages developed, despite their geographical distance from each other. They all struggled with many of the same profound issues, such as the nature and density of the self, the basis and practices of morality, and the sublime good of human life. About these men, Geering remarks:

> Certainly when one thinks of all that the subsequent world owned to them, it is surprising to find that Zarathustra, the Israelite prophets, Mahavira, Gotama the Buddha, Confucius, Lao-Tzu (or the author of the *Tao Te Ching*), and the Greek philosophers were all near contemporaries. Whether we regard as pure coincidence the almost simultaneous appearance of these men in some five or six areas which were geographically isolated from each other, or whether we interpret it as evidence of some underlying spiritual force (as some have been inclined to do), the fact remains that this period stands out as a kind of watershed in the history of religion and culture….It was just as if human-

kind's religious apprehension of the world underwent a giant turn on its axis.[7]

The changes brought about by the Axial sages, especially those made by the founders of the world religions, have significance for all people on Earth, without regard to particular creeds or dogmas. Through their insights, but always within the existing setting of their own culture, human consciousness was very much enlarged, and a movement began that brought about an age characterized as a *hinge* time.

Social and Political Situation of the Sages

What was happening in the time and surrounding areas of the sages that might have promoted their appearance on the Eurasian continent and influenced their prodigious output of creative ideas? To begin to answer this weighty question, we discuss some political and social developments that were occurring in the Axial centers during this period.

Urbanization and Mobility

The Axial Age occurred at a time and in areas of increasing urbanization and mobility. More and more, people were living in closer proximity to one another, in towns and cities. People, of course, lived in urban settings in pre-Axial times, but now this type of life accelerated and expanded. Urbanization was significant because it affected social structures and the human psyche. Frequently urban life disrupts a person's sense of identity and puts traditional values and beliefs in doubt.

Political and Legal Upheaval

The Axial centers were most often characterized by political and legal upheaval. For example, the Chinese Axial Age overlapped a violent epoch of Chinese history known as the Period of Warring States. India, Judah, and Iran underwent similar times of turmoil and transformation. Rapid political and social change and violence produces uncertainty and insecurity. But such times frequently are the most creative for religious and theological thought.

Characteristics of the Sages

Anxiety about Death

Sages in all the Axial centers became increasingly anxious about death and gripped by what, if anything, might lay beyond death. Persons of the pre-Axial civilization were, of course, not unconcerned about death, but since their sense of identity was rooted principally in their participation in the family tribe or clan, death could be accepted with the assurance that the family would survive one's personal demise. As the Axial Age dawned, attitudes toward death began to reflect a stronger concern about the experience of dying and the afterlife. More and more, death was regarded with dread, and speculation about what might lie beyond was filled with both hope and terror. Many possibilities for the afterlife seem to have been conceived: from ongoing existence in a place of delight; to life in a most unpleasant domain of the underworld; to rebirth in this life; or to decomposition of the body and the soul back to the elements of the Earth or to the resurrection of the dead at the end of time.

Full Self-Reflective Consciousness

Reflected in the shift in attitudes concerning death is the rise among the Axial sages of full reflective consciousness. Although much is known about the Axial Period—names and genealogies; accounts of conquests and migrations; the ruins of cities, temples, tombs; the remains of artifacts and weapons—our understanding of the experiences of the people of this ancient period is still shadowy. Robin Cooper remarks, "It is so difficult to imagine life in ancient times. People's minds, to the extent that one can glimpse their working through the dust of millennia, still seem somewhat strange, even alien. When is it that we can start to recognize the emergence of our own kind of consciousness? It seems to be in the axial age."[8] If the experiences of men and women in the Axial Period remain shadowy to us, there are, never-theless, parallels between their thinking and our own kind of modern consciousness. These parallels provide us with an access to understand-ing the human experiences of ancient times.

The Axial Period was not the beginning of self-reflective aware-ness; consciousness of the self as the originator of actions seems to have been a real capability much earlier. But from that pre-Axial level of awareness there evolved, in Axial times, an increase in self-critical thought. For the first time in history, men and women became aware they were thinkers: *human consciousness became aware of itself.* Words were found to describe, and thus to make more definite in the human mind, the concepts of the self. The subject who knows and wills was called *I.* The self as illuminated and known in self-reflective consciousness was called *me.* The self experienced a sense of individuality, of being a sep-arate, autonomous moral agent, accountable and responsible for one's own actions. And as human persons began to think of themselves as separate, autonomous individuals, death was experienced as a more dreadful reality. The awareness of selfhood promotes a feeling of isola-tion, or at least, a differentiation from the rest of the human commu-nity and the rest of reality. This makes it more difficult to accept death as a part of the natural process of living.

The Axial Age, then, was marked with the growth of self-reflective thought, and along with that state of awareness, the dread of death and the preoccupation about afterlife. And, as we shall see, some persons in this hinge period of history attained the level of full self-reflective awareness.

Critical and Innovative Thinkers

In contrast to the pre-Axial religions that were simply inherited from ancestors, the post-Axial religions are the work of critical and innovative founders. The few Axial sages, in a variety of places, were the first in history to dare to be individualists and to ask radical questions about their cultural inheritance. Although they were only a small minor-ity, they condemned, repudiated, and set to change the state in which they had found things.

In the Axial countries, a few men sensed fresh possibilities and broke away from the old traditions. They sought change in the deepest reaches of their beings, looked for greater inwardness in their spiritual lives, and tried to become one with a reality that transcended normal mundane conditions and categories. After this pivotal era, it was felt that only by reaching beyond their limits could human beings become most fully themselves.[9]

Study and debate evolved as important religious activities. There was to be no more blind acceptance of the status quo, and no more automatic fidelity to ideas received from the past. Truth was to be made a reality in the lives of the men and women who strove to achieve it. The spiritual revolts launched by the sages differed from each other greatly in degree, but each sage reflected critically on the past and created new formulations of the way in which humans could respond in faith to the ultimate issues of existence. There was certainly some continuity with what had gone before, but there was also an important element of discontinuity that allowed for creative change to take place.

Conjectures about Personhood and Search for Immortality

The growing sense of selfhood, the anxiety about life's transience and death, and the penchant for critical thinking stimulated the Axial sages to conjecture about the nature of the person and spurred them to search within themselves for something that might be able to endure the dissolution of the body, for something eternal or immortal. As a part of this quest, the Axial sages evolved a new way thinking about the world and the place of humanity in it. One of the first scholars to study the sociological dimensions of the Axial Age, S. N. Eisenstadt, calls this way of looking at life "transcendental consciousness," that is, the ability to stand back and look at the world more comprehensively, as a totality, not simply to accept the world as it appears or as tradition says what it is, but to examine it more reflectively and critically.[10]

This transcendental consciousness was one of the sources that led the Axial sages to be open to new experiences and interpretations of the

Sacred. In some cases they were not content to accept the old anthropomorphic gods and goddesses as the highest powers or realities of the universe. They often understood their experience of ultimate reality as an Absolute that transcended the ancient gods of the older, pre-Axial religions. They interpreted the impact on them of ultimate reality in sublime terms, such as the Hindu notion of *Brahman* and the Chinese *Dao*, so great that they exceeded the human capacity to think or to speak about them.

Rejection of Violence

One of the important factors that motivated the Axial sages' critical thinking and religious creativity was a visceral and principled rejection of the violence of their times. The spiritual revolution of the Axial Age occurred in the context of turmoil, migration, and conquest. The sages of the Axial Age did not work in serene, ideal circumstances; rather they responded to the brutal violence they witnessed around them. In each Axial Age case, revulsion from violence and hatred proved to be a significant catalyst of spiritual change; they developed their traditions in societies that were marked with rigid egotism and torn apart by violence and warfare. The sages were not utopian dreamers, but practical men; some were preoccupied with politics and government. In India, the Axial Age began when the ritual reformers started to remove the conflict and aggression from the sacrificial ceremonies. Israel's Axial Age began in earnest after the destruction of Jerusalem and the forced deportation of the exiles to Babylonia, where the priestly writers began to develop an ideal of reconciliation and nonviolence. China's Axial Age evolved during the Warring States Period, when Confucians and Daoists discovered ways to counteract widespread lawless aggression.[11]

Conclusion

The concept of the Axial Age affirms a concentration of events "in which outstanding individuals emerged and were able to become centers of new religious awareness and understanding, so that from their work have developed what we know today as the great world religions."[12]

The fact that it took centuries for the fruits of these pioneers to become widely disseminated, and that pre-Axial religions still continued in isolated areas, should not obscure the great significance of the religious founders and their work. As Karl Jaspers observed, "What the individual achieves is by no means passed on to all. The gap between the peaks of human potentiality and the crowd became exceptionally great at that time. Nonetheless, what the individual becomes indirectly changes all. The whole of human took a forward leap."[13]

Experiences of the Founders of the Post-Axial Religions

The next step in our efforts to comprehend the essence of post-Axial religion is to explore the fundamental religious experiences that appear to be commonly shared by the Axial sages. As we proceed with this study, we must be careful to avoid the dangers of simplistic overview. As Geering remarks, "Human history, human society and even the solitary individual, are always more complex than any of the patterns or schemes into which we to try to press them."[14] But if we allow for this caveat, there are some significant observations that may be made about our subject. As Jaspers comments, the paths of the Axial religions toward liberation and salvation "are widely divergent in their convictions and dogma, but common to all of them is man's reaching out beyond himself by growing aware of himself within the whole of Being and the fact that he can tread them only as an individual on his own."[15] While there must have been thousands of people in the Axial areas who started to reflect on their experiences, our concern here is the consciousness achieved by the minority, that is, by the Axial sages. They stood out because of the intense, vivid, and continuous quality of their critical awareness. As their thinking became more and more vital, they carried their discovery of the potential of awareness to the heights. "In the best of moments, the most quick-witted people attained full self-reflective consciousness."[16]

The founders were members of the intellectual elite, exceptional persons who played the various roles of prophets, philosophers, wise men, hermits, wandering ascetics, solitary thinkers, authoritative teachers, and theologians. They lived in several parts of the world and worked independently, all during the same epoch. "Through these men the human race took a giant step forward in self-understanding; and religion passed over an important threshold."[17]

The experience of each of the founders was certainly unique, but they do have fundamental similarities. What follows is a descriptive presentation (ideal type) of the essential religious experiences common to the founders of the world religions. Based on an empathetic understanding of pertinent documents and diverse practices, it intends to make those shared experiences more or less comprehensible. The phenomena we focus on here are not so much the concepts of the Axial sages' thinking, but rather their feelings of alienation from the world and the attitudes of awe, faith, and obedience that stirred in their depths as a consequence of their spiritual quest.[18]

Two Worlds: Temporal and Sacred

The founders experienced the world as awry. They became convinced that it had gone askew, become problematic; that life was defective, unsatisfactory, lacking. Along with others who took part in the transformation of the Axial Period, the founding sages were consumed with a sense of helplessness, obsessed by their mortality, and gripped by a profound terror and alienation from the world. In their experience of disillusion and malaise, they felt that the spiritual practices they inherited from their ancestors no longer worked for them. They were desperately in need of a new solution.

As the thinking of the Axial sages became more and more single pointed, the sages grew in self-awareness, and this lifted them above the tangible world in which they lived and experienced as awry. This transcendence enabled them to see more objectively both the world and themselves. What they perceived provoked terror as well as a sense of their own limitations, their powerlessness, the inevitability of their death, the arbitrariness of their human actions and social arrangements. As their awareness sharpened even further, they began to catch sight of the Sacred: the entire stream of the transcendent order of reality, being as a whole, the single, originating, eternal absolute reality. The Sacred was revealed to the Axial sages, and they responded to that disclosure with feelings of awe, wonder, and fear.

They became conscious of two different and mutually exclusive worlds. There was the finite, physical, temporal world, in which they carried on life with its suffering and evil; this was the world in which they would die. There was the infinite, invisible, nonphysical, and timeless world where perfect bliss is to be enjoyed; this was the transcendent world of the Sacred. Experiencing a sharp disjunction between these two domains, they placed a high value on the transmundane world and reached out eagerly toward it. While their predecessors in pre-Axial times accepted life as it was and sought only to continue it on a stable basis, the Axial sages experienced the disturbing and yet uplifting thoughts of a limitlessly better possibility.

> In light of the Sacred and the possibilities it offered, the sages appraised their present defective, unsatisfactory life. Whereas in the various forms of pre-axial religion there had always been a realistic awareness of suffering, insecurity and mortality, in the great post-axial traditions these are now thought of in terms implying a contrast with something fundamentally different—whether that different state lies in the future (as also perhaps in the remote past) or in the unrealized depths of the present moment.[19]

A Rude Awakening

This growing consciousness of the Axial sages, the start of their full self-reflection, must have been a rude awakening. For the sight it opened to their perception was likely to have been of the great gulf between the newly discovered self and the dark mass that lay beyond the edge of their new awareness. This was their experience of consciousness not-yet-fully illuminated; their realization of being only partially aware of themselves, of other people and nature, only partially aware of the Sacred. This was, indeed, a rude awakening. For it deepened their primordial feeling of alienation, of painful separation, and it produced within them the need of salvation.

They yearned to cross the divide, to heal the separation, and to experience full awareness. They yearned to fill in the chasm between the mundane and the transmundane worlds, to rise above the tragic enigma of the immediate passing world and death, so as to experience another world transcending time and space. They became increasingly aware of these spiritual needs and placed strong emphasis on satisfying them. Striving to overcome alienation, reaching out for completeness and union with the Sacred became their ultimate concern.

Search for Salvation

How they dealt with the problem of alienation was the hallmark of the Axial sages. Their names survived because they recognized the profound implications of their growing awareness and satisfied their spiritual needs in ways that led to the creation of new forms of religion and philosophy.

> They started to explore the regions of human experience opened up for the first time by self-reflective consciousness, to expand the light of awareness so that it took in more and more of the domains of mind and the world. Not dimming that torch beam into pre-consciousness, not jealously hoarding the small golden disc of first illumination, they shone it around a bit, even spreading the light out in a widening cone.[20]

Expanding their awareness, they moved to the border between conscious and unconscious. "This border is the zone of further exploration. Evolution always works at the edge of awareness, testing and extending boundaries, and finally transcending them."[21] In search of salvation, they reached out toward things of the transmundane world.

The Sacred Within and the Response of Faith

As they strove for the Sacred, the sages became more aware of the finiteness of the world in which they lived and of their own human limitations. This led eventually to a discovery within themselves of new strengths and new possibilities. They began to experience in the depths of their humanity something absolute, something sacred. This was the first time in history humans gained awareness, and a structured conception, of a sacred reality deep within them. This is the "true self"[22]: beyond the fluctuation of mere sensory impression and deeper than the flux of everyday experience; a core self bound to and concealed within the body, laden with instincts and only dimly aware of itself.

> What is new about this age…is that man becomes conscious of Being as a whole, of himself and his limitations. He experiences the terror of the world and his own powerlessness. He asks radical questions. Face to face with the void he strives for liberation and redemption. By consciously recognizing his limits he sets himself the highest goals. He experiences absoluteness in the depths of selfhood and in the lucidity of transcendence.[23]

The Sacred was then, the sages realized, not only of the transcendent world; it was also of the specifically human within them, making it possible for them to transcend themselves in the experience and knowledge of the Sacred.

And now, by moving from the sacred true self within, they reached out and attained the summit of consciousness. There at the heights of transcendence, they saw things as they truly are, they grasped the fundamental structures of reality and participated actively in salvation. By the light of the sacred core within them, they awakened fully to the revelation of the Sacred and were enabled to embrace that holy disclosure in a faith imbued with awe and trust. In light of that disclosure they saw, even if only dimly, that the Sacred is not *a* Being separated from the human person. The Sacred, rather, is *Being Itself*, permeating the person while at the same time transcending him or her. The Sacred permeates the very core of the human as the transcending force or condition making possible the experience and knowledge of the Sacred; the Sacred is the source, sustainer, and final perfection of human beings. Consequently, the human person stands alone in the whole of the cosmos as the one being who is absolutely oriented toward the Sacred, and whose very definition and essence are determined by this orientation. Human beings are alive by a sacred principle that transcends them, over which they have no power, and that summons them to surpass themselves in religious activity.

The Common Characteristics of Post-Axial Religion

The sages of the Axial civilizations responded in faith to the revelation of the Sacred. Their religion was what they *did* about their faith. It was their faith expressed and embodied in a structured complex of beliefs and convictions, historically grounded myths, rites of self-surrendering devotional worship and supplication, interior journeys of prayer, meditation, and contemplation, social organizations, lifestyles, and works in conformity with ethical codes.

Ethical Component

The religious traditions founded by the sages were significantly different in many respects from their pre-Axial counterparts. The sages still valued ritual worship, but they gave it a new ethical significance and established morality as an indispensable component of the spiritual life.[24] The religious tradition of the Axial Age insisted on the great importance and value of compassion. When they looked for the cause of violence in the human psyche, the Axial sages delved into their interior world and started to explore a realm of consciousness that hitherto had been undiscovered. There they saw that the cause of aggression was the ego, which is identified with one's deepest self; violence is rooted in egotism as well as in greed, selfishness, fear, despair, hatred, rage. So, despite some differences of emphasis, there was a remarkable consensus in their call for a turning away from selfishness and a spirituality of compassion.

Universal Concern

The Axial sages were not interested in providing their disciples with a little edifying boost after which they might return to their ordinary self-centered lives. Their objective was to set forth a cure for the spiritual malaise of the time and create human beings of a wholly different kind, persons with empathy and committed to charity, to loving kindness. When the Axial sages confronted aggressive, violent customs in the religious traditions and institutional practices they inherited, they did not pretend those practices were not there but worked vigorously to eliminate them. And in regard to the violent behavior of the people in their societies, the most gifted of the sages realized that prohibiting brutal, violent conduct required more than issuing external directives; these would not impact the profound areas of the human psyche that lead to atrocious behavior. So in giving expression to their faith, the sages created programs of education and systems of prayer and action intended to touch the deeper, less conscious levels of the self. These are the "spiritual technologies" devised to overcome, on the one hand, the egotism largely responsible for violence, and, on the other, to promote sympathy, respect, and universal concern for humankind.

Furthermore, nearly all the Axial sages were convinced that an authentic spirituality could not confine its benevolence only to one's own people; a person's goodwill must extend somehow to the entire world. Each axial tradition devoted time to reflecting on the nature of goodness, and each evolved its own version of the "Golden Rule": *Do unto others what you would want them to do unto you*. What the sages created was a religious technology that utilized natural human resources and/or the grace of the Sacred to counter, on the one hand, egotism and its aggressive products and promote, on the other, sympathy, respect, kindness, generosity, universal concern.

A self-effacing, compassionate, and nonviolent lifestyle was just as important as participating in ritual worship and prayerful study of sacred scriptures. Even the god, Indra, was required to change his belligerent way of life and live as a humble Vedic student before he could comprehend the deepest truths of the tradition. Before an Indian aspirant could undertake a single exercise of mystical meditation, he was obliged to become proficient in *ahimsa*, the practice of nonviolence, never engaging in antagonism in a single word or gesture. Until this was an integral part of his very being, his guru would not allow him to proceed with his meditation. It was not a question of first establishing a reflective, critical belief in God and then living an ethical compassionate life. Spiritual practice of self-surrender to the Sacred and liturgical worship as well as sympathetic love for others were each an important component of an integral religious life.

Tolerance of Suffering

In their teaching about ethical behavior, the Axial sages insisted that relating to others with compassion and loving kindness must be done even in the midst of one's own suffering. Suffering, they claimed, was an inevitable fact of human existence. To retreat from this fact, to deny that it has anything to do with oneself, to cultivate an intentionally positive attitude that excludes anybody's pain but one's own—this may be a tempting choice, but for the Axial sages it was not an option. Persons who deny the suffering that marks all human life would be acting like false prophets. One can develop an empathetic compassion for others only if one admits one's own pain.

Self-Transcendence and Salvation

While the methodical cultivation of the spirituality of loving kindness for others, a mindset different from egotism and violence, would by itself engender an alternative, consciousness of self-transcendence, it was the integral whole of religious life that would lead to salvation. The impetus behind these religious expressions—creative, innovative paths that are widely divergent in their convictions and dogmas—was to satisfy the various needs of the Axial sages and their followers. Ultimately, this was to overcome alienation, achieve self-transcendence, and fulfill their need of salvation. Salvation, on one level, is bridging the chasm between the mundane and transmundane worlds and experiencing union with the Sacred already in human history. This temporal awareness of wholeness—experienced, for example, as surrendering to the Sacred in faith, hope, and love; or coming to oneself with Being; or as *unio mystica* in the disappearance of subject and object or in the coincidence of opposites—is reached by various paths or religious activities established by the Axial sages; they are known as the way of works, the way of devotion, and the way of knowledge.

The sages saw that, as a result of living the spiritualities they founded, they and their followers were introduced to a different and transcendent dimension of human experience. It was an *ekstasis,* a "stepping out" from one's habitual, self-bound consciousness that enabled them to apprehend a reality they called God, *nirvana,* Brahman, *atman,* or the Way of Heaven. They transcended themselves and were living beyond the confines of egotism. At the ultimate level, salvation is release from this world and lasting union with the Sacred in the world to come. Most often in the traditions of the Axial sages, this is not reached by human religious activity, but comes solely from the bestowal of the Sacred.

Notes

1. Karl Jaspers, *The Origin and Goal of History*, trans. Michael Bullock (New Haven: Yale University Press, 1953), 19.

2. Karen Armstrong, *The Great Transformation: The Beginning of Our Religious Traditions* (New York/Toronto: Knopf, 2006), xii.

3. John Hick, *An Interpretation of Religion: Human Responses to the Transcendent* (New Haven and London: Yale University Press, 1989), 29.

4. Ibid., 29.

5. Ibid., 31.

6. Ibid., 29.

7. Lloyd Geering, *Christian Faith at the Crossroads: A Map of Modern Religious History* (Santa Rosa, CA: Polebridge, 2001), 15–16.

8. Robin Cooper, *The Evolving Mind: Buddhism, Biology and Consciousness* (Birmingham, UK: Windhorse, 1996), 122–23.

9. Karen Armstrong, *Buddha* (New York: Viking, 2001), 12.

10. S. N. Eisenstadt, "Introduction," in *The Origins and Diversity of Axial Age Civilizations*, ed. S. N. Eisenstadt (Albany: State University of New York Press, 1986), 1–25.

11. Armstrong, *Great Transformation*, xiv.

12. Hick, *Interpretation of Religion*, 31.

13. Jaspers, *Origin and Goal of History*, 4.

14. Ibid., 21.

15. Ibid., 4.

16. Cooper, *Evolving Mind*, 128. Full self-reflective awareness includes being present to one's self as a subject, as an agent, as a center of experiences; recognizing that one's own self is autonomous and separate from other selves around one and is able to make deliberate decisions; being able to attend to the working of one's own mind, as well as to sense experience; possessing qualities like sympathy for others, a sense of the purpose of one's activities, and a creative imagination. The stage of full self-reflective consciousness enables a person to conceive of himself or herself as an independent agent with the faculty of knowing and choosing in accordance with his or her individual character. It gives a person the possibility of thinking problems through.

17. Geering, *Faith at the Crossroads*, 20.

18. Ibid., 17.

19. Hick, *Interpretation of Religion*, 33.

20. Cooper, *Evolving Mind*, 132.

21. Ibid., 134.

22. James Martin, *Becoming Who You Are: Insights on the True Self from Thomas Merton and Other Saints* (Mahwah, NJ: Hidden Spring, 2006).

23. Jaspers, *Origin and Goal of History*, 2.

24. Armstrong, *Great Transformation*, 390–99.

PART TWO

HISTORICAL DEVELOPMENT AND THE DEFINING CHARACTERISTIC OF THE POST-AXIAL RELIGIONS

From our study of the experiences of the Axial sages—the founders of the post-Axial religions—we have seen that the central, defining, and comprehensive reality they sought for themselves and for the adherents of the religions they founded was that of self-transcendence and salvation. While the adherents of the pre-Axial religions had been solely concerned with fulfilling humankind's basic, mundane needs of food, protection, and reproduction, the Axial sages, in contrast, were convinced that human beings do not live by bread alone; rather they need to nourish their spirits by communion with the transcendent, eternal world of the Sacred. Benjamin Schwartz notes:

> If there is nevertheless some common underlying impulse in all these "axial" movements, it might be called the strain towards transcendence....What I refer to here is something close to the etymological meaning of the word—a kind of standing back and looking beyond—a kind of critical, reflective questioning of the actual and a new vision of what lies beyond.[1]

This new striving involved a questioning of the actual mundane or worldly dimension of reality and a new perception of the sacred order that lies beyond it.

What the Axial sages experienced was the appearance of the Sacred: the single reality above, beyond, and over all tangible, visible, immediately available realities; beyond the physical, the psychological, the political, the economic, the cultural—the eternal, originating reality to which all other realities are oriented. The Sacred the Axial sages got sight of, and to which they aspired, was, in fact, the Absolute, the Transcendent.

In light of this new vision of the Sacred, the Axial sages, and the persons they impacted, asked new and radical questions about themselves, their world, and the cultural tradition they had inherited from the past. As a consequence of this critical reflection, humankind began to perceive the relation between the mundane and sacred orders and to consider the problem of how to breach the distance between them. The problem they pondered and made efforts to solve was the challenge of salvation: how to unite this temporal world with the world of transcendence. They were aware of the past and believed that human beings had forgotten the fundamentals of human existence, and consequently the world had gone askew. Convinced of a sacred, absolute reality that transcended the confusions of this world, they sought to unite the conditions of daily life with the Transcendent and thus transform their present life into something radically and limitlessly better. In all the forms of post-Axial religion, the sacred Transcendent is that which makes possible a transformation of our present existence, whether by being drawn into fellowship with the transcendent Thou, or by realizing our deeper self as one with the Real (the Sacred), or by unlearning our habitual ego-centeredness and by becoming a conscious and accepting part of the endlessly interacting flow of life that is both *samsara* and *nirvana*.[2]

Religion consequently underwent an historical development and was transformed from a nature-oriented, pre-Axial type to a salvation type. Since the Axial Age, the ultimate concern of religions has been centered on the transmundane world and the fulfillment of the spiritual needs of transcendence, transformation of present existence, enlightenment, release, and salvation. For the first time in history, there is a conviction embodied in these religious traditions that the ultimate concern of human beings is no longer only with this world, but is rather to ensure, in another world that transcends time and space, the ultimate salvation of one's inner, true self. "From the point of view of [post-Axial religion] a man is no longer defined in terms of what tribe or clan he comes from or what particular god he serves but rather as being capable of salvation. This is to say that it is for the first time possible to conceive of man as such."[3] The quest, then, for salvation is the comprehensive, multidimensional structure of humankind's search for liberating union with, and self-discovery in, the Sacred, a characteristic that most distinguishes the post-Axial religions from their predecessors. This structure, in its fullest developed form, includes a self-transcending interior movement from egotism to a religious-ethical life of compassionate loving concern for all human beings, and of loving surrender, in history and at the end of time, to the Sacred.[4]

How this pursuit of salvation—this soteriological structure—came historically to characterize these religions is the main topic of the following seven chapters. The growth of religion from focus on this mundane world to the transcendent domain was not a solidly fixed design; it was a composite of changes or movements within a fluid medium, "like changes in the patterns of a river surface resulting from inflow from new sources."[5] The creative period of the Axial Age was not a clean break with the past; rather it was prepared for and anticipated by earlier movements, and since then has always been modified by elements of pre-Axial religions persisting within each of the great world religions and within the secular cultures today. Therefore, we trace the progressive development of each religious tradition from *pre-Axial roots* to its transformation as a *post-Axial religion*. What follows is not an exhaustive exploration of the religions, but rather a study that intends to make comprehensible the historical context in which each became shaped, in different specific configurations, by the soteriological quest, along with some other traits of the post-Axial religions.[6] Since an understanding of the historical development of this specific characteristic of the religions, and their other related attributes, is a vital preliminary to attaining our ultimate theological appraisal of them, it is explored extensively in the next seven chapters.

Notes

1. Benjamin I. Schwartz, "The Age of Transcendence," *Daedalus: Wisdom, Revelation, and Doubt* (Spring 1975), 3.

2. John Hick, *An Interpretation of Religion: Human Responses to the Transcendent* (New Haven and London: Yale University Press, 1989), 33.

3. Robert N. Bellah, *Beyond Belief: Essays on Religion in a Post-Traditional World* (New York and London: Harper & Row, 1970), 33.

4. Hick, *Interpretation of Religion*, 36.

5. Ibid., 29.

6. The chapters of part two are drawn from the following sources: Karen Armstrong, *The Great Transformation: The Beginning of Our Religious Traditions;* David S. Noss, *A History of the World's Religions* 12th ed. (Upper Saddle River, NJ: Prentice Hall, 2007); T. Patrick Burke, *The Major Religions: An Introduction with Texts* 2nd ed. (Malden, MA: Blackwell Publishing, 2004); "Introduction to the Prophets," *The New Jerusalem Bible* (New York: Doubleday, 1985; *The HarperCollins Dictionary of Religions* (San Francisco: HarperCollins Publishers, 1995); ed. John Bowker, *The Oxford Dictionary of Religions* (Oxford: Oxford University Press, 1997); Mark W. Muesse, *Religions of the Axial Age: An Approach to the World Religions*, parts 1–2 (Chantilly, VA: The Teaching Company, 2007); Paul J. Griffiths, "Rehabilitating Truth," review of *Truth and Tolerance: Christian Belief and World Religions*, Joseph Cardinal Ratzinger, *First Things*, May 2005 49–52; "Shinto," *Wikipedia:* http://www.en.wikipedia.org/wiki/Shinto; "Japan's Religion and Philosophy," *AsianInfo.org:* http://www.asianinfo. org/asianinfo/japan/religion.htm; Michael Pye, "A Tapestry of Traditions: Japanese Religions," reproduced from R. Pierce Beavers et al., *Eerdmans Handbook to the World's Religions* 1st American Edition (Eerdmans Publishing Company, 1982): http://www.sg.emb-japan.gojp/JapanAccess/religion.htm; "Religion in Japan," *Wikipedia:* http://www.en.wikipedia.org/wiki/Religion in Japan.

Chapter Three

ZOROASTRIANISM

To set the background for our study of Zoroastrianism and then of Hinduism, Jainism, and Buddhism, we focus first on the stepping stones to these traditions, that is, the ancient Aryans[1] and their pre-Axial religion.

The Aryans: An Ancient People

We begin with Central Asia in the millennium before the Axial Age by examining the cultural and religious practices of an ancient, loose-knit network of tribes that inhabited, from about 4500 BCE, the steppes of southern Russia, east of the Volga River and north of the Caspian Sea. Today this area is roughly the Ukraine to west Kazakhstan. Five thousand years ago, this territory was for the most part barren desert that had little rainfall and that suffered severe cold winters and unkind summers. A great deal is not known about these people of the Central Asian steppes in the pre-Axial period. But there is a consensus among scholars that they shared a common culture and identified themselves as the Aryans. Their name meant something like "noble" or "honorable" and, therefore, was not an ethnic or racial term but rather an assertion of their tribal pride. Because they spoke a language that would form the basis of several Asiatic and European tongues, they are also identified as Indo-Europeans. In the middle of the third millennium BCE, some of the tribes began a gradual migration to northern Europe, the northern Mediterranean region, as far west as Ireland, and southward to Iran and India. Careful analysis of the languages as diverse as Icelandic, German, Gaelic, Latin and Greek, Russian, Persian, Sanskrit, Sinhalese, and English has determined that these languages derive from what was once a single language. Over a period of time, the descendents of these Central Asians dispersed through Eurasia, and this single language developed into the dozens of tongues and dialects that are referred to as the Indo-European family of languages.

Of the several groups that migrated from the Central Asian region, we are most interested in those who traveled southward into regions now occupied by the countries of Iran and India. To distinguish this group from the other members of the Indo-European peoples, we refer to them as *Indo-Iranians*. These people remained together on the Caucasian steppes until about four thousand years ago, when they slowly drifted apart and migrated in two separate directions. The Iranian branch entered into and remained in Iran, while some of them ventured further into Mesopotamia, the area of present-day Iraq. The Indo branch immigrated into Afghanistan and then into the Indus Valley, gradually expanding across northern India. As the Indo-Iranians separated, their languages evolved from one another, but because they were similar enough, communication was still possible. The Iranian tribes spoke a dialect we call *Avestan* because now it only exists in a collection of sacred scriptures known as the *Avesta*. The group that migrated to India spoke a form of the language we now know as Sanskrit.

When each group arrived at its final destination, they called their new territory "the land of the nobles." For the sake of clarity, we use the term *Indo-Aryans* to refer to the group that settled in India and the word *Iranians* to identify the group that ended up in Iran. In what follows we focus on these two groups before they split, when they were united in Central Asia and beginning their southward movement. For this period we simply call them the Indo-Aryans.

Indo-Iranian Life and Religion

What we know about the Indo-Iranians comes mainly from two sources: the *Rig Veda*, the oldest extant Indo-European text, and the *Avesta*, a somewhat later text from Iran; both were originally kept in oral tradition. Because these documents were composed before the split, they communicate not a small part about the life of the Indo-Iranians. These people lived peacefully together and shared the same culture and religious traditions until about 1500 BCE.[2] They were arranged into tribes with no formal governing structures. As nomadic and semi-nomadic shepherds and cattle herders, they wandered about in relatively small areas, seeking pastureland for their animals. Because they had no real enemies, and no desire to conquer new territories, they were a peaceful people with a static, sedentary existence. Since they had not yet learned to tame horses, the earliest Indo-Iranians did not travel far, and they knew nothing about the kind of warfare that the horse made possible for other ancient societies. It seems they existed for centuries with hardly any significant cultural changes.

As much as it can be reconstructed from our limited resources, the simple and serene religion of the Indo-Iranians was based on a commonsensical view for people living in a harsh environment of Central Asia. Like other pre-Axial peoples, they had their gods, their beliefs about the nature of the world, and their rituals that enabled them to understand and influence those gods and that world.

The gods were of several kinds, related to the various aspects of everyday life. Especially important to the common people were the gods who controlled parts of the natural world, like the Sky and the Earth, the Sun and the Moon. In addition to these gods of nature, the deities associated with ritual practices were particularly important, namely the Fire, the Water, and a vision-inducing substance called *haoma* in the Avestan dialect and *soma* in Sanskrit. These divinities had special significance for the priests.

A third category of divine beings was the *ahuras* in Avestan, or *asuras* in Sanskrit, words that simply mean "lord." The greatest of the *ahuras* was Mazda, the Lord of Wisdom. Later, in the Zoroastrian religious reform, we will see how Lord Mazda is given a very prominent role, becoming the most important god of all Iranians. And finally, there were many lesser divinities called "the shiny ones": *deva* in Sanskrit and *daeva* in Avestan. The shiny ones represented such qualities as courage and justice.

In addition to this complex world of spirit and gods, the Indo-Iranians believed in a more abstract and impersonal principle of order. Those who spoke Sanskrit called it *rta,* and the Avestan speakers referred to it as *asha.* Both words signify a type of natural law that preserved cosmic order, maintaining the sun on its path and the seasons following in proper sequence. *Rta* and *asha* had a moral as well as a cosmological dimension, and in this sense meant an absolute principle for appropriate human behavior and for divine behavior, since the deities themselves were also obliged to conform to *rta* and *asha.*

Conformity to the moral law promoted harmony and well-being for the individual and for society. But the principle of order was opposed by another power that accounted for disharmony and chaos; by the Iranians it was called *druj.* Since these two principles were diametrically opposed to one another, the Indo-Iranians thought it necessary to help maintain and strengthen *asha,* the element of order. They were convinced they could do this by means of ritual. Proper observance of the religious rites thus enhanced the force of *asha* and promoted harmony in the world. This is one instance of the pre-Axial practice of cosmic maintenance, founded on the responsibility that people experienced for collaborating with the processes on which their lives depended.

Indo-Iranian Creation Story

We observe how these ritual practices promoted social and cosmological harmony. To understand pre-Axial rituals in any culture, it is important to have a grasp of its belief about the origins of the world as treated in its cosmologies or creation stories. Those who perform religious rites often understand themselves as reenacting the divine work of creation and thereby renewing creation. To illustrate this, we consider the world's creation taken from the Avestan texts and then show its relationship to ritual practices.

The Indo-Iranians' creation story in the Avestan version states that the Earth was created in seven stages. First, the sky was depicted as a gigantic inverted bowl made of beautiful stone. Second, water was created, covering the bottom of the sky shell. Third, solid earth was brought into being, floating on the water. In the fourth, fifth, and sixth stages, life was added in the form of one plant, one animal, a bull, and one man with the name of Yima or Yama. In the seventh stage, fire was added. In a last act of creation, the gods performed the first ritual sacrifice. By crushing and dismembering the plant, the bull, and the man, they created new life. The world now was populated and began the course of *asha* by means of death and reproduction.

Indo-Iranian Rituals

In a setting of rituals of various sorts, the Indo-Iranians reenacted the primordial sacrifice to preserve the cosmic and moral order and to ensure that new life properly replaced the old. The rituals performed were of many types, from the simple to the complex.

Those that were the simplest were offerings of libations to the gods of Water and Fire. In the arid and cold regions of Central Asia, the importance of these two elements is evident. Water was given a libation of milk and plant leaves to symbolize the animal and vegetable domains. These libations gave back to the divine powers the necessary elements that they needed to continue productivity and harmony. The Water goddess was fortified by these gifts. Fire had great importance for warmth in the cold of winter and for the cooking of food stuffs. Offerings to Fire, like libations to Water, were from the two realms: incense and wood from plants and animal fat from cooked meat. Melting fat made the flames blaze up, strengthening the fire.

The most sacred of the fire rituals often involved blood offerings, usually of goats, sheep, or cattle. This was done to replenish the energies the gods used to maintain world order and to obtain from them other practical goods. It was believed that the sacrifices placed an obligation on the deities worshiped to respond with benefits of purely material and mundane value, such as wealth, health, abundant harvests, and security. It should be noted that since they felt very close to their cattle and desired to respect the sacred life that united all creatures,[3] the ritualistic slaughter of a beast was executed in a humane manner, and its spirit consecrated to the sacred archetypical domestic animal. Consecrated and cooked meat offered to the gods was then eaten by the participants of the sacrifice. Because of their respect for animal life, the Indo-Iranians ate only consecrated meat of their domesticated animals. Even before killing a wild animal for food, hunters said prayers to assure the safe return of the animal's sprit to the Soul of the Bull. The Aryans would never lose this deep respect for the *spirit* that they shared with others, and this would become an important principle of their Axial Age. And as they came to realize that it was necessary that other creatures give up their lives in sacrifice so that others may live and the cosmos continue in existence, self-sacrifice became highly valued. No progress, material or spiritual, could be made without self-sacrifice. This too would become one of the principles of the Axial Age.

The priest conducted rituals that also involved a beverage known by *soma* in Sanskrit or *haoma* in Avestan. This substance, regarded as a deity, was found in a special species of plant whose identity is unknown today. Soma's properties induced in those who imbibed it to feel ecstatic, liberated from their ordinary world and transported to the realm of the gods. By drinking soma, the Indo-Iranians experienced what they believed to be the apex of existence: a temporary ecstasy that gave a sense of immortality, freedom from suffering and fear, communion with the gods and the spirits, and intense pleasure. Soma, then, was the means of expanding the mind to ponder the deepest possibilities of human existence; it gave a glimpse to the Indo-Iranians of a life free of suffering and fear. In the centuries to come, those who inherited their traditions would endeavor to seek similar experiences by means of meditation and ascetic practices rather than by physical substances.

Conclusion

We have now come to that time in history that marks the eve of the Axial Age, even though further developments in Indo-Iranian religions will occur before it dawns. But we are now able to make some statements about Indo-Iranian religion and culture that will facilitate our understanding of the Axial transformation that will come about in Iran and later in India. We have seen that the main purpose of religion for these peoples at this time was to collaborate with the gods and goddesses, or with an abstract impersonal principle, in the processes and functions of life. They were convinced that they experienced a close affinity with various aspects of the natural and divine worlds, and that it was necessary for them to do their part in keeping both the natural and social worlds in good working order, and it was clear that they had a close relationship with other aspects of the natural and divine worlds.

As supported by religious practices that promoted cosmic maintenance and keeping the world working in an orderly fashion, their culture was fairly conservative and not especially interested in change. Critical thinking and innovation in such societies tended to be viewed with suspicion and frequently looked upon even as sacrilegious since it represented departure from the primordial acts of the gods.

Indo-Iranians on the Threshold of the Axial Age

In spite of the conservative forces operative in the Indo-Iranian culture, the way of life of these people did eventually undergo dramatic changes. We discuss these changes now and their consequences for religious life on the threshold of the Axial Age.

Aggression Begins

As the Indo-Iranians drifted south from the Central Asian steppes, they came in contact with one of the great civilizations of the ancient world, that of the highly advanced people of Mesopotamia. Around 1500 BCE, they began to trade with them, and from them they learned about the making of bronze weaponry and how to domesticate the horse and how to construct and use war chariots. As they mastered the skill of taming the wild horses of the steppes and harnessing them to their chariots, they experienced the exhilaration of mobility and long-distance travel. And thus the tranquil and serene life of the Aryans came to an end. Their access to the chariot and the implements of war completely disrupted their once-stable culture. A new method of livelihood now surfaced to supplement the passive tending of sheep and cows; this was stealing sheep and cows. Many of the later Indo-Iranians became cattle rustlers who conducted fierce attacks on neighboring settlements, engaging in raiding and stealing cattle and crops.

Violence escalated on the steppes and a heroic age began. "Might was right, chieftains sought gain and glory; and bards celebrated aggression, reckless courage, and military prowess."[4] The Sanskrit-speaking Aryans, who had become cattle rustlers, no longer cherished the values of their old religion concerning reciprocity, self-sacrifice, and kindness to animals. Their new fundamental purpose was to gain wealth and glory. For a long time, cattle and sheep had been the measure of prosperity among the Indo-Iranians. In addition to providing meat and milk, the animals were the source of leather and bones for tools, dung for fire, and also urine for the consecration of sacred implements used in rituals.

The violence of raiding not only changed the economy of the Indo-Iranians, it also upset their moral concerns and respect for the law. The pillaging cattle rustlers showed little concern for the weak and defenseless; whole villages might be destroyed in an afternoon just to enhance another clan's livestock holdings. As a result of this new way of life, there emerged a third class of individuals alongside the priests and the producers: the warlords and professional warriors. This new class soon became known for their love of rough living, hard drinking, and gambling. "There was an excitement and a thrill to living on the edge and outside the constraints of conventional society."[5] New gods who were more acceptable to the rising warrior caste began to appear and even dominate the forms of religion. Their hero was the god, Indra, the slayer of dragons, who rode in a chariot upon the clouds of heaven. As they fought, killed, and stole, they experienced themselves as one with Indra and the aggressive *devas* who had founded the world order by force of arms. Actually, by the time the *Rig Veda* got to India, Indra was already the dominant divine being. More than one-quarter of the one thousand hymns of praise are addressed to him alone.

Not all of the Indo-Iranians took on the cattle-rustling and village-pillaging style of life. And in fact a new type of nomenclature entered the vocabulary to identify and distinguish the two types of people. In ancient Iran, those who were the wicked ones, devoted to the way of disorder, were called *drujvants;* those who followed the old way of order, the path of stability, were call *ashavans.* The *ashavans* were shocked by the violent aggression of their kin. And because they believed that events on Earth always reflected cosmic events in the heavens of the gods, they concluded that the terrifying raids must have a divine prototype. Their fellow Aryans who hustled cattle and fought according to the model of Indra must be his earthly counterparts.

Zoroastrianism

Zoroastrianism was once the dominant religion of much of Greater Iran. Until about 2002 (CE), most of the published estimates for the world total of Zoroastrians were 100,000 to 125,000. Recent publications of many major encyclopedias and world almanacs indicate a population of 2 to 3.5 million.[6] Small Zoroastrian communities are found in India, Pakistan, and Iran, as well as major urban areas in the United States, Canada, the United Kingdom, Australia, and a worldwide diaspora. There are two main groups of persons who are adherents of this tradition: those of Indian Zoroastrian background, who are know as *Parsis* (or *Parsees*), and those of Iranian background. They are numerically small, but their influence in the present-day world is more than proportionate to their number. And from a historical point of view, the religion founded by Zoroaster is of inestimable significance.

Zoroaster is a later Greek translation of *Zarathustra*. Little is known about him. The leading scholar in this area, Mary Boyce, dates him around 1200 BCE. Most recent scholars place him somewhere before the beginning of the Axial Age. He lived in the eastern area of present-day Iran and came from a modest family living in semi-nomadic conditions, at a time when the cattle rustlers and outlaws were in the prime and *druj*, the principle of disorder, appeared to be dominating *asha*, the principle of order and harmony. Except from much later traditions and legendary sources, all the information we have about Zoroaster is from a text called the *Gathas*, or the verses, which are a part of the oldest *Avesta*, the basic scripture of Zoroaster's religion. It is believed that these verses were composed by Zoroaster himself as he was moved by forces of inspiration. They are written in an archaic dialect very close to the Sanskrit of the *Rig Veda*; they are not sermons and didactic statements but rather spontaneous prayers addressed to the deity.

Zoroaster: Priest and Prophet

The *Gathas* indicate that Zoroaster was a priest, an authorized specialist. He believed that Mazda was the greatest of the *ahuras*: he was the single divine transcendent source of everything that was good, Lord of Wisdom and Justice, different in kind from any other divinity.[7] In Mazda's retinue there were seven luminous beings—the "Holy Immortals"—who were also divine, each manifesting one of Mazda's benign attributes. It is probable that Zoroaster came to this position by reflection on the creation story, which claimed that in the beginning there had been one plant, one animal, and one human being. It was logical to assume that originally there had been one god.[8]

According to tradition, at the age of thirty he had a compelling mystical experience in which he was led into the presence of Ahura Mazda and six other resplendent beings known collectively as the *hepatad*, the "seven." There he was graced with a special disclosure that persuaded him that he had a new life goal, a new vocation: this was to oppose the popular polytheism of his time and to effect a religious reform, to call his people to practice a true and final religion based on faith in Mazda.

Zoroaster's response to his new life goal was both conservative and revolutionary. As a priest and prophet faithful to the tradition, he urged his fellow Iranians to return to a respect for the principle of good order and harmony. As an innovator, however, he added a new perspective to the traditional worldview that made it an extremely engaging vision of the world. His innovative theology of reform had two principle dimensions, both directed to simplification. First, with passion he urged worship of Ahura Mazda as the superior deity, greater even than Varuna, the other *ahuras*, and the seven luminous beings. He claimed that the other *ahuras* and divinities were simply emanations or partial manifestations of Mazda, who was the only uncreated God and the agent of the seven stages creation theme.

Monotheistic Tendency

His second innovation was to simplify the pantheon by attributing specific moral characteristics to the other deities. All the beings that constituted the ensemble of spirits, *daevas* and *ahuras* were now plainly associated either with good or with evil. Because the *daevas* like Indra were worshiped by cattle rustlers, whom Zoroaster called the "Followers of the Lie," he reserved the word *daeva* exclusively for the wicked gods and the word *ahura* for the gods who were good and just. In accord with this theological simplification, he also declared the existence of an independent evil deity among the *daevas,* an entirely evil supernatural being called *Angra Mainyu,* or later by the name of *Ahriman.* The source of everything evil was Angra Mainyu, the wicked deity believed to be equal in power and opposed to Lord Mazda. Angra Mainyu had inspired the cruelty of Indra and the cattle raiders, who allied themselves with him and decided to fight alongside him in his battle against the good. Zoroaster therefore conceived of two superior beings, one completely good and other completely evil, hooked in mortal battle since the beginning of time, each one fighting for victory of his principles and powers.

Zoroaster's faith, then, was in several deities, but nevertheless, there was a monotheistic tendency in his religious convictions. For Lord Mazda was believed to be the Supreme God, the first deity to exist, the creative source of the Holy Immortals, who were of "one mind, one voice, one act" with him and fought with him in war against the forces of evil (identified in later time with Satan).[9]

Fundamental Moral Option

In line with his experience of the good and the evil transcendent deities, he taught that each human being must make a choice between one or the other. Persons are not able to avoid the responsibility of associating themselves with good or with evil, and they are obliged to live accordingly. As the *daevas* had made a choice, individual human beings are also faced with a similar decision. Everything resolved to a simple, uncomplicated choice, a fundamental option. Are you on the side of the good or of evil? It should be noted here that this is one of the points at which Zoroaster anticipates the transformation of the Axial Age. Repeatedly, as our study of the religions of the Axial Age continues, we encounter this call to make a decision, fundamentally to align one's life with the good or the evil as it is experienced and conceived of by the Axial sages. It is a situation in which demands are made on persons as individuals to accept responsibility for the moral quality of their words and actions.

In cooperation with Lord Mazda, men and women were to oppose the violence that had destroyed the peaceful world of the steppes and to resist all forces of evil. A new era had dawned; everybody, gods and humans alike, were obliged to make a fundamental choice between good and evil. Good persons must no longer invite Indra into the sacred precinct and offer sacrificial worship. Instead their calling was to defeat the *daevas* and their wicked henchmen, the cattle raiders. Only with the power of Mazda could peace, justice, and security be secured in the steppes. While he continued in his life to receive the revelations of

Mazda, this initial visionary experience was a principle turning point in his life; it transformed him from a priest to a prophet.

The command given to Zoroaster was to mobilize his people in a holy war against the terror and violence of their environment and the evil in the human soul. While human beings are vulnerable to the suggestions of the evil forces, they are also endowed with freedom to determine their own actions, and therefore they are able to choose between right and wrong. It was Mazda's will and their religious duty to transcend their human weaknesses, believe in him, and freely choose what is good and virtuous. The eternal fate and salvation of each person would be determined by the choices he or she made between good and evil.

In the religion established by Zoroaster (which was originally called *Zarathustrianism*), life was now seen as a battlefield in which all persons had a role. This basic message and theology of Zoroaster were reinforced by the various rituals of Zoroastrianism. Men and women who had committed themselves to Mazda were to purify their environment from dirt and pollution. In their efforts to separate good from evil, they would liberate the world for Lord Mazda. They were to pray five times daily and counter the influence of evil by meditating on the menace of evil and falsehood. In their reflections they would see that the world was in a period of raging cosmic conflict, racing toward an apocalyptic conflict. Prayer was to be performed standing in the presence of fire. If the devotee was outside in natural setting, the fire might be the sun. The sun had now become closely connected with Ahura Mazda. Like their Indo-Aryan relatives, the Iranians followed the custom of keeping the sacred fire continuously lit. These fire rituals were actually a part of the Zoroastrian practice of purification. The elements that made up the world need to be made clean and uncontaminated. The Zoroastrians also celebrate seven major festivals, associated mainly with the rhythms of agricultural life.

Zoroaster believed that individual persons would be judged on the fourth day after their death. Those who were judged good were to be led to the heavens across a wide bridge. There in the heavens they would enjoy the company of Mazda and the other *ashavans*. Those who were judged evil were obliged to cross an extremely narrow bridge. Without fail, they tumbled as they crossed and landed in the abyss of hell, where they suffered painfully for their sins in the place ruled over by the Evil One.

Apocalyptic Conclusion

A final cosmic destiny was also envisioned by Zoroaster; the assignment to heaven or to hell was only temporary. He believed the history of all humankind was directed in a specific direction toward a unique end. In a final battle it was anticipated that Ahura Mazda would bring the present world order to an end and save all of creation by a complete triumphant victory over evil and establish a reign of right and truth. There would be a general resurrection, and in a final judgment the eternal fate of each person would be determined by the choices he or she had made between good and evil; the wicked would be wiped from the face of the world and, along with the evil god, Angra Mainyu, sent to hell. The universe would be restored to its original pristine condition. Those human beings who had been observant of the divine will and were saved would be rewarded with everlasting life in heaven in union with Mazda; they would be like gods, free from sickness, old age, and mortality.

Zoroaster was unlike his contemporaries around the world in that he saw time moving forward in a linear fashion, from a beginning to a final apocalyptic conclusion. The end of the world would come in the universal battle between good and evil to a final climax. Then the forces of good would prevail and the devil would be completely crushed and banished from all existence. The Evil One and his associates, as well as hell and all its dwellers, would be exterminated, and paradise would be established on Earth.

It is possible that Zoroaster connected this vision of the final end with a bodily resurrection of the dead; those who had initially gone to heaven would return to Earth to continue life, joined again with their material parts. It seems too that Zoroaster anticipated the coming of a savior or apocalyptic judge who would play a role in the final drama. The Avestan texts allude to this future redeemer as a *saoshyant*. The *saoshyant* would be born of a virgin who had conceived by bathing in a lake in which Zoroaster's semen had been miraculously preserved.

Zoroaster's Innovative Concepts

These ideas—a grand cosmic struggle between good and evil, time progressing toward a final apocalyptic climax, the appearance of a redeemer-judge, the resurrection of the dead, and the need of humans to choose sides—all comprise Zoroaster's innovative concepts. "We can't say for certain that all these ideas originated with him; perhaps he was in conversation with like-minded persons or with ancient traditions. But we can say that it was through Zoroaster's influence and prophetic message that these ideas were widely decimated among the Iranians."[10] Mark W. Muesse points out the features that made Zoroaster's vision so compelling to many of his contemporaries:

> First, Zoroaster's vision implied a decisive role for human beings. To Zoroaster, people were not the pawns of the gods. The gods did not intervene and fool with the lives of hapless human beings. Persons had a choice to make, and that choice was essential. It determined the individual's future and shaped the cosmic drama itself. The gods were at war, and human beings had to act to ensure the side of right prevailed. In this way Zoroaster greatly elevated the importance of human moral responsibility.[11]

On the whole, the call to this kind of personal choice and obligation is an innovation in the history of religions because it is connected with fresh ideas about what it means to be human. For Zoroaster, the moral and religious decision of the individual now determines the status and quality of his or her personal destiny. The future existence of a person, especially in the world to come, depends on one's behavior here and now in history. So to the simple choice concerning the decision for the good or for evil, Zoroaster added another reality. The individual's ultimate destiny was dependent on the choice he or she made. He was of the conviction that a person's final end as a human being was contingent on whether he or she opted for the wholly good Mazda or the wholly evil Ahriman. This idea is something new for the times and common across the axial centers.

It should be noted that while we are with Zoroaster, we are in pre-Axial times, just on the threshold of the Axial Age. And for that time in history the notion of the moral choice and its consequences for the future constituted a remarkable concept. The first atypical element about it is its implication that the individual person in fact has a destiny beyond this historical life. Before the dawning of the Axial Age such a belief was not widely accepted. It is true that some may have had the belief that prominent individuals like the king were favored with a life after death. But even these notions were rarely well defined and clearly developed. With the coming of the Axial Age, however, the thought that individuals might have a destiny in a world to come came to be more commonly accepted.

But even more unusual was Zoroaster's claim that one's prospects for a life hereafter were contingent on the quality of one's moral choices. Even in those civilizations that held to a conception of an afterlife, very rarely was one's destiny dependent on one's moral behavior. An individual's existence after death might be predicated on the effectiveness of ritual practice, whether or not one had pleased the gods with sacrifices of enough quality, or perhaps on the doing of exceptional deeds, such as heroic bravery in battle. But seldom do we find the claim before the Axial Age that the individual's destiny is contingent on moral decision and behavior. This is in fact one of the important themes of the Axial transformation.

Mark W. Muesse also underlines the important way Zoroaster's vision gave meaning to human suffering and promised ultimate reward for it.

> Those suffering from an unkind fate from thieves and cattle rustlers, from illness and deprivation could see their plight in much larger context. Their anguish and misery was part of a grand drama involving the entire world and was not just bad luck or random happenstance. For their suffering the righteous would be given ample reparations. Immortal life in paradise—free of any and all evil—would suffice to make earthly suffering seem insignificant by comparison. And they would be satisfied by the sense the evil ones, too, would receive their just deserts.[12]

Foreshadowing the Axial Age

Zoroaster's teaching was based on a cosmic combat between good and evil, a traumatized vision that was vengeful and filled with imagery of burning, terror, and extermination. It inspired a militant spirituality. In this sense it participated in the piety of pre-Axial religion. In making a cosmic agon between good and evil central to his message, Zoroaster belongs to the old spiritual world. However, because his vision was passionately ethical, he did look forward to the Axial Age. For he tried to bring some morality to the ethos of war: heroes were to make efforts to counter aggression and not to terrorize their fellow creatures; the holy warrior was dedicated to peace; those who opted to fight for Lord Mazda were characterized by the virtues of patience, discipline, courage; they were to defend all good creatures from the assaults of the wicked. When Zoroastrians defended the weak, cared for their cattle, and purified their natural environment, they became bonded with Mazda and joined the struggle of the Immortals against the Hostile Spirit. Consequently, because of his strong emphasis on ethics, Zoroaster foreshadowed the Axial sages who came centuries later and made efforts to counter the cruelty and aggression of their time by promoting spirituality based on nonviolence.

Opposition, Growth, and Impact

In spite of its being rooted in ancient Aryan tradition, Zoroaster's vision was received with strong hostility. The people of his time found it too difficult, and some were shocked by his belief that all persons, not just the elite, could reach salvation. The established religious authorities opposed his teaching because it threatened to undermine their own traditional doctrine. After years of preaching to his own tribe, Zoroaster gained only *one* convert! Eventually he departed from his village and found a patron in the chief of another tribe, who established the Zoroastrian faith in his territory. One tradition states that Zoroaster was killed by rival priests who were furious because of his rejection of the old religion. By the end of the second millennium BCE, the Avestan Aryans had migrated and settled in eastern Persia, where Zoroastrianism became the national religion.

It should be noted that parallels exist between Zoroastrianism and some of the doctrines of the Middle Eastern religions. In Judaism and

Christianity, parallels may be found with Zoroaster's doctrine of transcendence and salvation: the end of the world, the resurrection, heaven and hell, immortality, the last judgment, and God's operation through the Spirit. In the beliefs of Islamic Arabs, parallels can be observed with the vision of the approaching last judgment foretold by Zoroaster, and then by Jews and Christians. One may wonder whether the parallels among the traditions are coincidental or whether there has been some actual historical influence from one tradition to the others. This has been, and still remains, a controversial issue. Some scholars working in this area propose that formative Judaism, Christianity, and Islam were shaped directly or indirectly by the more ancient Zoroastrian beliefs. "This influence," states Mark Muesse,

> is difficult to document and prove conclusively because the case is based largely on circumstantial evidence. There are no passages in the Bible or the Qur'an that quote from the Gathas or even paraphrase it....Early Jewish and Christian theologians probably never read any of the Zoroastrian scriptures because most of Zoroaster's religion remained in oral tradition for centuries.[13]

We may hold that if there was infiltration of Zoroastrian ideas, perhaps it occurred in a less formal way as Jews came into contact with Zoroastrian adherents and engaged in conversation and trade with them and observed their practices. In any case, there are no valid grounds to detract from the conviction of Jews, Christians, and Muslims that their religions are unique and of divine origin.

With the rise of Islam, the twelve hundred years of Zoroastrian imperial history came to an end in the seventh century CE. Within one hundred years of the Arab conquest, many Zoroastrians departed from Persia. In the tenth century, a band of Zoroastrians sought religious freedom in India, where they are known as *Parsis*, people of Pars (Persia). There the original teaching endures to the present. And Zoroaster is often revered more than a prophet, almost as a manifestation of the divine. For all Zoroastrians, he is the great role model, the strong defender of the true faith, the uncompromising enemy of evil, and the supporter of all that is good. In modern times it is estimated, as we have seen, that there are 2 to 3.5 million Zoroastrians in the world.

Notes

1. Here the term *Aryans* is to be distinguished from the same term as used by Adolph Hitler. He twisted the theories of the German archeologist and ethnohistorian Gustaf Kossinna (1858–1931) to put forward the Aryans as a master race of Indo-Europeans, who were supposed to be of Nordic appearance and directly ancestral to the Germans.

2. Mary Boyce, *Zoroastrians: Their Religious Beliefs and Practices* (London, Boston and Henley: Routledge & Kegan Paul, 1979), 2; Peter Clark, *Zoroastrianism: An Introduction to an Ancient Faith* (Brighton, Portland, UK: Sussex Academic Press, 1998), 18.

3. Mircea Eliade, *The Myth of the Eternal Return, or Cosmos and History*, trans. Willard R. Trask (London: Routledge & Kegan Paul, 1955), 1–34.

4. Karen Armstrong, *The Great Transformation: The Beginning of Our Religious Traditions* (New York/Toronto: Knopf, 2006), 7.

5. Mark W. Muesse, *Religions of the Axial Age: An Approach to the World's Religions* (Chantilly, VA: Teaching Company, 2007), part I, 39.

6. *Major Religions of the World Ranked by Number of Adherents*. Available at: http://www.adherents.com/Relgions_By_Adherents.html.

7. Clark, *Zoroastrianism*, 4–6.

8. Boyce, *Zoroastrianism*, 20–23

9. *Yasna* 19:16–18. Quotations from the Zoroastrian scriptures are taken from Mary Boyce, ed. and trans., *Textual Sources for the Study of Zoroastrianism* (Totowa, NJ: Barnes & Noble Books, 1984); cited in Armstrong, *Great Transformation*, 8. The term *Yasna* refers to the Zoroastrian daily liturgy of preparation of *haoma* and offerings to Fire and Water; the term, as used here, also refers to the title of the text recited in the ceremony.

10. Muesse, *Religions of the Axial Age*, part I, 55.

11. Ibid.

12. Ibid., 55–56.

13. Ibid., 57.

Chapter Four

HINDUISM

From Iran we move to South Asia and the pre-Axial culture of what came to be northwestern India. We first examine the indigenous Indus Valley culture, whose religious practices were centered on goddess worship and fertility rites. Then we go on to study the migration of the Indo-Aryans, the descendents of the Indo-Iranians who traveled to South Asia and encountered the Indus culture. We examine the elements of both Indus and Indo-Aryan religions to prepare for the examination of the Axial transformation of the Indian religion. The meeting of these traditions—that of the Indo-Aryans and that of the Indus Valley culture—produced deep changes for the Indus religion and ultimately provided the basis for the Hindu family of religions.

We start with a sketch of India prior to the Axial ferment to help us understand the transformations that led to the birth of Hinduism, Buddhism, and Jainism. We look at the Indus culture and civilization that flourished along the Indus River Valley at least fifteen hundred years before the Indo-Aryans migrated into what is now Pakistan and the Punjab regions of India. This civilization was in decline by the time the Aryans settled in this area, around 1500 BCE.

Indus Valley Culture

The Indus civilization was the largest of the ancient world. Archeologists have uncovered more than seventy cities in an area about the size of Texas. The largest of these urban centers, remarkably well planned and organized, may have contained as many as fifty thousand inhabitants at one time. From the absence of any significant weapons among the archeological artifacts, we infer that the Indus civilization

63

was relatively peaceful. It is also evident that agriculture was the basis of their economy, along with trade with the Mesopotamians living along the Tigris and Euphrates rivers. In regard to our knowledge of their religion, we have only informed speculation on the material artifacts of the ruins. No textual evidence is available to corroborate scholarly inferences.

We are able to say that religious practices of the pre-Axial Indus dwellers were significantly concerned about the functions of sexuality and procreation, and that concern, mixed with fascination and anxiety, most likely encompassed the human, the animal, the plant, and the divine realms. It may be that a mother goddess, and perhaps animals themselves, were worshiped to help ensure fertility and fecundity on all levels of life. And finally, the design of the cities and ritualistic practices indicate a deep preoccupation with maintaining restraint and order.

This sketch of the Indus religions suggests that beliefs and practices were oriented toward the present historical life on Earth and not toward a life hereafter. Nothing in the ruins indicates that the Indus dwellers thought much about an afterlife or even pondered about what might be in store for the individual beyond death. Ritual practices and sacrifices appear to be exclusively for the purpose of maintaining order in the here and now. Religion served a conservative function in this culture; it was aimed at keeping the world as it is by harnessing its powers and respecting its boundaries. And for a millennium and a half, the Indus religion succeeded at achieving this goal. Little seems to have changed in the life of this civilization during its life span of fifteen hundred years.

The Indus culture was already in decline by 1500 BCE, and it did reach an end about the time the "Indo" branch of the Indo-Aryans, with their predilections for war and conquest, migrated gradually and relatively peacefully into the Indus region. With the Indus people who still remained there, the Aryans probably coexisted for a time. As we have seen, the Indo-Aryans were initially pastoral nomads, and by the time they entered India, they were skilled in horsemanship, the use of chariots, and the manufacturing of bronze. They organized themselves in tribes led by chieftains and referred to themselves as the "Noble Ones," the literal meaning of *Aryan*. From this point on in our study of India, instead of the compound Indo-Aryan, we will use the term *Aryan*, since that is how they designated themselves.

When the Aryans migrated into India, they brought with them a belief in a pantheon of gods, an understanding of human beings, a worldview and a set of rites based on their revealed scriptures, the *Vedas*. In the discussion that follows, we focus on the integral Indian religious heritage as it evolved from the religion of the Vedic Age to its maturity as classical Hinduism. This development is traced in the following sacred writings that follow in historical succession, and that together make up an important portion of the collection of Hindu scriptures: the *Vedas*, the *Brahmanas*, the *Aranyakas*, the *Upanishads*, and the *Bhagavad-Gita*. As we explore this evolution, we shall see how India's major spiritual tradition gradually took on the comprehensive soteriological characteristic of a post-Axial religion.

Rig Veda

The Ritualists

During the second millennium BCE, some of the Sanskrit Aryans had begun a migration to the south and eventually colonized the Indus Valley. There, as their warriors carried on exploits of stealing the cattle of the indigenous communities, their learned elite, the *rishi*, composed the earliest hymns of the *Rig Veda*. These compositions express the religious genius of their authors; they are considered to be the most prestigious portion of the Vedic scriptures, as well as the foundations of the Indian Axial Age and the later Hindu religion. The Vedic scriptures are regarded today by traditional Hindus as the oldest and most sacred scripture, the written expression of divine revelation, containing the profound secrets of the universe. According to traditional belief, the *Vedas* have no author; they were revealed to certain ancient sages by reality itself. The oldest of the *Vedas*, the one most pertinent for our purposes, is the *Rig Veda*. It contains more than a thousand hymns to various god and goddesses. Its origin is pre-Axial and is generally considered to date between 2300 and 1200. The hymns were preserved for centuries in oral tradition, and most likely were not written down until well after the Axial Age.

From these scriptures we know about the religion of the early Aryan colonizers of India. It involved ritual sacrifice to the gods for the purpose of obtaining from them the necessary goods for a comfortable and pleasant life in the present time. The gods, known in Sanskrit as *devas*, were believed to dwell on Earth, in the heavens, and in the midspace between heaven and Earth. It was understood that most of the *devas* had specific functions or domains associated with them. For instance, Indra, the supreme deity, was the god of war who led the Aryans into battle and was looked upon as the model soldier. As understood by Zoroaster, Indra was one of the main *devas* related to chaos and evil. Indra also ruled over the waters of heaven that brought the rains and monsoons. Agni was the divine fire who inhabited the Earth in the domestic fireplace, the hearth. He was also found in midspace as lightning and in heaven as the fire of the sun. Agni was versatile and acted as the mediator between the gods and humans and therefore had a place in the Aryan religious rites. There was also Surya, the god of the sun; Yama, the king of death; Ushas, the goddess of the dawn; Kubera, the *deva* of wealth and prosperity. In addition to these deities, there were a whole host of lesser divine beings of different ranks and qualities, including the *asuras* whom the Aryans considered evil.

The heavenly wars between the various deities were ritually reenacted by the Aryans in their cattle raids, and in this process they made their warfare into holy sacrificial offerings that transformed and united them with Indra. Their sacrificial rites, which legitimized and gave sacred significance to the destructive cycle of raid and counter-raid, were severely aggressive and competitive. They were sometimes occasions of solemnity but also of rowdy carnivals. The ancient Vedic religion was inspired by ceaseless migration, violent ritualistic action, cattle raiding, and appropriation of new territory.

The Self-Understanding of the Aryans

From the structure and performance of the rituals, the Aryans gained an understanding of the meaning of being human. For instance, in the few hymns of the *Rig Veda* concerning death, we get some sense of the Aryan perspective on the human self and the meaning of human life. In those hymns we see that the Aryans regarded death as an occasion for sadness and grief, since life on Earth was precious and something to be held on to for as long as possible. But there is no indication that death terrified the Aryans. Nothing in the *Vedas* indicates that life after death might be unpleasant and tortuous.

But in the *Vedas* we see a rather wide-ranging conjecture about the possible fates of those who undergo death. In one verse, the individual who has died is believed to travel to heaven, carried along by the fires of cremation, where he or she is united with the ancestors and the gods in a pleasant postmortem life. In another verse of the same hymn, the individual dissolves into the elements of the natural world. Still later, according the same hymn, the body of the deceased person is "cooked" by the funeral pyre to prepare it for a sacrifice to be consumed by the gods. In other Vedic hymns, it is suggested that the soul goes down to the underworld ruled by Yama, the god of death. The *Vedas*, then, do not agree about the final destination of human beings. Nor do they give a consensus about what determines one's final end. It appears, sometimes, that the correct performance of sacrifices and other rituals is what decides one's destiny. Sometimes other deeds are decisive, such as fighting in a battle or giving gifts to the priests. Sometimes it seems that one's final end has no relationship at all with how one lives his or her life. It is quite clear, however, that the *Vedas* make no unambiguous and sure pronouncement that an individual's destiny is related to moral choices in the way that Zoroaster linked moral decision and destiny.

The Rituals of the Aryans

We investigate now the dimension of Aryan religion that unites the divine and the human realms. Rituals, central to Aryan life, gave meaning to everything from the creation of the universe to the death of the individual. They are at the very heart of pre-Axial religious life in ancient India. They provide us with the basis for understanding the dramatic transformations that occur as the Axial Age begins.

In our first look, previously, into the religious environment of ancient India, we observed a world of gods and goddesses controlling the various aspects of life that were of special concern to the inhabitants of the Indus Valley and their Aryan successors. The interest of the Indus dwellers and the Aryans had in their gods appeared to focus on the ways these powerful beings could help sustain and enhance life on Earth. Gods and goddesses were called upon to facilitate reproduction, render aid in battle, and stave off sickness.

Their rituals were supported by a complex belief structure. Hymn 121 of the tenth book of the *Rig Veda* illustrates this complexity in a creation story about Purusha, the massive cosmic man, who was larger than the physical universe itself, and the primordial sacrificial victim. In this hymn the *rishi* expressed ideas that would become one of the seminal myths of the Indian Axial Age. There he conveyed a vision of a creator god who rose from a primal chaos, a personalized form of the brahman, whose name was Prajapati, the All. Prajapati was identical with the universe; he was the power that sustained it, the seed of consciousness, and the light that emerged from the waters of unconscious matter; but he also was a spirit that transcended all of creation. Immanent and transcendent, only he was "God of gods and none beside him."

To another *rishi*,[1] this seemed much too explicit. He claimed in the beginning there was nothing. There was no existence and no nonexistence, neither death nor immortality. But how could this confusion become ordered and viable? The poet concluded that there could be no answer to this question. So he and his audience were reduced to silence.

Finally, in the famous Purusha Hymn, a *rishi* reflected on the ancient creation story of the Aryans and established the foundation for India's Axial Age.[2] He remembered that the sacrifice of the first man had brought the human race into existence. Then he described this primordial Person (Parusha), walking voluntarily into the sacrificial ground, reposing on the freshly strewn grass, and permitting the gods to kill him. By this act of self-surrender the cosmos was set in motion. The Parusha himself was the universe. From his corpse everything was generated: birds, animals, horses, cattle, the classes of human society, heaven and Earth, sun and moon. The great *devas*, Agni and Indra, even emerged from his body. But like Prajapati, he was also transcendent. In this sacrifice, unlike the agonistic rituals of the warriors, there was no fighting. Purusha surrendered himself without a struggle.

Parusha and Prajapati were remote, obscure figures, with no elaborated mythology. On the brink of the Axial Age, the sacred authors of India were moving beyond concepts and words into reverent appreciation of the ineffable. However, the Purusha Hymn indicates they were still inspired by the ancient ritual. Even though the rites were so dangerous and violent, they would be the inspiration of the great transformation in India. "By the end of the tenth century, the *rishis* had established the complex of symbols that would create the first great Axial Age spirituality."[3]

A particularly important feature of this Parusha creation story is the way it established reciprocal relationships among the sacrifice, the act of creation, and the elements of the created world. Since the sacrifice was the primordial mode of creation, sacrifice now became the method according to which creation would be renewed; it became the method to recreate and maintain the world periodically when it became necessary. Many persons in the ancient world believed that the powers responsible for the well-being of life often needed human assistance. The human and the divine worlds were in a symbiotic relationship. Each relied on the other for the maintenance of life. The performance of sacrifice, like the gods engaged in at the beginning of time, renewed and invigorated the world. In performing the sacrifices, the priests reenacted creation itself, and in so doing, they were made tantamount to gods.

The creation of the parts of the world out of the ritual dismemberment of the first man also implies a structure of relationships between the ritual and the greater world beyond it. In the creation myth, the seasons are identified with the components of the sacrifice; therefore, by manipulating those components of the ritual, the priests were in effect controlling the seasons themselves. Since everything was once connected to the Purusha, and because the Purusha is sympathetically united to the ritual, the performance of the ritual sacrifice was believed to have effects in the world beyond.

Finally, the creation myth of Purusha permits us to understand the caste system. Previously we saw the gradual development of the caste system among the Aryans, beginning with the distinction of priests and producers in the society of the earliest Indo-Aryans. Then we saw the addition of the warrior caste as the cattle-rustling and village-raiding life became popular, creating a society of priests, warriors, and producers, the ones in charge of raising crops and tending livestock. The fourth and lowest rank in the Aryans system was most likely made up of the indigenous people from the old Indus culture. So the story of the Purusha suggests that the classification of priests, producers, warriors, and servants was intended by the gods and embedded in the very fabric of the Universe.

The Shrauta Rites

The Aryans performed many different rituals to secure from the gods benefits for an abundant life in the world. But the most important were the *shrauta* rites, which required great skill and could be executed only by trained Brahmins with the necessary expertise. These *shrauta* rites were ordinarily performed for this-worldly aims. Those who paid for the sacrifices sought to enhance their relations with the gods in order to achieve greater success in business, to breed more and better cattle, to provide sturdy male children, and to promote health and longevity. The attainment of a happy afterlife in heaven also could be added to the supplications, but that goal seems to be secondary to the others.

In the early Vedic period, it was held that the sacrifices persuaded the gods to act on behalf of those who paid for the sacrifice. But over time, the sacrificial ritual itself came to be regarded as the real agent of transformation. Priests no longer considered themselves as persuading the gods to act in certain way. By manipulating the component objects of the sacrifice and especially by uttering the powerful words called *mantras,* the Brahmins came to believe that they themselves were controlling the cosmic powers. This belief seems to be the logical development of the concept of corresponding relationships between the ritual and the world. Eventually, the sacred words spoken during the ritual actions were seen as powerful in themselves. The very utterance of these words generated or gave access to the creative power of the sacrifice. The priests came to call this power *Brahman,* a word that means "that which makes great," and they came to regard themselves as the guardians of this Brahman. Brahman was not experienced as a deity, but rather as a power that was higher, deeper, and more fundamental than all the various gods. This holy force held the disparate elements of the universe together and prevented them from fragmenting. While it was an all-encompassing, ineffable reality, it could be encountered in religious rites.

Summary

We have seen some of the essential elements of the Vedic rituals. First, ritual is of immense importance in Vedic religion. It was the main means for appealing to the divine. Like most pre-Axial peoples, the

Aryans were not especially anxious about belief and doctrine. But they were greatly concerned about the correct performance of specific religious acts, because these ceremonies and sacrifices were essential to their well-being on Earth and perhaps had a bearing even on their destiny after death. Over time, these ritual observances came to be regarded as the special province of trained experts, Brahmins educated in the precise ways the ceremonies were to be enacted. And as these religious practices evolved and became more and more refined, the Indo-Aryans came to hold that the ritual themselves were powerful. It was not so much that the rites prompted the gods to act on human behalf; rather the rite itself, and especially the words of the ritual, came to be seen as the veritable agent of control. These traits, then, summarize the world of Indo-Aryan religion near the end of what is conventionally called the Vedic period of Indian religious history, between 1500 and 800 BCE.

The Indian Axial Age Begins

We go on now to consider the factors that mark the end of the Vedic era, the advent of the Axial Age, and the beginning of classical Hinduism. It is not that one era superseded the other. The advent of the Axial Age did not mean that Vedic religion was no longer operative, that its practices faded into oblivion. The Vedic traditions were retained and still observed. A more accurate way of understanding this development is to suggest that as classical Hinduism arose, religion in India expanded and was enlarged. The older Vedic concepts and practices were preserved and to some extent reinterpreted; a new system of ideas and interests from other sources were added to the old; and the amalgam that resulted was what we call Hinduism. The appearance of classical Hinduism, therefore, does not mean the disappearance of pre-Axial Indo-Aryan Vedic religion, but changes, nevertheless, did occur.

These changes were motivated by several factors, many of which appear to be characteristics of Axial changes throughout the world. One of the most important of these changes is the spreading of the Indo-Aryans into the Gangetic plain of northeastern India beginning around 1000 BCE. This extension of Aryan culture involved what may be called the second urbanization of India. The Aryans started to give up the nomadic way of life, settle down in towns and villages, and began agricultural pursuits. This development eventually resulted in a period of greater material progress and put the Indo-Aryans in substantial contact with non-Aryan peoples.

These fundamental sociological and economical changes were related to certain development in the Indo-Aryan religion, a development effected by the Indian ritualists who by the ninth century BCE took on the function of *reformers* whose task was to reshape the liturgical life of their people.

Brahmanas

The Reformers

In doing their work of ritual transformation, the reformers inaugurated India's Axial Age. They belonged to the Brahmin priestly caste that had arisen in the late Vedic period. The work they accomplished is preserved in a body of scriptures, the *Brahmanas*, technical ritual documents compiled between the ninth and seventh centuries. The new rites of the reformed liturgy have several new, significant features.

Elimination of Violence

First, from the rites they inherited, the reformers eliminated any practice that would lead to violence. At this time the life of the Aryans had become more settled. Rather than cattle raiding, the production of agricultural goods became the focus of the economy, and consensus was developing that the warlike cycle of raid and counter-raid should come to an end. So the reforming Aryans wanted a religious practice that inflicted no harm or injury on any of its participants. The sacrificial victim was put away as painlessly as possible in an area outside of the holy area, and any gesture of aggression toward human beings was forbidden. "Already at this early date, the ritualists were moving toward the ideal of *ahimsa* ('harmlessness') that would become the indispensable virtue of the Indian Axial Age."[4]

Internalization

Second, the new rites of the reformers focused on an internalization of the sacrificial action. In a story told by the ritualists that became a charter myth of their movement, Prajapati fought with Death in the performance of a sacrificial rite, competing against him with the use of the usual chariot races, dice games, and musical contests. Death was soundly beaten by Prajapati, who refused to fight with the traditional weapons. Instead he used the new ritual techniques, and not only defeated Death, but swallowed him up. Death had been eliminated from the sacrificial arena, and like the patron in the reformed rites, Prajapati found himself alone. In the process of making Death a part of himself, Prajapati had internalized and therefore mastered it. Death no longer needed to be feared. By making Prajapati swallow Death, the ritualists directed attention away from the external world and into the interior domain. The ritualists concluded, therefore, that there was no ritual competition, and Prajapati had become the archetypal sacrificer.

In the performance of the new reformed rites, human sacrificers must follow the example of Prajapati. Anybody who imitated him would not overcome Death by competing against his opponents or by fighting and killing. Death would be conquered only when the sacrificer would internalize it and take it into his own being by means of the rite. In this way Death was absorbed into the very self *(atman)* of the sacrificer. "Death becomes the self of him who knows thus; when he departs from this world, he passes into the self and becomes immortal, for Death is his own self."[5] By taking death into his own being instead of projecting it onto others, the sacrificer would become one with the sacrificial offering. "Dying a symbolic death in the new rites, he would offer himself to the gods and—like the animal—he would experience immortality: 'Becoming himself the sacrifice,' one ritualist explained, 'the sacrificer frees himself from death.'"[6] This internalization was yet another feature of the Indian Axial Age.

Mindfulness

The third feature of the new rites was the requirement that the sacrificer had to be fully aware and understand what he was doing. It was of no avail simply to go through the motions in a mindless manner. He had to be conscious of the fact that he was, in effect, identified with the animal victim and was therefore offering himself to the fire. And he had to be mindful of the fact that he was one with Prajapati, who had commissioned the ritual. The sacrificer therefore was aware of having abandoned the profane world or mortality and having entered the divine realm. He could declare, "I have attained heaven, the gods; I have become immortal." What is new is that the sacrificer was to be mindful of these links by means of his participation in the rites and by his own mental effort. By means of the mental activity of the sacrificer, he left behind the frail particularity of his profane existence to become one with the divine.

Promotion of Interior Life and Development of the Inner Self

The fourth feature of the reformed liturgy, closely related to the third, was the fact that it led the sacrificer into the interior world and promoted his becoming more reflectively self-aware. The focus of the old, pre-Axial rites was on the gods, and their goal was to acquire material goods, cattle, wealth, and status. But the reformed rites, since they strongly emphasized the sacrificer's mental state of awareness, redirected the sacrifices from their original orientation to within the sacrificer and the formation of his inner self, the atman.

Fundamental to the ritual reform of the priestly caste was the conviction that human beings were frail creatures easily prone to fragmentation. Born defective and unfinished, they could build themselves to full strength and maturity only by means of the religious rites. By the correct and mindful performance of rites the sacrificer reconstructed his self, his atman, so that it could live on after his death. This mysterious reality of the inner self came to be identified by the reforming priests as the essential, eternal core and unique element of the human person. Eventually this led, in some of the later texts, to a revolutionary proposal: for a person expert in ritual lore, solitary meditation could be just as effective in building up the atman as participation in the external rites. The well-versed individual, then, did not need to take part in external liturgy at all. By interior or spiritual meditation this person could create his or her own divine atman and find the way to heaven.[7] And once the atman had been created within the sacrificer, the ritualists argued that it became a permanent and inalienable possession, making him an equal to the gods, not needing to worship them anymore. All that was necessary was to speak and act according to the truth and thus be filled with the power and energy of the Brahman.[8]

Conclusion

Thus the Axial Age of India had begun. By meditating on the inner dynamic of the ritual, the reformers had begun to look within. The emphasis on being aware and knowledgeable of the meaning of the rites and the promotion of reflective consciousness would be an important continuing development of the Axial Age. The reform that had begun with the elimination of violence from the sacrificial rites had led the Brahmins and their lay patrons in the unexpected direction of the journey within to the inner self and the development of a more interior spirituality. Their budding profound concern here was *not* to assure an abundant material existence in this world, but to *transcend* the world and themselves in search of personal liberation.

Aranyakas

The Renouncers

In the Ganges region of north India, life was becoming more settled, and the householder, the family man, had become the mainstay of society. He was allowed to have a sacred fire in his own home; there he could perform the daily rites that were scaled-down versions of the reformed public liturgy and that could build up an inner self capable of surviving death and living in the world of the gods. But some men took the extraordinary step of leaving their families and households, renouncing society, and withdrawing to the forest where they lived rough, ascetic lives. These *renouncers* became central to India's spiritual aspirations and the chief agents of the next stage of the Indian Axial Age.[9]

The reformers of the rites had taught that a person's atman, his inner self, was identified with Prajapati; it was the sacrifice, so why engage in other external motions? The renouncer did not give up sacrifice but made it an interior act. In effect, he was asking, What is a true sacrifice? Who truly is the Brahmin...the priest who performs the external rite, or the renouncer who carries the sacred, sacrificial fire with him wherever he goes?[10] The renouncer effected a transition from an externally structured religion to an interior one enacted within the self. According to the claim of the ritualists, the sacrificial rites created the divine, eternal self; the entity sacrificed was the atman; the rites contained the power of the Brahman. But the renouncers claimed that one's atman was able to give access to the power that held the universe together. The holy life of renunciation and asceticism would unify the renouncer to the Brahman that was mysteriously embodied within his atman, the essential core of his being. The rationale for the rigorous holy life of the renouncers was expressed in the *Aranyakas,* the "Forest Texts" that developed an esoteric interpretation of the old rites. Fasting and celibacy were no longer only a preparation for the ritual sacrifices, as in the old Vedic religion; they were the ritual activity itself.

Upanishads

The Forest Wanderers

We go on now to consider yet another advance in Indo-Aryan religious thinking and a further stage of the development of the Indian Axial Age. In the later Vedic period, it seems that the people began to experience growing doubts about the effectiveness of their traditional rituals. These questions about the rituals seem in part to be associated with the resentment of the middle castes in regard to the power of the Brahmin priests and their monopoly of ritual performance. However, it may be that even deeper than this was the emerging awareness that what the rituals sought to achieve—an abundant material existence in this world—was not all that valuable. The aspiration was to renounce the world in search of personal liberation.

We see these doubts arising in a collection of writings known as the *Upanishads*, profound spiritual literature from the end of the Vedic period and the dawning of classical Hinduism. In these scriptures, written most likely by forest wanderers of the Brahmin and Kshatriya castes, the old Vedic religion of India came of age. The crowning achievement of these unknown but prominent Axial sages, endowed as they were with considerable talents for philosophy and poetry, was a series of books completed from 700/800 to 300. *Upanishad*, which means "to sit apart" (in the forest, away from the workaday world), connotes the secret teaching a person receives at the feet of a spiritual teacher or guru. Among several things, the writing began to reevaluate the Vedic ritual practices. One story in the collection includes a dialogue between a young Brahmin, Machetas, and Yama, the king of Death. As a result of an interesting set of circumstances, Machetas is sent to the underworld, where Yama grants him three wishes. For his third wish, Machetas asks Yama to explain what happens when a person dies, an apparently simple petition to make to the god of death. Yama, however, is reluctant to respond to this simple question. The dialogue goes on in this manner:

> Nachiketas says: When a man dies, this doubt arises: some say "he is" and some say "he is not." And Death responds: Even the gods had this doubt in times of old; for mysterious is the law of life and death Ask for another boon. Release me from this. Nachiketas: This doubt indeed arose even to the gods, and you say, O Death, that is difficult to understand; but no greater teacher than you can explain it, and there is no other boon as great as this. Death says: Take horses and gold and cattle and elephants; choose sons and grand-sons that shall live a hundred years. Have vast expanses of land, and live as many years as you desire. Or choose another gift that you think equal to this, and enjoy it with wealth and long life. Be a ruler of this vast earth. I will grant you all you desire. Ask for any wishes, however, hard to obtain...and I will give you fair maidens with chariots and musical instruments. But ask me not, Nachiketas, the secrets of death. Nachiketas responds: All these pleasures pass away, O End of all! They weaken the power of life. And indeed how short is all life! Keep your horses and dancing and singing. Man can-

not be satisfied with wealth. Shall we enjoy wealth with you in sight? Shall we live while you are in power? I can only ask for the boon I have asked....Solve then the doubt as to the great beyond. Grant me the gift that unveils the mystery.[11]

As an alternative to answering the question, Yama offers the young Brahmin the gifts of wealth and longevity on Earth. These were likely what the Indo-Aryans considered the highest goods of life, and precisely what the Vedic rituals were supposed to secure. But Nachiketas refuses these gifts in favor of his desire to know about the afterlife.

This story indicates that an important shift has occurred among the adherents of Indian religion. It was not that the Aryans believed the old rituals were not effective, but that what the rituals provided, such as riches and long life, now were regarded with significantly less favor and maybe even a touch of contempt; for ultimately they were not so important. Furthermore, for the first time in early Indian literature, we have begun to notice an expression of anxiety about death. Nachiketas wants to know whether after death the individual exists or not. Urgency and intensity mark his question, and he refuses to let the god of death dismiss his inquiry. Nothing like this is found in the early texts; in the *Rig Veda* there is no agreement about the ultimate destiny of human beings and no sense that the Indo-Aryans were deeply concerned about the afterlife.

At this point we find ourselves in the midst of a transition in Indian religious history. We have begun to observe the close of the Vedic Age and the dawning of the era of classical Hinduism, a period that coincides with the Axial Age. There is, of course, no identifiable moment in time when it can be definitely said that the Vedic period has ended and the classical period has begun. The Vedic traditions were for the most part retained and embraced by the rising Hinduism. The stage is now set for significant change. Questions that are now appearing here and there—questions about the ultimate fate of human beings, about the nature of the afterlife and the absolute reality of the entire universe—these questions will take center stage in the next phases of Indian religious history. We know about these phases because they are accounted for in the *Upanishads*.

Unlike the authors of the *Vedas* and *Bramanas*, who had an optimistic, world-affirming outlook, the pensive sages of the *Upanishads* found the human condition sad and disheartening. As we explore the writings of these pensive authors, we see that in their experience the world was flawed and the cause of suffering. With disdain for the formal, ritual sacrificial worship urged by the pre-Axial scriptures, they searched instead for interior, mystical experiences. Their concern was not to assure an abundant material existence in the world but to transcend the world and themselves in search of personal liberation. Sacrificial worship might ease the anxieties of those who feared or hoped in the gods, but it did not satisfy the doubtful sages of the Axial Age. It should be noted that even though many of the gods worshiped and practices observed in the *Vedas* and *Bramanas* were abandoned later in classical Hinduism, these early Vedic writings retained scriptural status throughout the later centuries and became deeply rooted in the fabric of India.

The Evolution of Classical Hinduism

What distinguishes the classical Hindu era is the reorientation of religious practices to new concerns and new beliefs. This evolution occurred over a two-hundred-year span, beginning around 800 BCE and continuing on to about 600. The old Vedic ritual system that had dominated Aryan religion for centuries came under close critical examination, and Indian religious life began to change in a dramatic fashion.

Some reflective persons increasingly spoke of doubts about the kind of goods the Vedic rituals were able to produce. The Indo-Aryans still valued long life, health, material prosperity, and children, the kind of benefits the rituals were expected to bring. But now some thoughtful persons had begun to consider these elements of the good life as less important in the scope of the large picture. Sages were wondering if only such good things were all there was to life, or does human existence have some meaning and value that transcends the acquisition of these benefit? As the Aryans began to profit from greater material success as they settled down in villages and became farmers, these questions came up more frequently. As subsistence needs receded into the background, issues of a philosophical or transcendental nature seem to have come more to the fore.

The increase in material well being does not wholly account for this philosophical turn, but surely it played a part....For a variety of reasons, growing numbers of individuals in northern India at the time we're considering were asking the same questions: Is this all there is? Is there something more to life than simply satisfying our desires, and if so, how do we find it?[12]

Death, Samsara, Karma

Closely associated with these questions was a growing concern with death and the ultimate destiny of the individual person. In the Vedic period, the Indo-Aryans were not without concern about death, but their interest was not a significant preoccupation or a matter of great passion. Death did not provoke terror, nor was it the object of intense speculation. It was simply a reality of life, and the meaning of life seemed to be to enjoy what the world had to offer before death was encountered. There were some passages in the *Vedas* that suggested that there may be some form of existence beyond the death of the individual, but this was not at all a consistent or widespread belief. The clear and definite emphasis throughout the *Vedas* was on the total enjoyment of the benefits of this earthly life. But as the Axial Age comes fully to the fore, the issue of death becomes a reality of unprecedented and intense pondering.

One of the many ideas about death being discussed among the philosophically minded individuals is of particular significance for later Hindu thinking. Surely an important number believed in heaven, where individuals experienced a pleasant and permanent existence among the gods and ancestors. And heaven could be gained by performing the appropriate sacrifices and rituals. Yet now, at the end of the Vedic Age and the beginning of the Axial Age, doubts began to cloud the picture of the afterlife. In the later portions of the *Vedas* there are explicit suspicions about the permanency of life in heaven once it has been achieved. In these texts, there is a fear that one might initially reach heaven only to lose it again through death. The word *redeath* now enters the religious vocabulary to describe a situation in which a person dies and ascends to heaven, exists there for a time, only later to die again, this time dissolving into the elements of the natural world.

It is likely that the idea of redeath was an intermediate step toward the development of the notion of reincarnation, or what is known also as the transmigration of the soul. The idea that the individual self undergoes a continual series of births, deaths, and rebirths seems to have come up for the first time in India at the start of the Axial Age. It is not known with certainty just how the belief in reincarnation appeared and then became widely accepted throughout India. But in India the notion of rebirth was so widely accepted that it became the fundamental assumption of nearly all religions and philosophies, including Hinduism, Buddhism, and Jainism. The word used by these traditions to denote the endless series of births, death, and rebirths is *samsara*, literally meaning "wandering," and suggesting a kind of aimlessness to the process. It implies that the given world of common sense or ordinary experience is only provisional, not relevant in an ultimate sense. To consider it as ultimate is to delude oneself and thus be trapped in a cycle of rebirths. Only when one comes into union with Brahman, the Truly Real, can one have access to genuine self-transcendence and liberation. Otherwise, one must travel the journey of worldly life, being reborn.

No mention of transmigration is made in the *Vedas*. The first place in the ancient Indian texts where a clear idea is found about transmigration is in the *Upanishads*. By the time the *Upanishads* appear, the concept of rebirth had begun to enjoy a widespread acceptance. Even so, we do not find a clear or systematic understanding of the nature of the process in these writings. But as the Axial Age progresses and the *Upanishads* are further developed, many of the precisions about samsara are attended to and refined. One of the most important is the idea of *karma*.

To the Indian view of rebirth, karma adds a unique and unusual perspective. While the idea of rebirth is not exclusive to India, the belief that one's future incarnation is dependent on the ethical quality of one's behavior in this life is a distinctive Indian contribution. Like Zoroaster and the religions influenced by him, the *Upanishads* make a person's moral behavior the decisive element in human destiny. It is karma that determines the form and rank of one's next birth. Essentially, karma refers to the actions that a person performs and the consequences of those actions. These consequences or effects, considered as part of the act itself, will at some point return to the agent, to the one who performed the act in the first place. In short, the idea of karma means that every person gets what he or she deserves. It is a principle of absolute justice, and the process by which it operates is ineluctable and impersonal, like the law of gravity operating on physical bodies. There is no god or divine being administering justice. It just happens to be the way the world operates. In fact, according to Hinduism, even the gods themselves are subject to the law of karma. No one can escape the consequences of his or her actions.

As the doctrines of samsara and karma took hold and became universally accepted, the general mood of India changed and became depressed. The people felt doomed to one transient life after another. The Vedic rituals could not provide a solution; not even good karma could save them. The best the old rites could offer was a rebirth in a world of the gods, but in light of the new doctrines, this could only be a temporary release from the relentless suffering and death. The *Upanishads* did promise final transcendence and salvation, but they were *not* for everyone.

Summary

We have seen that Axial Age speculation in India produced important new ideas. The individual is consigned to an endless series of births, deaths, and rebirths that are governed by moral deeds. As the idea is developed in greater detail, it gains wide acceptance throughout the Indian populace. But it also generates new challenges for the way Indians think about their lives. The older Vedic beliefs that maximized the comforts and pleasures of earthly existence fade away, and new concerns emerge about how to face the world of samsara.

The Quest for Liberation

The ideas of rebirth and karma may have emerged independently of each other; but if this be the case, during the Axial Age they became inextricably linked in Indian spirituality, and this gave birth to a new attitude toward life and the world. At first, rebirth and karma were not consistently understood by the sages who wrote the *Upanishads*. Over time, however, a basic pattern of belief developed among the sages who were pondering on these matters. As we have seen, that pattern involved the ethicization of rebirth, the concept that moral deeds determine the level of one's reincarnation. Good behavior brings about a favorable rebirth; evil behavior results in an unfavorable rebirth. The doctrine of karma means that the level of a person's rebirth is in his or her hands. Karma raises the individual to be the master of his or her destiny. What happens to a person is the consequence of that person's own choices and behavior. Similarly, a person's present condition was shaped by the deeds previously performed. So like Zoroaster, the *Upanishads* place the importance of personal, moral responsibility on a high level.

Speaking of a good or bad rebirth implies a hierarchy of being. An individual might be reborn on any level of the hierarchy, from plant life to the various ranks of animal life to the human realm. And the human domain, of course, is stratified from low caste to high caste, and then to the levels of the deities. On what level a person is reborn depends on the amount of his or her good or negative karma. To have a favorable, high rebirth—that is, to be reborn as a god or a Brahmin or, in some senses, simply as a human being—is extremely rare and demands a great deal of karmic merit. For the vast portion of our infinite number of rebirths, most individuals have been reborn as insects or other animal forms. Because it is such a demanding feat, to have achieved a human rebirth in this life is almost a miraculous event.

What makes rebirth on the human level favorable is not just its rarity but also the meaning it has in light of the big picture. Human beings, more than animals or even the gods, have the most favorable opportunity to affect their future existence. One of the causes that results in persons being reborn a great number of times on the animal level is that animals simply are not able to generate much good or negative karma. And this means that such nonrational beings are not in a position significantly to influence their rebirth one way or another. But human beings, due to their rational makeup, have practically limitless chances to act morally, that is, to produce deeds that have karmic relevance. To waste or misdirect this precious human life would be a tragic mistake.

Especially for those living in the West, one of the first facets of the notion of rebirth that has to be grasped is that samsara is not a desirable situation. Most people who hold to the belief in reincarnation do not desire to be reborn. In spite of how confident one may be that his or her good conduct is sufficient to merit increasingly better rebirths, eventually there comes the realization that even the best possible lives are filled with suffering, pain, grief, and must one day end in death. Therefore, simply attaining the apex of the great chain of being cannot be the final goal. Even at the acme of the hierarchy, rebirth continues without end. The positive karma a person has acquired will eventually be exhausted, and reincarnation is inevitable and with it the suffering that is part of every life. Hindus generally believe that the individual person will by his or her own experiences in due course become convinced of the futility of samsaric existence. Finally, a person will realize that he or she must seek for the ultimate purpose of life, that is, liberation from samsara all together. Hindus call this *moksha*, salvation, the complete release from reincarnation. Seeking a favorable rebirth, therefore, can only be a preliminary goal. A person aspires to maximize his or her good karma, persistently improving rebirths until one has achieved a life in which realizing *moksha* is a possibility.

From the samsaric point of view, existence does not seem to be so pleasant. To be sure, life in the world has its pleasures: the warmth of family and children, the joys of eating good food and seeing beautiful sights, the love of friends and companions. But now from the samsaric standpoint, from the point of view of endless number of previous lifetimes and the prospect of infinitely more, this world does not carry quite the same attraction for Indians in the Axial Period as it did to the Indo-Aryans centuries before. Recall the words of Nachiketas to the king of Death: "All these pleasures pass away, O End of all! They weaken the power of life....Man cannot be satisfied with wealth. Shall we enjoy wealth with you in sight? Shall we live while you are in power?"

How to Achieve Moksha

So belief in, and the experience of, samsaric existence bring about a new religious problem: How to live in such a way as to achieve *moksha* and escape the endless round of rebirths all together? This was the problem and the challenge of the Indian religion of the Axial Age. Virtually every religious sect and movement throughout the course of the history of India, and there have been many, attempted to understand and solve this issue.

As the idea of samsara developed and became more and more accepted during the Axial Age, it produced a widespread movement of individuals who were convinced that the most important thing to do in life was to find liberation from samsaric existence. Consequently, they left their homes, families, and occupations to seek a homeless and ascetic way of life that would lead to escape from rebirth. They engaged in one form of discipline and now another, adopting this doctrine and then that. It was at this time that many of the practices that have come to be associated with Indian religion were developed, such as meditation, and hatha yoga, and the countless varieties of self-denial and self-mortification, from fasting to celibacy. While this movement included men and women of all ages and from all castes, it tended to attract persons from the middle castes especially. For the most part, this activity occurred in the years between 800 and 400 BCE, and in the plains area of the Ganges River, in northeastern India, where the Indo-Aryan culture had expanded many years earlier.

This expansion into the Gangetic area was previously referred to as the second urbanization of India. Aryan culture became more settled as villages and towns developed. And as farming and commerce flourished, people came to enjoy material prosperity. Several small republics and small kingdoms were established. It was an era of economic, social, and religious ferment, a decisive period for the development of Indian culture.

This was a world of change, when traditional practices and doctrines were no longer taken for granted. In this area of India, the Brahmin priests ceased to have the power and prestige that they had enjoyed in earlier years. And without doubt many of those who joined the movement in search of escape from samsara began to experience dissatisfaction with the ordinary domestic existence and a yearning for high adventure. In a life of renunciation they saw their only hope for a life of freedom and fulfillment. For this reason, those individuals who took on the homeless and ascetic life—the *samanas*—did not do so simply to escape a world they found distasteful, but because they saw in it their only possibility for a life of freedom and fulfillment. Mark Muesse states:

> I would characterize the new axial outlook in India as ultimately optimistic, despite its negative assessment of the phenomenal world. Although the world as we know it is indeed

a vale of tears, the sages were saying, by perfecting the spiritual life, the samsaric realm might be conquered and an even greater bliss enjoyed. That was the conclusion of the individual who left home because it was cramped and dirty, the man who later became known as the Buddha.[13]

Many of the renouncers, the *samanas,* who sought *moksha* in this very lifetime, lived alone in caves or in the forests, or with their families in ascetic communities; many wandered from village to village. These ascetics and sages were common sights in the villages and towns. Frequently persons who remained householders sought them out for advice; they supported the renouncers by giving them food, clothing, and shelter, and in doing this they believed they were meriting good karma. The ordinary householder might assist the *samanas* now in this life, hoping that in a future lifetime others would help them in their efforts to attain *moksha.* So while liberation from samsara is the widely accepted ultimate religious goal, not everyone seeks it in this life. It should be added that so large and familiar was this countercultural movement of the *samanas* that they were virtually seen as a fifth caste, alongside the priests, the warriors, the producers, and the servants.

Acquiring Knowledge

While the way of life and beliefs of this fifth caste varied widely, they were of one mind in their quest for liberation from the severe sense of suffering associated with their understanding of samsara. They were united in yet another way: in the conviction that the path to freedom lay in acquiring knowledge. Their life of renunciation was considered as a required means for removing the impediments that might hinder them from gaining the extraordinary knowledge that led to *moksha.* The quest for this knowledge to freedom was of such great consequence and so demanding that all concerns of the world had to be set aside.

The knowledge they sought had two qualities. First, it was not simply the knowledge of ritual action and sacred words that was being sought. At this point, the sages wanted to know the profound reality that was at the foundation of ritual practice, and that was equivalent to the reality that was the foundation of the whole of life. They aspired to know the world's fundamental basis, to grasp reality's elemental nature. They desired to know the whole of reality by understanding its deepest principles, the principles that illuminate everything. The tendency to see the world not as a collection of unrelated objects and beings but as an integral whole that can be understood by knowing its fundamental basis became so pervasive in the Axial Age that we can designate it as one of the salient characteristics of this era. The sages desired to understand it all—the way to final liberation, the answer to life's deepest questions, the knowledge of the secrets of the universe itself—not because they valued knowledge for its own sake, but because knowing the fundamental basis of existence could bring, they believed, true freedom and fulfillment. Zoroaster had provided such knowledge to his followers with his vision of life as a cosmic battle between good and evil, a view that furnished a comprehensive framework for interpreting every dimension of existence and provided a practical manner of orienting people's lives.

The second quality of the knowledge sought by the north Indian *samanas* was that it was extraordinary, esoteric: to be acquired by rigorous methods of asceticism and meditation, not gained from reading books. This form of knowledge in Sanskrit is *jnana*, which is closely related to the Greek word *gnosis*. This was a supramundane kind of knowing, accessible in principle to everyone but acquired only by those willing to make the sacrifices necessary to get it. And despite difficulty or costs, many of the ascetic seekers claimed to have discovered what they were looking for.

Conclusion

We have now set forth the fundamental predicament or problem of Indian religion, and we are in a position to begin an examination of some of the responses proposed by the ancient *samanas*. In what follows we study the solutions offered by three of the most important and enduring schools of thought emerging from the north Indian renaissance. The first is the Vedanta, the views offered by the *Upanishads* themselves and that provide a basic theological foundation for Hinduism. Then we take up Buddhism and Jainism, two traditions that reinterpret the problem of samsara and then propose an alternative response to the approaches of classical Hinduism.

The Vedantic Solution

Hinduism, Buddhism, and Jainism each claimed that the apparently unending cycles of existence were the basic existential problem, although they did interpret differently the details of rebirth. They all were convinced, furthermore, that human beings were able to escape the cycle of rebirths as long as individuals were willing to dedicate themselves to the task. And they agreed that the task was an arduous one. Yet, in spite of these shared convictions, they each proposed diverse solutions to the problem of samsara. We examine these various approaches and movements, beginning with Vedanta, the perspective offered by the *Upanishads*. The *Upanishads* were the first documents that communicated the new problem for the Axial Age, and they were also the first texts to propose a solution to that problem. In the course of time, Hinduism embraced other spiritual paths and added them to its vast repertoire of practices and doctrines, so the Vedanta is not *the* Hindu solution. It is one among several, and it does not even represent the most popular form of spirituality in present-day Hinduism. Nonetheless, despite its minority status among modern Hindus, the Vedantic way was critical to the genesis and subsequent growth of Hinduism. Since it develops many of the fundamental ideas accepted by practically all forms of Hinduism, its theological perspectives shape the religious lives of those Hindus who do not explicitly practice them.

While hundreds of *Upanishads* were written, only a few came to the fore as especially important and influential. These focus on a profound religious goal: the search for intuitive knowledge of ultimate truths, insight into the transcendent behind the countless particulars of reality, liberated life in conformity with the demands of the Absolute. External ritual action was replaced by rigorous mystical introspection. This was looked upon not as an innovation but as the fulfillment of the ancient tradition. One of earliest texts was the *Chandogya Upanishad*. It emerged seamlessly from the *Bramanas,* and was, like the *Aranyakas,* an esoteric section added onto a *Brahmana* commentary of the different priestly schools. It was set in a social context that was at the very beginning of the process of urbanization.[14]

Chandogya Upanishad

This *Upanishad* expresses the heart of the Upanishadic vision. No longer was the focus on the gods outside the worshiper or on the external performance of a rite; rather, the sage was required to direct his attention within himself and on the interior meaning of the rite. He had to know what he was doing, and this sacred knowledge would lead him to *Brahman*, the ground of being, the transcendent reality that is the source, the foundation, and the "stuff" of everything. According to some *Upanishads*, this transcendent reality is ultimately a supreme Person; for others, it is an ultimate transpersonal Absolute. The *Upanishads* were also concerned with the atman, the self, which was identical with the *Brahman*. If the sage could discover the inner heart of his own being, he would automatically penetrate into the ultimate reality and free himself from the terror of mortality. Since most Aryans lacked the talent or desire to undertake this long and arduous journey, they continued to worship and sacrifice in the former traditional manner.

After pondering the heart of the Upanishadic vision, we go on now to gain a more analytical understanding of these famous writings. In them the sages aspired to unravel the profoundest mysteries of the universe. They desired to understand two elements: the fundamental nature of *ultimate reality*, the fundamental power or principle underlying the totality of the universe; and the fundamental nature of *the self*, what lies deep within the individual as his or her essence. If they came to an apprehension of these Absolutes, they believed they would be endowed with the liberating knowledge that would bring the samsaric cycle to an end and fill them with complete ecstasy.

Nature of Selfhood

The majority of the religions and theologies-philosophies of the past three thousand years have claimed that the human essence is a reality that transcends the material body. The most common name given to this essence is probably *soul*, that aspect of being that animates and gives life to the body and signifies what a human truly is. The Sanskrit word was *atman*. *Atman* was an ancient Vedic term that was associated, in the early texts, with the breath, and that was then reinterpreted and redefined by the sages of the Axial Age. The sages of the *Upanishads* identified the soul as an immortal substance, something that transcends the body and survives death. Part of their experience and interpretation of the atman was the increasing anxiety about the fate of the individual at death, one of the major themes of the Axial transformation.

If not the body or its breath, what in fact constitutes the human essence? What really is the soul? Practically all the Upanishadic writers hesitated to identify the soul with mind or consciousness. Soul for them was something that existed beneath or beyond the mind. Some of the sages concluded that what is beyond the senses and the mind itself is not accessible by sense or thought. Therefore, they concluded that the atman must be imperceptible and beyond comprehension. While the soul dwells within the body, it is distinct from the body and all its parts; and since it transmigrates from body to body in the process of rebirth, it must also be immortal. The soul does not come into being at a specific moment; it is not created; it simply always has been.

While the Upanishadic thinkers are not of one accord in regard to the specific details of the views of the human self, they all agree on the general understanding that distinguishes a *higher* self from a *lower* self. The lower or phenomenal self is associated with the body and the senses and the mind. These aspects are all transitory and moral. The higher self, the atman, is distinct from these other elements by virtue of its eternal and spiritual nature. What brings suffering to human beings is confusing the higher with the lower self.

Yajnavalkya of Videha

One of the most important sages in the development of the early *Upanishads* was Yajnavalkya of the kingdom of Videha, a frontier state on the most easterly point of Aryan expansion in the seventh century BCE. Like all Upanishadic sages, he was convinced that there was, as it were, an immortal spark at the core of the human person. It participated in, and was of the same nature as, the immortal Brahman that sustained and animated the entire cosmos. Since the spark was an immanent presence in all human beings, it could be discovered in the depths of the self, the atman. For Yajnavalkya, the atman was the transcendent agent behind all the senses and was therefore free from external ritual, ineffable and beyond description. Yet the goal of the new Upanishadic spirituality was, indeed, knowledge of the unknowable atman.

Yajnavalkya led his disciples in the long slow quest for self-discovery: systematically removing layer after layer of superficial knowledge; perceiving ordinary realities as manifestations of the absolute; discovering modes of being that were different from a person's normal consciousness, dominated by sense perceptions and rational thought; achieving a state of unified consciousness and the loss of all sense of duality; and seeing, finally, that the core of the self was not the individual "I" that manages one's daily life and is hemmed in by physical needs, desires, and fears, but an ultimate reality in its own right. This was the inner person that was behind and that controlled the *I* of mundane experience. It was the experience of being at one with the inner core of one's being; of being calm, composed, cool, patient, and collected because one is in the world of the Brahman. Suffused by the immortal, fearless Brahman, one is free from evil, free from stain, free from doubt. Because one knows the immense and unborn self, unaging, undying, immortal, and free from fear, one knows the Brahman and is released from terror and anxiety.[15] Yajnavalkya believed that persons who know this—who had realized and gained the sacred knowledge of their identity with Brahman—would go to *Brahman* at death, taking their knowledge with them. By means of Vedic liturgical rites, a person built up a self that would survive in the world of the gods. But for Yajnavalkya, the creation of an immortal self was not attained by external rites but rather by this carefully acquired sacred knowledge.

This arduous journey in search of the self was one of the clearest expressions of a fundamental principle of the Axial Age. "Enlightened persons would discover within themselves the means of rising above the world; they would experience transcendence by plumbing the mysteries of their own nature—not simply by taking part in magical rituals."[16]

Ultimate Reality

The Indian sages desired to understand not only the nature of the self but also the very essence of ultimate reality, the fundamental power or principle supporting the entire universe. Similar to their quest for the soul, the sages' pursuit of ultimate reality was grounded on a concept from the old *Vedas*, that is, the Brahmins' speculation about what made the sacrificial ritual effective. The Brahmins used a specific technical term to identify the mysterious power that lies hidden within the ritual; they called it *Brahman*, and the Brahmin priestly caste believed their main function was to ensure the proper application of this power. In the Axial Age the quest for liberating knowledge came to focus on discovering the true essence of this Brahman power. This focus followed a logical development: the ritual and its sacred words had always been understood to be associated with greater cosmological and moral realities beyond the simple ceremony itself. The myth of the sacrifice of the Purusha, discussed earlier, suggested that society, the various elements of the world, the ritual practices, and the Sanskrit language itself were all mystically interconnected. Finding the deep meaning of ultimate reality in the Brahman power was the natural outcome of this Indian line of thinking. By the Axial Age the sages had come to understand that *Brahman* meant more than the power of the ritual; it now was reinterpreted as the ultimate reality itself.

While the authors of the *Upanishads* were not in total agreement as to the exact nature of Brahman, the following elements are those on which they agreed. All through the *Upanishads* it is held that Brahman is one, single, undifferentiated unity, without parts or divisions. In various other passages, Brahman is credited with creating and sustaining the life of the entire universe. It is stated that Brahman, even though imperceptible, does permeate all things; does include good and evil, yet transcends both; is beyond morality altogether. Therefore, Brahman encompasses the whole of reality, and yet at the same time surpasses it. Absolutely nothing is beyond the scope of Brahman. Brahman is not a being, and surely not a personal being. Brahman would be more accurately described as the Absolute or Being Itself. Hindu theologians came to state that Brahman was *nirguna*, that is, without qualities. Gradually the Upanishadic sages came to realize that Brahman was ultimately unknowable, at least in the traditional sense of that word; Brahman was beyond conception and perception so these faculties were ineffective in discovering the absolute reality. What they searched for was the most profound kind of knowing, a comprehension of reality that can be best labeled as mystical or ineffable.

Identity of Soul and Ultimate Reality

As the sages of the *Upanishads* went further on their search for knowledge of the human essence and of ultimate reality, a new intuition enlightened their awareness and was manifested in the later *Upanishads.* The sages came to the conclusion that what is labeled the human soul is in fact identical with ultimate reality itself. They are one and the same. The *Chandogya Upanishad* claims, "This is the Spirit that is in my heart, smaller than a grain of rice or barley, or a grain of mustard seed, or a grain of canary seed. This is the spirit that is in my heart, greater than the earth, greater than the sky greater than heaven itself, greater than all these worlds."[17] What is meant here is that the atman and the Brahman are consubstantial, two names for the same reality. The true self is indeed ultimate reality. Brahman-atman is the only reality there is. It is hard to imagine a more exalted view of humanity. This assessment of the self seems almost diametrically opposite to that of mainstream of Western monotheism, in which God is viewed as wholly other than humanity.

Despite the *Upanishads'* exalted view, the soul nevertheless is convinced that it is in an endless cycle of birth, death, and rebirth. Like many Eastern and Western traditions, the classical Hindu view understands that the embodied soul is not at rest; it is not in its true home. So how can it be reconciled that, on the one hand, true selves are identical with the ultimate reality, and yet, on the other hand, they undergo the rounds of endless rebirth?

According to the *Upanishads*, ignorance, the human misperception of reality, is the cause of samsara. *Maya*, a veil over reality, accounts for human ignorance. It causes individuals to perceive plurality where in true reality there is unity. Human beings experience and interpret the world as composed of a multitude of realities rather than the one reality that is. They are deceived by *maya* to think of themselves as separate entities, as individuals separate from one another and separate from ultimate reality. *Maya* causes persons to forget who they truly are and prompts them to identify with their lower selves. Lower selves, however, are ultimately not real because they are inconstant and transitory. Until persons fully recognize the truth about Brahman and atman, they continue to suffer on the wheel of samsara because they continue to generate karma that ties them to the phenomenal world. As persons believe themselves to be distinct individuals, they tend to think and behave in self-centered ways, generating desires and deeds that perpetuate the illusion of the separateness from Brahman. And this attitude of separateness brings about fear and hatred of others, the greed for material things, as well as ultimately the fear of death. The *Maitri Upanishad* states,

"Whenever the soul has thoughts of 'I' and 'mine,' it binds itself with its lower self, as a bird with the net of a snare."[18] The very desire to be special is the cause of human suffering.

But if Brahman is beyond the powers of perception and conception and language, how may one come to the liberating knowledge of ultimate reality? How may one penetrate the *maya* that deceives the mind and causes unhappiness?

The One and the Many

According to the teaching of the *Upanishads,* it is not sufficient for the mind to grasp the ideas of atman and Brahman. Simply comprehending the identity of self and ultimate reality in the traditional conceptual way does little good; it must be apprehended by the very core of one's being. Only then does it become knowledge that leads to *moksha.* Unless a person attains this deep, existential understanding, he or she persists in a life of self-centeredness and desire, engendering the karma that binds one to samsara.

We examine now what the sages of the Axial Age considered it took to acquire this exceptional kind of understanding, and what the alternatives were for those who discovered that this approach was too difficult or simply unappealing. Attaining the total mindfulness of Brahman and atman requires, first of all, a reorientation of how truth may be discovered. The Vedantic perspective insists that the truth is not out there, but within one's deepest self. The *Chandogya Upanishad* states, "He who has found and knows his Soul has found all the worlds, has achieved all his desires."[19] To discover one's self is, in effect, to discover ultimate reality there by the means of meditation.

Meditation

One of the aims of the introspective disciplines of Hinduism, particularly meditation, is the discovery of the divine within. It is likely that meditation was practiced in India long before the Axial Age. Artifacts discovered in the ruins of the Indus culture represent individuals in what seems to be a traditional meditative posture. The *Vedas,* as well, suggest that the Indo-Aryans may have engaged in a type of meditation. By the Axial Age, meditation had come to eclipse ritual as the central discipline for samanas seeking *moksha.*

The various *Upanishads* propose different methods for practicing meditation, but there were some characteristics they all shared. It was of prime importance to restrain the body and quiet the mind to attain a state of inner serenity. The mind was to be focused on a particular object, such as the breath, or on an external object or internal image, or a mantra, a special word repeated silently to oneself. This focus of the mind promoted concentration and the avoidance of sensations and thoughts that distracted from the goal of the practice. It was held that over time, serious and persistent meditation would result in a range of experiences, including visions, ecstasies, the intensification of awareness, and the transcendence of ordinary thoughts and imaginings. By means of the persistent use of meditative techniques, a person aspired to gain access to the higher self, to the atman.

The practice of meditation was enhanced by efforts to dissociate from the lower self that is habitually mistaken for the true self. The aim here was to close off ways that led seekers astray, holding them in the trap of *maya.* Some ascetics committed themselves to silence because knowledge of Brahman was beyond language. Some attempted to overcome attachment to the material world by vows of poverty, and fasting, and celibacy. Others practiced mortification of the body. The purpose of all these practices was to discipline the ascetic to renounce all attachments that promote a sense of individuality or separateness from the rest of reality. In order to attain awareness of the higher self and its identity with Brahman, it was necessary to relinquish all selfish desires. The supreme teaching of the time insisted that desire creates karma, and karma binds one to samsara.

Encounter of the True Self

The Upanishadic sages taught that to encounter the true self meant to see that there was nothing to desire and nothing to fear. Since the atman was immortal and consubstantial with ultimate reality itself, there would be no reason to want or fear anything. And because one lacked for nothing and feared nothing, following this path to its end resulted in a deep sense of serenity and a joy beyond all earthly pleasures. There would be no rebirth, since there would be no clinging to life; there would be no fear of dying, only a state of equanimity in face of the world. This was to experience *moksha* in one's historical lifetime. It is the awareness of one's unity or identity with Brahman. This is less an achievement and more the simple apprehension of truth. The soul does not need to unite with Brahman because it already *is* Brahman; it only fails to recognize that. *Moksha* is seeing the light, becoming aware that one is united with Brahman.

The *Upanishads* inspired subsequent generations of sages to continue to work through and reinterpret their essential features. Three subschools of Hindu thinkers were based on the *Upanishads,* also called the *Vedanta.* Two of Hinduism's greatest philosophers, Shankara and Ramanuja, both post-Axial sages, were founders of Vedantin schools. But the importance of the *Upanishads* goes well beyond providing material for subsequent philosophers. The importance of these writings

> to the overall Hindu tradition was more a matter of establishing the key elements that provided Hinduism with many of its characteristic features: the belief in the unity and incomprehensible nature of ultimate reality; the conception of *samsara, karma, atman* and *moksha;* and the sense that the world and ourselves are not really the way they appear.[20]

New Perspective and Practices

The Vedantic approach to the seeking of *moksha* was not congenial to the religious sensibilities of everyone. As Hinduism developed during the course of the Axial Age, it continued to add new perspectives and practices to accommodate the beliefs and tastes of individuals. Ultimately, Hinduism became a structured family of religions, but without a set of beliefs every Hindu was expected to accept. Hinduism is distinct from religions that require doctrinal purity. From the beginning, it has accepted differences rather than exclude them. It has always been aware that people are at diverse stages in their spiritual journeys, and that beliefs and practices for some persons might not be appropriate for others. The *Rig Veda* insists, "Truth is one; but the wise call it by various names." Hinduism has and continues to give significant latitude for individuals, enabling them to take from its rich source, according to their stage of development, and in a way congenial to them.

It is not surprising that many Indians found the way of the *Upanishads* to knowledge and *moksha* simply too rigorous and unappealing as a way of life. Some may be attracted by the mystical tradition of imageless contemplation in silence, but most religious seekers call for some concrete symbols and words to channel their spiritual energies. It seems that most people need thinking, concepts, and images to nourish their devotional lives. Therefore, most Hindus preferred a more traditional type of spirituality, one that focused on the worship of a personal god or goddess rather than the highly abstract and impersonal Brahman.

The Shvetashvatara Upanishad

From around 300 to 220 BCE a religious revolution was afoot in India. The people who felt excluded from the demanding mysticism of the *Upanishads* and the world-renouncing ascetics began the process of creating a spirituality based on their own experiences, one suited to *their* way of life. They needed a less abstract and more emotive religious practice. So from their own religious experiences and spiritual needs they developed devotion to a deity who was a manifestation of Brahman and who loved and cared for worshipers.[21] This led to the appearance of brilliantly painted temples, colorful processions, popular pilgrimages, and devotion to the images of a multitude of exotic deities.

The first sign of this development can be seen in the *Shvetashvatara Upanishad*, composed probably in the late fourth century BCE. Here Brahman, the absolute reality, was identified with its personal manifestation, Rudra/Shiva, who would liberate the devotee from the painful cycle of samsara. When worshipers experienced union with God—*moksha* or salvation—they would be enlightened and see the deity within themselves. In the very last verse of this *Upanishad*, an important new word is found: bhakti ("love"; "devotion"). It explained that the liberation or *moksha* it described would arise "only in a man who has the deepest love *(bhakti)* for God and who shows the same love toward his teacher as towards God."[22] The central act of *bhakti* was self-surrender: devotees ceased from resisting the Lord God, and aware of their helplessness, were confident that God would help them.

At this early stage, the way of *bhakti* devotion was in its infancy. A later, crucial text—the *Bhagavad Gita* of around 200 BCE to 200 CE—developed the theology of the Shvetashavatara in a new direction that profoundly affected Indian spirituality.

Bhagavad Gita

This is one of the great texts of Hinduism, written down at the end of the Axial Age or shortly thereafter. It probably has been more influential than any other Indian scripture. A dialogue between a warrior named Arjuna and the god Krishna—an avatar or embodiment of Vishnu, who was Brahman—the *Bhagavad Gita* takes one through the many practices of Hinduism, including Vedic rituals, karma and morality, meditation and yoga, and devotion to the gods. One of the main themes is that while these spiritual disciplines are beneficial, the best of all is devotion to God. Near the end of the scripture, Krishna encourages Arjuna to focus his mind, will, and heart on devotion to god and let go of everything else. By this heartfelt devotion, Arjuna—and any devotee—will find liberation from samsara.

Whereas other writings confined salvation to a few gifted ascetics, the religion of the *Bhagavad Gita* was for *everyone*. Anybody could love and imitate the Lord Krishna, and therefore Brahman, and learn to transcend selfishness in *bhakti* worship and in the ordinary duties of everyday life and thus find access to *moksha*. As *bhakti* devotion to one of the principle manifestations of Brahman, especially Shiva and Vishnu, developed, it was defined as the passionate longing for the Lord from one's whole heart; the love of the Lord would take people beyond their selfishness, make them "perfect, immortal, satisfied, attaining which a person does not desire anything, does not hate, does not exult, does not exert himself or herself (in furtherance of self interest). Having known that, a person becomes intoxicated, becomes motionless, and becomes one who enjoys the self."[23] Consequently *bhakti* was another way of emptying the heart of egotism and aggression. Those who could not model their lives on an interior, intellectualized, mystical paradigm could imitate a deity whose love and selfishness were easily apparent. Between 200 BCE and

200 CE there was a powerful explosion of *bhakti* faith in India that reflected the aspiration for a more intimate, personal, and emotional spirituality.

Two Paths: Way of Devotion and Way of Knowledge

Seeking union, by the way of mystical knowledge, with Brahman—the ultimate reality without qualities—quite plainly did not satisfy the religious aspirations of many. This, however, was not really a problem because the emerging Hinduism did not require uniformity of practice and belief. Heartfelt devotion to and worship of personal deities continued without abatement in the Axial Age; it became even more popular near its end, and afterward, with the writing of the *Bhagavad Gita*, the most frequently read Hindu scripture.

The fact that two paths have coexisted—the way of heartfelt devotion to the gods and the Upanishadic way of mystical knowledge in search of realization of Brahman—calls for a reflection on the relationship between these two very different religious practices. The way of knowledge is based on the conviction that Brahman, the ultimate reality, is totally immaterial and beyond concepts, words, and images. Yet it must be said that India is a land of an astounding array of divine icons. There are pictures and statues of members of the Hindus pantheon everywhere one goes: in the public buildings, on buses, in the taxis and rickshaws, at the tea stalls and shops, on the sides of road. The gods and goddesses cast a watchful eye over everything. The casual observer could hardly guess that the ultimate reality of Hinduism was incomprehensible and beyond image.

The mystical and the devotional practices of Hinduism have coexisted because the theology of Brahman was refined to incorporate the extensive numbers of gods and goddesses who are venerated all throughout India. Hindu theologians introduced another dimension to the theology of Brahman, and thus they provided a way for those devoted to the gods and the seekers of mystical union with Brahman to understand themselves as relating to the same ultimate reality. While the *Upanishads* do focus on the incomprehensible nature of Brahman, later religious thinkers proposed that Brahman *is,* in a sense, knowable and can thus be represented and made comprehensible—not entirely of course, but partially. Consequently, in addition to the position that Brahman was *nirguna* —that is, without qualities and beyond the mind's grasp—later theologians put forth that Brahman was also *saguna,* with qualities, and consequently able to be conceived and perceived. It was possible for the formless and the infinite to take form and finitude. According to this belief, the many gods and goddesses of popular devotion were so many manifestations of the one inconceivable ultimate reality. By means of a heartfelt devotion to any of the deities (who were really manifestations of Brahman), the individual devotee relates to ultimate reality. Each god or goddess serves as a channel to the ultimate reality, mediating the absolute sacred to the believing devotee. Thus, Hinduism supplied the theological foundations for its broad tolerance and inclusive outlook.

Even though the Hindu pantheon is immense, individual Hindus do not render worship to all the gods. Each devotee chooses a personal deity. Frequently this personal god is the deity venerated by one's family or village. But an individual's decision to worship a specific god is exclusively his or her own, and it may be based on a special attraction that one experiences for a particular god. Devotees worship their chosen deity as indeed the supreme god, but they do not feel compelled to deny the reality of the other gods or the supreme of these gods for their followers. In India, a land of 330 million gods, the traditional number of the Hindu pantheon, this is how Hindus can understand themselves to be qualified monotheists.

Conclusion

We have examined two different theologies and practices that arise in the Indian Axial Age: the first is a mystical theology according to which ultimate reality transcends the reach of the mind; and the second, a theistic outlook according to which the divine can be represented by symbols and images, permitting the devotee to relate closely to God by devoted acts of reverence and love. Followers of these ways may claim superiority for his or her particular way, but both approaches have been embraced by the greater tradition of classical Hinduism.

Classical Hinduism

On the foundation of the faith and practices expressed in sacred writings referred to previously classical Hinduism arose. This ancient religion of India is not a single cohesive tradition, but rather a family of religions. Through all the Hindu family runs this unifying theme, which is characteristic of the Axial Age: spiritual salvation or liberation, the most important value to seek in life, requires transcending the ego either in self-giving to the divine Lord, the Supreme Person, or in achieving union with the ultimate transpersonal Absolute.

In this view, human beings in their true nature are *already* one with the eternal being of Brahman, the universal Self. Their existence as separate egos is illusion; their ultimate identity with the Sacred is at present obscured by the empirical ego, the self-possessing *I* that encases and conceals the inner self. This *I* is the samsaric illusion of *maya*, the world of perpetual change and unfulfilment through which the soul passes in the course of many earthly lives until it attains to liberation. Thus salvation is the freeing of the eternal self—which is ultimately identical with the divine reality—from the confining and distorting influence of the succession of its false egos. How to come to a realization of this eternal soul and how to liberate it from its real or imaginary connection with the psychosomatic entity that thinks, wills, and acts, is from the time of the *Upanishads* onward the central challenge facing the Hindu religious consciousness.

Hindu tradition *ultimately* identifies three ways to final liberation. These are not mutually exclusive but rather represent different emphases that are appropriate for different types of personality or even for the same person at different times. One way is the *Path of Knowledge* (spiritual insight). On his path one strives to come to experience and realize with one's total being the great truth: *tat tvam asi*, "That thou art" (You are that Supreme Brahman), the identity of one's deepest inner self with the eternal and universal Self.[24] This is a knowledge that can only be achieved by intense meditation and the hard-won negation or transcendence of the ordinary conscious ego. Eventually, after long years, perhaps many lives of perseverance, a person may finally attain to salvation and become a soul liberated from the illusions of ego-centeredness while still in this world. This path is generally chosen by those who leave the householder stage and an active life in the world for an existence centered on spiritual reflection.

Another way to salvation is the *Path of Action or Works*. Traditionally this path, which is available to the householder, involves performing the prescribed rituals in worship, mostly of the lesser deities, and observing the moral norms and social regulations of one's status in the elaborate caste system. The important element called for here is action with inner detachment, with a lack of concern for the fruits of one's actions.

Finally, there is the *Path of Devotion or Bhakti*. This is self-giving devotion to the transcendent sacred reality as encountered in one of the principle deities. As a loving commitment to a divine Lord and Savior, it has been followed by Hindus in the broad devotional stream of both Vaishanavite and Shaiviate religious life. It involves a movement from self-centeredness to centeredness in the Transcendent, a radical reentering in the divine Other. It is expressed in intense personal love and gratitude, often in devotional temple worship, in personal testimony and dedicated missionary witness, in a life spent in the service of the Lord. "In all of these it involves a transposition of the individual's existence from a state of self-centeredness to a new centeredness in the Real experienced and responded to as the divine Thou....The point to be stressed here is that as a way of conversion from self-centeredness to God-centeredness *bhakti* is a form of human transformation."[25] The Hindu way of devotion has it parallels in Christianity, Judaism, Islam, Sikhism, and the Jodo sect of Buddhism.

Conclusion

This brings to a close our look at the emergence of Hinduism in the Axial Age. In chapter 5 we begin to explore another movement that begins in the ferment of northern India and develops into Buddhism and Jainism.

Notes

1. *Rig Veda: A Metrically Restored Text with an Introduction and Notes,* eds. Barend A. van Nooten and Gary B. Holland (Cambridge, MA: Harvard University Press, 1994), 10.29.

2. Ibid., 10.90.

3. Karen Armstrong, *The Great Transformation: The Beginning of Our Religious Traditions* (New York/Toronto: Knopf, 2006), 25.

4. Ibid., 79.

5. *Shatapatha Brahmana* (SB) 10.5.2.23; 10.6.5; cited in J. C. Heesterman, *The Broken World of Sacrifice: An Essay in Ancient Indian Ritual* (Chicago and London: University of Chicago Press, 1993), 57. The *Shatapatha Brahmana* is one of the prose texts describing the Vedic ritual associated with White Yajur Veda. It is notable as one of the oldest prose Sanskrit texts altogether. Linguistically it belongs to the Brahmana period of Vedic Sanskrit, dated to the first half of the first millennium (roughly 800 BCE).

6. SB II.2.2.5; cited in Armstrong, *The Great Transformation,* 80.

7. Thomas J. Hopkins, *The Hindu Religious Tradition* (Encino, CA, and Belmont, CA: Dickenson, 1971), 36–37.

8. Heesterman, *Broken World,* 216.

9. Paul Dundas, *The Jains,* 2nd ed. (London and New York: Routledge, 2002), 17; Steven Collins, *Selfless Persons: Imagery and Thought in Theravada Buddhism* (Cambridge, London, New York: Cambridge University Press, 1982), 64.

10. Collins, *Selfless Persons,* 56–60.

11. Mark W. Muesse, *Religions of the Axial Age: An Approach to the World's Religions* (Chantilly, VA: Teaching Company, 2007), part I, 89–90.

12. Ibid., 97.

13. Ibid., 114.

14. Patrick Olivelle, ed. and trans., *Upanishads* (Oxford and New York: Oxford University Press, 1996), xxix.

15. *Brihadaranyaka Upanishad* (BU) 4–4.23–35. References to the *Upanishads* are taken from Olivelle, *Upanishads.* The *Brihadaranyaka Upanishad* is one of the older, "primary" *Upanishads.* It is contained within the *Shatapatha Brahmana,* and its status as an independent *Upanishad* may be considered a secondary extraction of a position of the *Brahmana* text. It is therefore one of the oldest texts of the *Upanishad* corpus, possibly dating to as early as the ninth century BCE.

16. Ibid., 131.

17. *Chandogya Upanishad* 3. 14. *The Upanishads,* trans. Juan Mascaro (Middlesex, UK: Penguin Books, 1965), 114. This text is one of the oldest (perhaps *the* oldest) "primary" *Upanishads.* Though there are some one hundred *Upanishads,* only ten are principle. These are known as the *Dashopanishad* and

known for their philosophical depth. Along with the *Brihadaranyaka Upanishad,* the *Chandogya Upanishad* is an ancient source of principal foundation for Vedantic philosophy.

18. *Maitri Upanishad,* 3.2. Ibid.

19. *Chandogya Upanishad,* 8.4.1. Ibid.

20. Klaus K. Klostermaier, *A Survey of Hinduism,* 2nd ed. (Albany: State University of New York Press, 1994), 221–27.

21. Muesse, *Religions of the Axial Age,* part I, 142–43.

22. *Shvetashvatara Upanishad* 6:23. Olivelle, *Upanishads.* This text is one of the "primary" *Upanishads.*

23. Cited in Klostermaier, *Survey of Hinduism,* 222.

24. *Chandogya Upanishad,* 6:14. *The Upanishads,* trans. Juan Mascaro.

25. John Hick, *An Interpretation of Religion: Human Responses to the Transcendent* (New Haven and London: Yale University Press, 1989), 39–40.

Chapter Five

BUDDHISM AND JAINISM

Hinduism Challenged

In India in the late fifth century BCE, a spiritual vacuum arouse out of a complex matrix of factors that challenged Hinduism and give rise to Buddhism and Jainism. The first factor was that of a spiritual malaise. By this time, the doctrines of *karma* and *samsara*, which had been controversial at the time of Yajnavalkya, were universally accepted by the people.[1] "Bad" karma meant that individuals would be reborn as slaves, animals, or plants. "Good" karma would ensure their rebirth as kings or gods. But this was not a fortunate occurrence: even gods would exhaust this beneficent karma, die, and be reborn in a less exalted state on Earth. As this teaching took hold, the mood of India changed, and many people became depressed with the fear of being doomed to one transient life after another. Not even good karma could save them. As they reflected on their community, they could see only pain and suffering. Wealth and material pleasure were darkened with the grim reality of old age and mortality. As this gloom became more and more intense people sought to find a way out.

People became increasingly unsatisfied with the old Vedic rituals that could not provide a solution to this problem. The very best these rituals could do was provide a rebirth in the domain of the gods, but this could be only a temporary release from the relentless and suffering-producing cycle of samsara. Some even rejected the spirituality of the *Upanishads,* which was not for everyone. It was a full-time task, demanding hours of effort each day, and it was incompatible with the duties of a householder. And at this time the revolution that produced bhakti devotion as the universally accessible means to salvation had not yet taken place. So, because of the prevailing malaise of doom and despair, many people in India were looking for a spiritual solution and longing for a *jina*, a spiritual conqueror or a Buddha, an enlightened one who had woken up to a different dimension of existence.

Social, Political, and Economic Change

In addition to the spiritual malaise of this time, there was a social crisis. The people of northern India were undergoing major political and economic changes. The Vedic system had been the spirituality that supported a highly mobile society, constantly engaged in migration. But the peoples of sixth and fifth centuries were settling down in increasingly larger communities that were focused on agricultural production. There was also political development. The small chiefdoms had been absorbed into the larger units of kingdoms. As a result, the *Kshatriya* kingly warrior class had become more prominent. The new kingdoms stimulated trade in the Ganges basin. This generated more wealth, which the kings could spend on luxury goods, on their armies, and on the new cities that were becoming centers of trade and industry.

This new urbanization was another blow for Vedic spirituality, which was not well suited to urban culture and civilization. The kings began to shrug off control of the priests, and the urban republics tended to ignore the Brahmin class altogether and put a limit on the traditional sacrifices. The lavish sacrifices had been designed to impress the gods and enhance the prestige of the patrons. By the fifth century, the eastern peoples realized that their trade and culture brought much more wealth and status than the Vedic sacrifice rites. Instead of conforming to the old traditional ways, the new cities encouraged personal initiative and innovation; individualism was replacing tribal, communal identity; the lower classes of the Vedic system were acquiring wealth and status that once would have been inconceivable.

These massive social changes brought about by urbanization were unsettling and left many people feeling disoriented and lost. The tensions were especially acute in the East, where urbanization was more advanced and where the next phase of the Indian Axial Age began. Here, life probably was experienced as particularly ephemeral, transient, plagued by disease and anomie, confirming the now well-established belief that life was *dukka*, suffering. The urban class was ambitious and powerful, but the gambling, theater, prostitution, and spirited tavern life of the towns seemed disarming to the people who still trusted in the older values.

Radical Dissent

Life was becoming more and more aggressive than before, in strong contrast to the older ideal of *ahimsa* that had become so crucial in north India. In the kingdoms there was infighting and civil strife. The economy was moved by greed and rugged competition. Life was experienced as even more violent and terrifying than when cattle rustling had been the backbone of the economy. The Vedic religion impressed people as increasingly out of touch with the violence of contemporary public life. People needed a different religious situation.

These ideas of radical dissent, along with the spiritual malaise and social, economic, and political crisis of the time, formed the complex matrix from which Buddhism and Jainism emerged during the Axial Age to vex the course of Hinduism. The founders of these religions, Siddhattha Gotama and Mahavira, provided alternative solutions to what had become the central problem of Indian life: how to find self-transcendence and salvation from the continual cycle of rebirths in the frightening and suffering-producing world. The Buddhists and Jains, of the warrior tribes and the *Kshatriya* caste, were more than ready to contest the Brahmins' claim to cultural control. They did not appreciate either the social or the religious implications of the Brahmins' teaching. Among the ranks of the Buddhists and Jains there were persons of brilliant mind for whom the costly sacrifices prescribed by the priests were not satisfactory. They and others like them had no interest in priestly sacrifices that did not immediately give them solace or fulfill their spiritual needs; they sought near-at-hand practical modes of release from their growing sense of the essential misery of existence. Like the authors of the *Upanishads*, they considered the world flawed and a cause of suffering. So they rejected the religion controlled by the Brahmins as being ineffectual for souls inwardly pained. Their radicalism was in their rejection of the sacrificial system of the *Bramanas* as well as their refusal to give the Brahmins first place of prescriptive rights in their urgent search for ways to liberation from the plight of suffering and the cycle of rebirths.

Buddhism

Buddhism emerged from the complex matrix of radical dissent, spiritual malaise, and the social, economic, and political crisis of the Indian Axial Age. About its founder, the Buddha, historians are confident of a few key facts. He was born into the family of King Shuddhodana and Queen Maya about the year 566 BCE in a region of the Indian subcontinent that now lies in southern Nepal. This date has been questioned recently by a group of historians who place his birth in the fifth century BCE. Most scholars now think that the Buddha in fact lived around 490 to 410. He was a member of the Shakya tribe, his clan name being Gotama, his given name Siddhattha. It is common to refer to him as *Siddhattha Gotama* or, more commonly as *Shakyamuni*, "The Sage of the Shakya Tribe." He was one among the thousands of brave individuals who searched in the northeastern forests of India to end samsara, the transmigration of life, during the Axial Age. Like many others, Gotama had become convinced that conquering the suffering of samsaric existence was the highest aspiration of life. Nothing else was of equal importance. And like others, he willingly gave up everything to attain that goal.

He departed from his princely existence and began his search for salvation as a wandering mendicant. For six years following his departure from palace life, he made serious efforts to attain his spiritual goal. As he engaged in this quest, he came to the conclusion that the philosophy of the Brahmins was unacceptable and their claims unsubstantiated. He also denied the saving efficacy of the *Vedas* and the ritual observances based on them. But he did take up the options available to him for practicing the ascetic and contemplative disciplines. Quickly he mastered the extreme ascetic method for reaching union with Brahman but found it did not bring him what he was looking for. After many years of frustrating searching, he decided to abandon the well-trodden spiritual paths passed on to him by his teachers and to devise his own path. Within a short time after this decision, he went to a nearby river, cleansed himself of the dust that had accumulated on his body for many months, and then ate a bowl of milk rice. According to his new, self-taught approach to the spiritual journey, he would have to care for his body because physical well-being was necessary to pursue liberation from samsara. The traditional harsh forms of self-mortification he had followed previously had to be abandoned. Shortly later, on the evening of the full moon in the month of Vesakha (which is between April and May) he sat beneath the *bodhi* tree near the village of Bodhgaya in the present Indian state of Bihar. Resting in the shade of that tree released an old memory of sitting under a rose-apple tree as a child during a clan agricultural festival. Gotama recalled that as his father was engaged in a ceremonial plowing action, he became restless and bored. And with nothing else to do, he began to pay close attention to his breath. In those moments, he experienced a heightened sense of awareness and a pervasive serenity that diminished his boredom and restlessness. Remembering that time of his childhood, Siddhattha thought that this gentle practice of awareness meditation might be useful for the spiritual practices he wanted to devise for himself.

This form of meditation was different from the practices of his teachers in that it emphasized the quality of *mindfulness*. While the goal of other meditations was to become absorbed in exceptional states of mind, *his* mindfulness meditation aimed at attaining a heightened awareness of the immediate present moment, so that one became attentive to what was occurring in the mind, the body, and the external environment and observing these processes without judgment. By putting aside goals and releasing preconceptions and judgments, the Buddha believed the mind would become more open to insight into the nature of the world and self. Gotama sat beneath the huge tree, practicing his meditation, and vowed not to leave the spot until he realized the liberating knowledge he had sought for so many years.

In his mindfulness he scrutinized his behavior, carefully noting the ebb and flow of his feelings and sensations as well as the fluctuations of his consciousness. He made himself aware of the constant stream of desires, irritations, and ideas that coursed thorough his mind in the space of a single hour. By this introspection, he was becoming acquainted with the working of his mind and body in order to exploit their capacities and use them to best advantage. Finally, at dawn, he was convinced that he had attained the knowledge that liberates and conquers samsara. At this moment Gotama earned the title, the *Buddha*, which means the "awakened one."

For forty-nine days, the Buddha enjoyed his liberation. He then decided to teach others the knowledge with which he had been enlightened. He found five former disciples and delivered to them a discourse that is sometimes called the "Buddha's First Discourse and Turning the Wheel of Dhamma." This formal talk consisted of a concise formulation of the insights that he had received under the bodhi tree. It contained what the Buddhist tradition calls the "Four Noble Truths," considered by many to be the essence of Buddhism. Most of the Buddha's subsequent teachings might be considered explanations or amplifications of these basic points. As the four truths are discussed here, other teachings in the Pali scriptures will be used to clarify them.

The First Noble Truth: Suffering

The first noble truth is that life is *dukka*—suffering—and that craving for things of the world is responsible for suffering. It was not only the traumas of old age, sickness, and death that made life so unsatisfactory. "Human existence was filled with countless frustrations, disappointments, and its nature was impermanent. Pain, grief and despair are *dukka*," he explained. "Being forced into proximity with what we hate is suffering; being separated from what we love is suffering; not getting what we want is suffering."[2] Suffering includes a whole range of human experiences from the usual events of getting sick, growing old and dying, to not getting what we want and getting what we do not want. Suffering is the fundamental quality of the whole of existence. The very makeup of human existence is entangled in suffering. The whole of human life—not only certain occasions—is suffering. In his mindfulness he also observed how one craving after another took hold of him, how he was ceaselessly yearning to become something else, go somewhere else, and get something he did not have.

We might ask, Why did the Buddha teach that suffering is comprehensive and constant and not simply episodic in human life? Mark W. Muesse suggests the reason the Buddha taught this "is because we do no fully appreciate the extent to which we suffer or feel the unsatisfactoriness of existence."[3] The First Noble Truth is not a statement of a self-evident fact of life; rather, for individuals it is a challenge to discover for themselves the depth and breadth of *dukka* by the means of introspection and observation. The Buddha himself hinted at much when he said, "'This Dhamma that I have attained is profound, hard to see and hard to understand, peaceful and sublime, unattainable by mere reasoning, subtle, to be experienced by the wise.'"⁴ Muesse adds, "I would even go so far as to say that one cannot realize the nature and extent of *dukka* until the moment of complete awakening, as the Buddha himself did on the full moon of Vesakha. The true depth of suffering can only be seen from the perspective of the enlightened mind."⁵ Recognizing that suffering is manifested not only in particular experiences, but in the whole of existence requires persistent and attentive awareness.

The Second Noble Truth: The Cause of Suffering

In the Second Noble Truth, the Buddha states that the root of suffering is desire, or craving. This aspect of the Buddha's teaching distinguishes it the most from other religious perspectives.

The cause of suffering is *tanha*, desire. Desires are problematic when they are self-centered and become intense craving: that is, when an object of desiring becomes a matter of necessity, as if our lives depended on it. Or when we already possess what we desire and believe that losing it would be devastating to our existence. And such craving can lead to the point where relationships to objects, people, values, beliefs, ideas, power, status, experience, and sensation have the nature of attachments or clinging. The problem is not with the objects of attachment themselves, but with the nature of a person's relationships to them, which can become addictions. Since everything in the world is of constant change, nothing can support a person's attachments; all things to which we become attached are subject to change, and this causes suffering. To allay this suffering we seek something else to cling to, but the more we try to secure happiness through acquisition the more we suffer. Attachment can also include an aversion to an object or situation, causing a negative relationship that is just as difficult to relinquish as an attachment. Both Hinduism and Buddhism recognize attachments as mechanisms that lead to samsara and suffering. The Buddha's answer to the dual dangers of attachments and aversion is equanimity, the Middle Way between the two extremes.

Now that the effects of *tanha* and attachments have been discussed, we ask in turn about their antecedent causes. What makes us have desires that become attachments? The cause is ignorance: ignorance of the true nature of ourselves and the world. We develop strong desires and attachments when we are ignorant of the fact that the world and self are really impermanent; they are not things, they are only processes. In the mind of the Buddha, change and impermanence are constant, persistent. Even solid objects are in constant flux. The Buddha viewed the cosmos as a complex arrangement of processes rather than a set of things. It is not only that things change, but that change is the only thing there is. Unlike the Vedanta tradition of Hinduism, the Buddha held that the soul or true self of the human person is impermanent.

No-Self *Anatta*

On his spiritual journey, the Buddha eventually became convinced that the ultimate cause of his suffering and unfulfilled longing was delusion about himself. He failed to see that he was selfless. The human person as "me" or "I" forms a distorting lens through which the world takes on a false character. In that lens the universe is misinterpreted as structured around "me," and the world process is accordingly experienced as a stream of objects of my desires and aversions, hopes, and fears that give rise to grasping. This covetousness expresses itself in egotism, injustice, and cruelty, in a pervasive self-regarding anxiety in face of life's uncertainties, in the inevitability of final decay and death—all of which comprehensively constitute the "suffering of human existence," *dukka*. The salvation Siddhattha searched for was liberation from the suffering caused by the powerful illusion of "me" or "self." It involved the recognition of his having *no* self: his selflessness. Being liberated from the illusory and falsely evaluating "me" was for him to exchange the realm of ego-infected consciousness for the sublime freedom of *nirvana*.

What the Buddha came to perceive and teach his followers about selflessness is called *anatta* in Pali. However, the Sanskrit term, *anatman* ("no-self") makes it evident that the Buddha denies the reality of the *atman*, the Hindu concept of the permanent, immortal, substantial soul or true self. Most interpreters of Buddhism hold that *anatta* was meant to be a doctrine or concept or an ontological statement-theory about the nonexistence of the conscious subject. But it is perhaps more appropriate to hold that it was intended to refer to an *anti-concept* as well as an

axiological or value-oriented, realistic prescription for a certain kind of moral practice.
It is more a denial of what humans ordinarily believe themselves to be.
Let us develop this position, first focusing on *anatta* as an anti-concept.

Anatta as Anti-Concept and Axiological Prescription

The Buddha held that the concept of the self can promote fruit-less speculation and contribute to humankind's suffering. Instead of putting forth another view of self, the Buddha simply indicates that the concept of the self is an inept way of thinking about human beings. While it is permitted to refer to the self reflexively, as in talking about ourselves, the Buddha insisted that we should never consider that it refers to anything substantial or permanent. However, one should not think that the Buddha denies human existence or suggests that human life is unreal or an illusion. *Anatta* means essentially that human beings do not exist in the way they think they do, that is, as separate, substantial selves. To hold this is to hold to an illusion, an unsubstantiated belief in the same way a rainbow is an optical illusion, created by the convergence of various conditions.[6] To the Buddha, atman is an illusion supported by changing conditions. That is why no one is able to iden-tify or pinpoint the soul or essential self. The Buddha taught that the problems of human beings arise when they ascribe reality to this illu-sion. Belief in a permanent, substantial self is the origin of suffering; it sets into motion a series of thoughts, words, and actions that bring on anguish and disappointment. The so-called self is not a thing; it is no-thing, nothing; it is insubstantial; it lacks permanence and immor-tality. The Buddha's denial of self states that no concept is able to express the reality of who we are. His intention is merely to attempt to disrupt human beings' old habits about who they are.

Instead of viewing individuals as immortal souls in perishable bodies, the Buddha saw the human person as a complex of intercon-nected and ever-in-flux energies or forces that he called the "Five Aggregates of Being." These are (1) matter, one's physical makeup; (2) sensation or feeling, the way one judges experiences as pleasant, unpleas-ant, or neutral (such judgments condition one's tendencies of attach-ment and aversion); (3) perception and apperception; (4) mental formations, the sources of desire, craving, and intention; mental formations are, in the Buddha's thinking, the sources of karma; therefore as long as there is craving, there will be rebirth; (5) consciousness, the process of awareness. There is nothing about these components that endures. All of them are in flux. Neither is there a permanent agent of subject that underlies these processes.

The Buddha's teaching, then, about *anatta* is an anti-concept. Furthermore, it is appropriate to understand it also as an axiological or value-oriented and practical ethical prescription about how one should direct his or her life in order to attain salvation. A person should live in a way that is selfless, that is, without being attached to the notion of "my self"—and this is truly a way of being that is "authentically myself." It is the distinctive and famous path to axial self-transcendence that Gotama personally chose to follow. It led to the overturning of the delusion of self and discovering nirvana, the Place of Peace, of inner freedom and the extinction of suffering.

The Third Noble Truth: The Cessation of Suffering

The Buddha's good news for humanity can be found in the Third and Fourth Noble Truths. The Third Noble Truth is direct and clear: "Now this, bhikkus, is the noble truth of the cessation of suffering: it is the remainderless fading away and cessation of the same craving, the giving up and relinquishing of it, freedom from it, non-reliance on it."[7] One does not have to suffer. If *tanha*, thirst or craving, is the cause of suffering, then clearly the solution is to cease from craving, and when persons end craving, attachments dissolve, and they are liberated from the cycle of suffering and rebirth. The reason to end craving is *nibbana*, in Pali, or *nirvana* in Sanskrit. *Nirvana* means the eradication of desire, the cessation of thirst, and the destruction of the illusion that one is a separate, substantial self. It is the end of suffering, the point where a person ceases craving for reality to be other than that what it is, radically accepting the way the world and the self truly are. The *method* for quenching thirst is set forth in the Fourth Noble Truth. But before we focus about the way to the goal, let us discuss the goal itself.

Nirvana is experienced at death, but a form of it can be realized in one's historical lifetime. One who achieves this is called an *arahant:* he or she has fully realized the truth of the Buddha's vision and is free from craving, aversion, and ignorance. *Arahants* continue to experience physical pain and other forms of old karma. However, even with physical pain, one does not suffer. Suffering is distinguished from pain; pain is a bodily sensation, while suffering pertains to the mental anguish that comes from resisting pain or merely resisting the way things are. The *arahant* does not generate new karmas but still must experience effects of the old ones. When at death nirvana is experienced, all karmic forces that sustain existence are dissipated, and the *arahant* is released from rebirth. The image that is frequently associated with final nirvana is a candle, the flame of which has gone out because the fuel and the oxygen have been exhausted. In a parallel fashion, without karma to perpetuate rebirth, the flame of the candle belonging to the *arahant* "goes out."

The Buddha's disciples, of course, were strongly interested in what occurs at final nirvana. One of the central issues of the Axial Age, as we have seen, was the matter of an individual's destiny after death. So the disciples were curious: whether an *arahant* exists after death or does not exist after death; or both exists and does not exist after death; or neither exists nor does not exist after death. But the Buddha refused to respond because knowing the answer was not essential to seeing nirvana, and dwelling on such questions was an obstacle to the goal. The Buddha was generally reticent about issues that were not essential to the termination of suffering.

It should be noted that, for the Buddha, freedom from suffering was not received as a grace or gift from God. Like the path of knowledge in Hinduism, the Buddha's Middle Way required great effort and discipline because human beings are the cause of their own suffering and only they themselves can find freedom from it. The Buddha only shows the way to that freedom.

The Fourth Noble Truth: The Eightfold Path to Enlightenment

In this final truth, the Buddha shows the way to enlightenment with an outline of what the discipline involves. "Now this, bhikkus, is the noble truth of the way leading to the cessation of suffering: It is this Noble Eightfold Path that is right understanding, right intention, right speech, right action, right livelihood, right mindfulness and right concentration."[8] The Noble Eightfold Path the Buddha followed and taught was in the middle between simply giving in to the sensual, vulgar desires of an ordinary foolish person and depriving oneself of even the very necessities of existence. Traditionally, the eight components of the plan of action have been divined into three sections: *conduct*, or developing ethical behavior; *concentration*, or developing the mind by meditation; and *study*, or cultivating the wisdom that enabled persons to see themselves and all things as they truly are. For this reason the Noble Path is sometimes called the "Triple Practice." By following his middle path and thus avoiding the two extremes, Gotama achieved, at Bodhgaya in Bihar, the enlightenment for which he passionately searched.

Right Understanding

The Buddha recognized that to begin engaging in the Eightfold Path requires some initial understanding of his teaching about the Middle Way and the Four Noble Truths, and that this understanding is achieved by study, discussion, and reflection. The result of such study and reflection is, however, only a glimmer of the truth that the practitioner sees that prompts him or her to take the path at the outset.

Right Intention

The interior motive bridges right understanding and the next division of the triple practice, developing moral conduct. Right intention involves the determination to practice specific virtues that neutralize the conditioned tendencies of individuals toward greed, hatred, and harming. The virtues that exert the counteracting effect are nonattachment, goodwill, and harmlessness.

Right Speech-Action-Livelihood

Developing moral conduct, the second part of the triple practice, is the chief part of the Buddha's path. This moral behavior is not commanded either by a god or by the Buddha. It is rooted, the Buddha believed, in the very nature of human beings. He also held that karma is generated only by intentional acts; the source of karma is the aggregate of mental formations, the idea of desire and intention. An appropriate way to discuss the moral dimension of the Buddha's teaching is to start with what he called the "Five Precepts":

1. "I will refrain from harming sentient beings."
2. "I will refrain from taking what is not offered"; that is, one promises not to steal or to covet.
3. "I will refrain from sexual misconduct."
4. "I will refrain from false speech"; not only lying and slandering, but also gossiping, cursing, loud talk, idle chatter.
5. "I will refrain from stupefying drink"; intoxicants.[9]

Right Mindfulness-Concentration

Virtuous moral behavior is central to the holy life, but the Buddha considered it equally important to discipline the mind. As self-absorbed habits hinder the basic compassion of the human heart, so misled habits of the thinking mind obstruct the ability to understand the world and the self as they truly are. For the Buddha, the mind meant the complex of thoughts, sensations, feeling, and consciousness that in each moment arise and fall away. The mind has great power and potential; however, in its unenlightened condition it is out of control, unruly and undisciplined. And to bring it under control requires skill, persistent training, and patience.

Right concentration involves the practice of meditation to strengthen the virtues of attentiveness and nonattachment. The Buddha intended the practice of meditation to heighten consciousness of the world and self by being attentive to the events of ordinary life in the present moment. The fundamental meditative practice, based on the Buddha's own experiences, involved attending to the breath and observing without judgment the coming and going of thoughts, sensations, feeling, and perceptions. As these phenomena come to awareness, the subject notes them and allows them to fall away without dwelling on them. Simply by being observant of the mind, the body, and the surrounding world, the Buddha held it was possible to gain an insight into the true essence of the world and the self, and on the basis of such insight to act and think accordingly. He believed this meditative practice would disclose the illusionary nature of self and the origin of suffering in the mind's tendency to thirst for new pleasures and to avoid unpleasant experiences. He also held that meditation could hold back the mind's inclination to make spontaneous judgments and to become absorbed in thoughts about the future and the past, all of which were considered to be unwholesome habits.

In the development of mindfulness and the practice of contemplation, the Buddha also fostered the skillful states of a lucid, conscious mind, completely alert, filled with compassion and loving welfare for all beings.[10] By performing these mental exercises at sufficient depth, they could, he was convinced, transform the restless and destructive tendencies of his conscious and unconscious mind. At each stage of his journey into the depths of his mind, he intentionally evoked the emotion of love and directed it to the four corners of the Earth without omitting a single plant, animal, friend, or foe from its embrace. This outpouring of loving kindness was a fourfold program. First, he developed an attitude of friendship for everything and for everybody. Next, he cultivated an empathy with their pain and suffering. In the third stage of his mindfulness, he evoked a "sympathetic joy" that rejoiced in the happiness of others, without envy or a sense of personal diminishment. Finally, he aspired to an attitude of complete equanimity toward others, feeling neither attraction nor antipathy.

This expression of universal love was a difficult challenge because it involved Gotama's turning away completely from the egotism that always is concerned with how other people and things might benefit or detract from the self. He was learning to surrender his entire being to others, and thus to transcend the ego in compassion and loving kindness for all creatures.[11]

Enlightenment

In the Buddhist tradition there are two levels of understanding. The first is attained by mere reasoning. The second form is the understanding that occurs in enlightenment; it is the content of enlightened experience. Gotama's great experience of enlightenment was the first most significant event in the history of Buddhism. His followers who follow his Eightfold Path aspire to achieve that same enlightened experience. When they arrive at this goal, then in light of the eternal reality of being itself—the transcendent stream of Universal Being—they see themselves and the world around them, as he himself saw, as passing, unsubstantial expressions of the Absolute. This is seeing reality as it is, unfettered by expectation, belief, or defilement of any kind. In this form of comprehension, one knows for certain the authenticity of the Four Noble Truths without reliance on authorities other than one's own experience. To comprehend the Buddha's teaching at this level means to live one's life in accord with the truth. One no longer seeks for or aspires to nirvana. Nirvana has been seen.

In written accounts of the Buddha's enlightenment, he is described as rapt in ecstatic joy, imbued with a compassionate love of all sentient beings, "as a mother toward the only child," and endowed with the equanimity of a perfectly liberated person. In monastic commentaries, this state of even-mindedness is described as the opposite of three kinds of experience: the pleasure that comes with attachment, the displeasure due to aversion, and an ignorant kind of indifference. What the Buddha experienced was nirvana: It transformed his life.

Nirvana

What was nirvana? It was the extinguishing of the fires of greed, hatred, and delusion, the elimination of the craving, hatred, and ignorance that subjugate humanity. And even though the Buddha was still subject to physical ailments and other vicissitudes, nothing could cause him serious mental pain or diminish his inner peace of complete selflessness. The Buddha would continue to suffer; he would grow old and sick like everybody else; but by following his Noble Eightfold Path, he had found the inner haven that enables a person to live with suffering, take possession of it, affirm it, and experience in its midst a profound serenity.

The Buddha was convinced that nirvana was a transcendent state because it lay beyond the capacities of those who had not achieved the inner awakening of enlightenment. And while no words could adequately describe it, in mundane terms it could be called "Nothing" since it corresponded to no recognizable reality. But those who had been able to find this sacred peace realized that they lived a limitlessly richer life.[12]

Later monotheists would speak about God in similar terms, claiming that God was "nothing" because "he" was not another being; and that it was more precise to state that he did not exist because human notions of existence were too limited to apply to the divine reality.[13] They would also state that a selfless, compassionate life would bring people into God's presence.

But, like other Indian sages and mystics, the Buddha found the idea of a personalized deity too limiting. He always denied the existence of a supreme being because such a deity would become another block to enlightenment. The Buddhist Pali texts never mention Brahman. Gotama's rejection of God was a calm and measured posture. He simply put the notion serenely out of his mind.

When Gotama made an effort to give his disciples a hint of what nirvana was like, he used both negative and positive terms. Nirvana was the "extinction of greed, hatred and delusion"; it was "taintless," "unweakening," "undisintegrating," "inviolable," "non-distress," "unhostility," and "deathless." Nirvana was "the Truth," "the Subtle," "the Other Shore," "Peace," "the Everlasting," "the Supreme Goal," "Purity, Freedom, Independence, the Island, the Shelter, the Harbor, the Refuge, the Beyond."[14] It was the supreme goal of humans and gods, an incomprehensible serenity, an utterly safe refuge. Many of these images are suggestive of words later used by monotheists to describe their experiences of the ineffable God.

The Buddha as Teacher

After the important event of his enlightenment, for nearly a half-century the Buddha traveled the Gangetic basin teaching his doctrine and building a community of followers. After his initial enlightenment at Bodhgaya, the second most significant occurrence in the history of Buddhism is Gotama's first sermon, which was given at Sarnath. In this presentation to his first five followers, he began to expound the Middle Path and the Four Noble Truths as the kernel of his awakening experience. The principle conception of his teaching was the doctrine of *anatta*, "No Self," and the invitation to his listeners to a way of life that leads to the Axial ideals of self-transcendence and salvation from the suffering and dissatisfaction that is part and parcel of human existence.

At the age of eighty, the Buddha peacefully died and passed into final nirvana. After his death, the Sangha or Buddhist community continued his teaching, and with grand success. They gathered together to consider how to preserve the Buddha's teaching. Early Buddhist councils led to the creation of authoritative texts and to the discussion of important doctrinal issues. This ultimately divided the community into several sects. Of the eighteen different varieties of Buddhist schools, only the Theravada school remains, making it the oldest extant Buddhist tradition. It probably represents the form closest to the way Buddhism was practiced around the time of the Buddha.

Around the first century CE the Mahayana form of Buddhism began to take shape in northwestern India; it added a substantially different dimension and new views about the Buddha and his role in making salvation accessible to humanity. New narratives were created that ascribed to the Buddha divine, godlike status. Mahayana developed the idea of the *bodhisattva*, an enlightened being who remained in the samsaric circle or in the heavenly domain in order to help others attain enlightenment and salvation. Mahayana was carried to China, Korea, and Japan. It eventually became the most popular form of Buddhism but has also fragmented over time into new schools. Out of the Mahayana emerged the third major form of Buddhism, the Vajrayana, practiced for centuries in Tibet and Mongolia.

Gotama's doctrine of "No Self" is at the heart of both the Theravada and the Mahayana schools of Buddhism. In Theravada there is a psychological realization of *anatta* which is the loss of "conceit of I am." This constitutes the attainment of the state of enlightenment, the state of be an *arahant*. In Mahayana the same concept of liberation from self applies, but here the aim is not to become an *arahant* but a *bodhisattva*, an enlightened person whose openness to the Transcendent is expressed in unlimited compassion for all sentient beings. For to live as a "self" is to seek happiness for oneself. But transcending the ego, becoming a manifestation of the universal Buddha nature, is to seek the happiness of all.

Today there are a total of approximately 329 million Buddhists in many areas of the world, including Sri Lanka, Burma, Thailand, Cambodia, Laos, China, Korea, Japan, Tibet, Mongolia, Europe, and the United States. One hundred twenty-four million Buddhists are of the Theravada branch; 20 million are of the Vajrayana; 185 million are of the Mahayana.[15] In chapter 7 we explore the Mahayana tradition in tandem with Shinto as these religions developed and are practiced in Japan.

Jainism

Almost all estimates indicate that there are 350 million Buddhists in the world today and fewer than 5 million Jains, almost all of them in India, mostly in Mumbai and other large urban centers.[16] While they account for less than 5 percent of the Indian population, their influence on the religious, social, political, and economic life of India has been, and is, quite out of proportion to their numbers. In Europe, largely in the United Kingdom, there are presently estimated to be 25,000 Jains. Some estimates suggest a similar number may be found in North America. There is a vast disparity in the number of Buddhists and Jains, but the two traditions share similar histories, beliefs, and practices. Both reject the authority of the *Vedas,* and both accept rebirth and karma and aspire to release from samsara.

Modern history specifies the origins of Jainism in the same cultural environment that gave rise to Hinduism and Buddhism. Jainism grew from the struggle for enlightenment of its main figure, Vardhamana Jnatrputra (c. 497–425 BCE), called the *Jina* ("Conqueror") or *Mahavira* ("Great Hero"). Sometimes he is referred to by outsiders as the founder of Jainism, but Jains themselves see their religion as a tradition going back dozens of generations before Mahavira. Devout adherents of Jainism insist that their religious tradition is eternal, based on truths that have no beginning in time. At certain moments in the universal life cycle, these truths have been forgotten and lost, but then rediscovered and reintroduced to humanity. When an Axial Age sage named Vardhamana Mahavira began to teach the doctrines of Jainism, he was only communicating a religion that had been taught many times before by others. Each of these former teachers was a *Tirkanthara,* a word that means "bridge builder" ("those who find a ford over the river of suffering"). The *Tirthankaras* were exceptional individuals who showed the way to salvation by their words and example. In the last turn of the universal cycle, there have been twenty-four *Tirthankaras.* The most recent was Vardhamana, portrayed mythically as being of supernatural birth and the twenty-third and last in a long line of *Tirthankaras.* He is not considered to be the founder of Jainism, only its reformer and reviver. It should be noted that there is no historical evidence to support the existence of the first twenty-two *Tirthankaras*.

Modern scholarship locates the origins of Jainism in the person of Vardhamana Mahavira of the Axial Age, who according to tradition was born into the *Kshatriya* in 599 BCE. Both Buddhist and Jain texts indicate that the Buddha and Mahavira were contemporaries living in the same region of northeastern India, in Bihar state. The texts indicate that they knew of each other but never actually met. However, if the Buddha in fact lived around 490 to 410, as most scholars now think, then the traditional dates of Mahavira would be inaccurate.

After the death of his parents, at the age of thirty Mahavira gave up his princely life and became a wondering monk in search of liberation from death and rebirth, following a harsh lifestyle as a *samana*, a renouncer of wealth and life in society. For the next twelve years, he practiced intense asceticism, including fasting for long periods of time, mortification of the flesh, meditation, and the practice of silence. He scrupulously avoided harming other living beings, including animals and plants. By dedication to these austere practices he merited a title given to him by his admirers, the *Mahavira*, meaning the "Great Hero." At the age of forty-two, after twelve years of uncompromising dedication to self-discipline, he believed he was simply the latest in a long line of *jinas* who achieved complete victory over his body and the desires that bound him to the world of matter and sin; he had crossed the river of *dukka* (suffering) to find access to liberation and enlightenment. In his enlightened state he attained a transcendent knowledge that gave him a unique perspective of the world. He was able to perceive all levels of reality simultaneously, in every dimension of time and space, as though he were a god. In fact, for Mahavira, God was simply a creature who had accomplished supreme knowledge by perceiving and respecting the single divine transcendent soul that existed in every single creature. This state of mind could not be described, because it entirely transcended ordinary consciousness. It was a state of absolute friendliness with all creatures, however lowly. He had crossed the river of *dukka* to find access to liberation and enlightenment.

For the next thirty years he roamed around the Ganges region teaching others his principles and practices for achieving liberation from samsara, for which he used both the terms *moksha* and *nirvana*. Like the

Buddha, he drew men and women and children from all social strata. His followers were called "Jainas," or now, according to a more modern pronunciation, "Jains," because they were disciples of the *jina*. Some legends indicate that at one point Mahavira had gathered more than 400,000 disciples. He organized his followers into an order of monks, nuns, and laypersons. To attain liberation, one had to become a monk because of the austere discipline required to achieve it. Laypersons expected to strive for *moksha* in a future lifetime when circumstances were more favorable for such a pursuit. His teaching became the basis of the *Agam Sutras,* one of the most important scriptures in Jainism. According to tradition, Mahavira died and attained final nirvana at the age of seventy-two, after thirty years of successful teaching and organizing. He is now, according to all Jain sects, at the top of the universe, where all perfect ones go, enjoying complete self-transcendent bliss in a state no longer subject to rebirth. After his death, the Jains would develop an elaborate prehistory, claiming that in previous eras there had been twenty-four of these ford makers who had discovered the bridge to salvation.

Mahavira taught his followers in conformity with this vision. Like Buddhists and Hindus, he appropriated many of the basic assumptions and beliefs circulating in the Ganges basin in the early Indian Axial Age, but he reinterpreted them to fit his particular enlightened view of the world. We now explore how Mahavira understood these concepts, including his idea of time, the structure of the world, the nature of the soul, karma, and the path to salvation.

Time

Mahavira was of the belief that the world was never created and will never be destroyed. Cosmic time, therefore, is infinite, but it does conform to a cyclical pattern. Each cycle has two half-segments, a period of decline and a period of ascendancy. Each segment is further divided into six unequal parts. The half-cycles are incalculably long. One half-cycle is a time of decline. During the first part of this period, people are very tall and live lives that are very long. They are exceedingly happy, wise, and virtuous, with no need of religion or ethics. All of their needs are provided by wish-granting trees. As the cycle proceeds, conditions become progressively worse. The world and life are gradually tainted with corruption and deterioration; ethics and religion are then introduced; writing is invented, since peoples' memories begin to fail. During these times the *Tirthankaras* appear. When the lowest point of the cycle of decline is reached, people will be only about three feet tall and live twenty years. Like animals, they will live in caves and pursue all sorts of immoral activity.

But as time reaches its lowest point, it begins to ascend, and the world becomes increasingly better. People then start to live longer, healthier lives, to conduct themselves in more compassionate ways, and to experience greater happiness. When this cycle reaches its apex, time begins again its downward motion. The pattern is repeated over and over again, forever. According to Jain belief, we are presently in the fifth stage of the cycle of descent, a period when things are bad and will become even worse. The current era began a little over 2,500 years ago and will continue for a total of 21,000 years. When this period ends, Jainism will be lost and will be reintroduced by the next *Tirthankaras* after the half-cycle of ascent commences again.

Structure of the World

According to the teaching of Mahavira, the physical world is made up of three levels: the underworld; the surface of the world, or the middle realm; and the heavens. In the underworld are a series of seven or eight hell realms, and each of these is colder than the next. The hell realms are for the punishment of the wicked as a means of purifying negative karma. The Jain hells are more like a purgatory than a location of ultimate condemnation. When souls have suffered sufficiently for their sins, they may be reborn in another realm. The middle level is the place of life; it is known by the name of *Jambudvipa*, or the island of the rose-apple tree. It is a name used also by Buddhists and Hindus. The upper level of the world is the realm of the gods. It has sixteen heavens and fourteen celestial abodes. And then, above the ceiling of the universe is a crescent-shaped structure where the *Tirthankaras* and the completely liberated souls dwell. This is the ultimate goal and destination of those who attain *moksha*.

Nature of the Soul

Mahavira, like the sages who wrote the *Upanishads*, believed that the soul was real, not illusionary as the Buddha thought. Mahavira considered the soul to be a living, luminous, and intelligent entity within the material body; it was unchanging in essence, but its characteristics were subject to change. It was also his conviction that there were an infinite number of souls, each an actual, separate individual. Therefore, Mahavira would not have accepted the Vedantic idea that soul and ultimate reality are consubstantial, since that view denies individuality. Furthermore, all souls are of equal value; one is no better than another. Souls may be embodied in gods and in humans, as well as in animals and plants, and even, according to some, stones, minerals, bodies of water, fire, and the winds. By the karmas of former lives they had been brought to their present existence. Therefore, all beings share the same nature and must be treated with equal respect and care that persons would want to receive themselves.[17]

Karma

In its pure state, the soul enjoys perception, knowledge, happiness, power, all of which are perfect. However, at the present time, all souls, with the exception of the completely liberated ones, are defiled because they are embodied and tainted with karma. The Jain understanding of karma is of a fine, material substance that clings to and stains the soul. Karmas are invisible particles, floating throughout the world. When a soul commits a karmic act, it attracts these fine articles, which adhere to the soul and weigh it down. These karmas accumulate and, in due course, color the soul. We cannot see a soul because of our defiled state; but if we could, we could with ease detect a soul's moral and spiritual quality. The souls that are worse are stained black, and the purest are white. And in between, from bad to good, the soul may be blue, gray, red, lotus-pink, or yellow. Like in Buddhism and Hinduism, karma determines persons' future births and keeps them bound to the material, samsaric world.

Since they are imprisoned in matter, souls do not enjoy omniscience as they do in their pure state. Karmic stains cause our perceptions to be distorted and our knowledge of the world limited. These distortions urge the soul to seek pleasure in material possessions and fleeting enjoyments, which further lead to self-absorbed thoughts and anger, hatred, greed, and other states of the mind. These, in turn, bring about the further accumulation of karma. Consequently, the cycle is a vicious one.

The limitations that result from karmic defilement also mean that we are unable to understand the great richness and complexity of reality. The Jains propose that reality is many sided; this means that the world is made up of an infinite number of material and spiritual substances, each with an infinite number of qualities and manifestations. Since the universe is complex and our knowledge is limited, all claims of truth must be tentative. The Jains refer to the principle as "non-absolutism," which means making no categorical or unconditional statements.

Path to Liberation

In Mahavira's teaching, liberation meant the release of one's true self from the constraints of body and thus the achievement of salvation, inner control, and transcendent peace of mind, enlightenment, all being the great values of the Axial Age. The path to liberation is simple. At first, preventing the flow of new karma and then, second, eliminating the old karmas that have already accumulated and weigh the soul down.

To attain the first goal, Mahavira urged his followers to fulfill five Great Vows. The first and foremost of these vows is *ahimsa*, to avoid harming any living beings. The Jains take this rule further than the Buddhists, who drew the line at sentient life, not at life itself. The Jains are convinced that even unintentionally injuring another creature causes negative karma. In line with these beliefs, Jains are vegetarians and refuse to use leather or other animal products. Most avoid agriculture, because the plow might inadvertently damage a worm, and other kinds of occupations that might cause harm to other forms of life. Some, especially the monks, use a cloth to cover a glass when they drink so as to strain out insects that may have fallen into the liquid; and they sweep the pathways before them to avoid stepping on bugs. *Ahimsa*, however, means more than avoiding physical injury to life. It also involves what the Jains call *ahimsa* of the mind and *ahimsa* of speech. The former is the practice of right thought. Evil thoughts are held to generate negative karma. The latter is speaking in a nonhurtful way, using kind, compassionate language.

Achieving salvation is centered on not harming one's fellow creatures. Until persons had acquired this empathetic view of the world, they could not attain salvation. Consequently, nonviolence was a strict religious duty. All other ethical and religious practices were useless without *ahimsa,* and this could not be achieved until the Jain had acquired a state of empathy, an attitude of positive benevolence, with every single creature. All living creatures should be of support and assistance to one another. They should relate to every single human being, animal, plant, insect, or pebble with friendship, goodwill, patience, and gentleness.

The other four vows are connected to *ahimsa* and the cessation of karmic accumulation. They are always to speak the truth; not to steal or take what is not given; chastity, which is understood as celibacy for the monks, and faithfulness in marriage for the laypeople; and last, nonattachment to people and material things.

Preventing new karmas from staining the soul is the first step to liberation; purification of the stains of old karmas is the next. Good deeds and asceticism are the principle means of eliminating the accumulation of karmas. Those who desired to attain perfect enlightenment must, like Mahavira, practice fasting, engage in certain types of meditation, penance, yoga, study, and recitation of the scriptures. These acts purge the soul of its karmic deposit. They lead to transcendence over one's own physical state and to a trance state marked by complete disassociation from the outer world. This trance state is believed to be like the one Mahavira entered into in the thirteenth year of his seeking and assured him of his final liberation.

The ultimate ascetic observance, assumed by many throughout history, is fasting to death. The fast is the symbol and producer of absolute renunciation. Before this point, the ascetic has abstained from all but food and water. And then in a profound meditative state, food and water are given up, ending for good all attachments to samsara. This fast is not considered an act of violence, but a gesture of compassion, because there is no anger or pain associated with it.

The purging of all karmas restores the soul to its pure, undefiled state. It then has perfect knowledge, perfect perception and power. It is no longer weighed down by the burden of its karma, so it ascends to the very ceiling of the universe, where it enjoys the bliss of nirvana in the company of other liberated beings.

Similar to the Buddha and the Upanishadic sages, Mahavira taught a path of self-salvation. Since each individual soul is responsible for its own karmas, only the individual person is able to reverse the karmic accumulations. The purpose of the monastic community was to provide a supportive context for the pursuit of nirvana. Because the Jain search for nirvana required a more austere asceticism than the Buddha's Middle Way, taking on the life of a monk or nun was more vital to the realization of nirvana in Jainism than in Buddhism. The monks were also responsible for safeguarding the Mahavira's teaching, first in oral tradition and then in writing.

Although there are in Jainism differences of doctrine and practice, they should not be overemphasized. According to the contemporary Jains scholar, Nathmal Tatia, all Jains agree on the central message of Jainism, which is nonviolence, non-absolutism, and nonattachment.[18] These basic observances are the elements in the Jain quest for personal liberation from samsara and the communitarian goal of peace throughout the world.

Conclusion

With this we conclude our study of Jainism and the Indian Axial Age. We next turn our attention to East Asia and ancient China.

Notes

1. Thomas J. Hopkins, *The Hindu Religious Tradition* (Encino, CA, and Belmont, CA: Dickenson, 1971), 50–51.

2. *Vinaya: Mahavagga* 16. This text is part of the *Vinaya Pitaka*, the *Book of Monastic Discipline*, which codifies the rule of the Buddhist order. Cited in Karen Armstrong, *The Great Transformation: The Beginning of Our Religious Traditions* (New York/Toronto: Knopf, 2006), 278.

3. Mark W. Muesse, *Religions of the Axial Age: An Approach to the World's Religions* (Chantilly, VA: Teaching Company, 2007), part 1, 175.

4. Ibid.

5. Ibid.

6. Ibid., part 2, 16.

7. Cited in Ibid., part 2, 23.

8. Ibid., 26.

9. Ibid., 28–29.

10. *Majjhima Nikaya* (MN) 38. Cited in Armstrong, *The Great Transformation*, 278. The Pali scriptures include four collections of the Buddha's sermons (*Majjhima Nikaya, Digha Nikaya, Anguttara Nikaya,* and *Samyutta Nikaya*) and an anthology of minor works, which include *Udana*, a collection of the Buddha's maxims, and the *Jataka*, stories about the past lives of the Buddha and his companions.

11. Hermann Oldenberg, *Buddha: His Life, His Doctrine, His Order* (London and Edinburgh: Williams & Norgate, 1882), 299–302.

12. Muesse, *Religions of the Axial Age*, part 1, 97–98.

13. Karen Armstrong, *A History of God: The 4000-Year Quest of Judaism, Christianity and Islam* (New York: Knopf, 1993).

14. *Sutta-Nipata* 43:1–43; cited in Armstrong, *Great Transformation*, 282. The *Sutta-Nipata* is an anthology of early Buddhist poetry.

15. Major Religions of the World Ranked by Number of Adherents. Available at: http://www.adherents.com/adh_branches.html.

16. Ibid.

17. Muesse, *Religions of the Axial Age*, part 2, 59–62.

18. *That Which Is: Tattvartha Sutra,* trans. Nathmal Tatia (San Francisco: HarperCollins, 1994).

Chapter Six

CONFUCIANISM AND DAOISM

East Asia before the Axial Age

Throughout most of its recorded history, China has been home to three major religions: Confucianism, Daoism, and Buddhism. Our concern in this chapter is the first two of these traditions as they developed in the Chinese Axial Age. To set the scene for our study, we look first, briefly, at the pre-Axial religious and cultural life of China as it was in prehistory, and then during the Shang and the Zhou dynasties.

Mythological Prehistory

The Chinese trace their history back five thousand years. While no written or archaeological evidence supports them, legends speak of the Era of Three Sovereigns and the Era of Three Sages several millennia before our current era. During these prehistoric times, the fundamental characteristics of Chinese civilization were established, including hunting and fishing, agriculture, boats and carts, religious ritual, silk, centralized governments, and writing.

These prehistoric eras hold significant symbolic importance for the Chinese because they explain why culture exists as it does, and they provide norms by which later people could evaluate their ideals and behavior. Confucius was of the opinion that the China of his day had drifted from the mores of an earlier golden age, and he believed that a return to the ways of old was the only choice for promoting moral harmony in society.

Shang Dynasty

The first period for which there is historical evidence is the Shang Dynasty, arising during the fifteenth or fourteenth century BCE in the northeastern region of China. The artifacts from this period supply a wealth of information about religious practices of the pre-Axial era. The most important of these practices was a type of divination, a form of communicating with the spirit world and predicting the future. The artifacts also indicate that the ancient Chinese were convinced that there was a close connection between the spirit realm (heaven, or *tian*) and the human realm (Earth, or *di*). Heaven and Earth were thought of as continuous realms in which the gods and spirits were immediately accessible to human beings. An important part of Shang religion focused on maintaining the harmony between these domains that was necessary for the well-being of everyone. One of the king's main functions was to preserve harmony.

Shang theology interpreted the divine as composing a heavenly court that was in parallel with the earthly royal court. Just as the king ruled on Earth by means of a bureaucracy of nobles, so the high god ruled heaven with his assistants and servants. *Shang Di* was the Lord Supreme who presided over many lesser divinities who held sway over the powers of the natural and human worlds. The Chinese prayed to them to bestow favors in matters of agriculture, hunting, military campaigns, and health and longevity. They related to their gods in a businesslike fashion, not desiring friendships or devotional intimacy with them. And there is no evidence that the gods were concerned with the moral behavior of human beings. Favors were not granted on the basis of virtuous conduct. The principle concern in the divine-human relationship was for the gods to receive pleasing sacrifices and worship and for human persons to receive divine assistance with the matter of life in the world. The Indo-Aryans at this same point in history were likewise concerned with meeting basic needs and leading lives of abundance more than developing morally or spiritually.

Ancestors also functioned in an important way in the religious lives of the pre-Axial Chinese, as they still do today. Deceased family members existed in the spirit world, and there they continued to exert influence on the living. Consequently, they were consulted on important family matters and venerated with sacrifices and gifts. Since burial of the dead was probably the earliest religious ritual, some of the first theorists of religion suggested that the reverence of ancestors may have been one of the earliest forms of religion.

Yet another factor that plays an important part in the development of the Axial Age thought is *de*, a word found inscribed on many of the ancient artifacts. *De* is translated as "virtue," although its meaning in pre-Axial China differs from that definition. The word *de* referred to a power or force produced by an act of compassion or by a pleasing sacrifice to a god or ancestor. The attitude with which the act was executed was most important. *De* born of an act of kindness was able to affect the lives of others positively, since a good act encouraged the receiver to act kindly. Those persons who benefited from acts of compassion felt indebted to the benefactors and would desire to repay them with a similar act of kindness, called *bao*. Acts of virtue are important in Chinese religion, for example, in regard to family obligations. Children are deeply indebted to their parents for giving them life. Since this debt can never be repaid fully, the only proper response is filial reverence. Including ancestors as an important part of the ongoing life of a family is connected with what the Chinese call "filial piety," or reverence for one's parents. The great significance of filial responsibility has been basic to Chinese culture throughout the Axial Age and up to modern times. The other aspects of the Shang religion have been preserved in some fashion through most of Chinese religious history.

Zhou Dynasty

In our first view of China's religious history, we discussed the important practices and beliefs of the pre-Axial period, including divination, ancestor reverence, ritual sacrifices, and gods, all of which endured into the Axial Age and up to modern times. Now we examine the transition to the Axial Age.

Scholars are not completely sure when the Shang Dynasty began, but we do know when it ended. In or about the year 1045 BCE, the Shang rulers were deposed by another aristocratic family, who founded the next period in Chinese history, the Zhou Dynasty. This period lasted, at least in name, some eight hundred years until it was supplanted by the Qin Dynasty in 221 BCE. This time frame means that the Zhou

Dynasty roughly spans the complete Axial Age. Consequently, it is necessary to discuss some of the political and cultural aspects of this period to help us understand its religious dimensions.

The Zhou were a people who ruled a principality in the Wei Valley. In 1045, the king of the Zhou invaded the Shang domain in the Yellow River Valley, and eventually the king's brother, the duke of Zhou, completely quashed the Shang, who then lost control of the central plain. When Prince Cheng, at a young age, became the new king, the duke of Zhou took on the prominent role as regent and devised a quasi-feudal system. The figures in the early history of the Zhou Dynasty, particularly the duke, came to be looked upon as the paragons of leadership and moral conduct by later Chinese, especially Confucius. Confucius even states that he had frequent dreams about the duke.

The duke of Zhou, who was regent of the empire when the young Prince Cheng assumed the throne, believed that heaven had given the ethical mandate to all the Zhou people; therefore the new king had the obligation to rely on the advice of his ministers. Cheng, however, was of the opinion that the mandate had been given exclusively to the king, who was thus endowed with a unique, mystic potency that give him the power to rule. So, because of this difference of views, the duke of Zhou was forced to retire in the city of Lu, which had been assigned to him as his personal fief. To the people of Lu, he became a hero; they revered him as their most distinguished ancestor. The duke's conviction that virtue was more important than magical charisma would become a highly cherished value of the Axial Age. But at this time the Chinese were not yet ready for this moral vision.

It appears that the Zhou rulers accepted parts of the Shang religion. Like the Shang kings, the Zhou leaders worshiped a high god in addition to the countless local spirits and divinities that made up the heavenly bureaucracy. In Zhou theology this Supreme Being was called *Tian*, a term that usually is translated as "heaven" in the Shang Dynasty. *Tian* was simply a generic term for the realm of heaven; however, in the Zhou period, the idea of Tian became more ambiguous. The Zhou people thought of Tian as a personal deity, a being conceptualized in anthropomorphic terms, like Shang Di has been understood in the Shang Dynasty. In fact, the Zhou rulers originally used the names Shang Di and Tian rather interchangeably to identity the highest god. Over time, however, the more impersonal associations came to be more prominent in Zhou theology, and heaven was regarded fundamentally as an ultimate principle. So *Tian* could now refer to both a personal god and an impersonal principle.

But the crucial difference between the Zhou and the Shang concepts of the highest power pertains to morality. As we have seen, in Shang theology the gods, from the highest on down, simply were not concerned with how human beings behaved toward one another. The gods did not make moral behavior a condition for granting favors. As long as the sacrifices were sufficient, they did not care about the moral quality of persons. But Tian did care. This attribution of moral characteristics represents an important shift from the pre-Axial understanding of the gods, and it is part of the general ethicization process that we have observed throughout the several Axial centers. The Zhou introduced an ethical ideal into their polytheistic religion that until that time had been unconcerned about morality. They came to believe that Tian, Heaven Most High, the god they worshiped as supreme, was not pleased simply by the sacrifice of pigs and oxen; he also required the compassionate and just *behavior* of his worshipers. They saw that God's command to them— "Heaven's Mandate"—included an ethical component. This divine directive, then, would become an important ideal during the Chinese Axial Age. If a ruler was selfish, cruel, and oppressive, heaven would not sustain him, and he would fall. If the ruler of a state was wise, humane, and truly concerned for the welfare of his subjects, people would flock to him from all over the world, and heaven would elevate him to the highest position.

But it is not completely clear just how far Tian's moral concerns extended. For instance, it is not clear if heaven were interested in how the ordinary Chinese man related to his wife or how she behaved toward her neighbor. It is evident, however, that heaven had an interest in who the ruler was and how he treated his subjects. This is known because a new concept begins to appear in the Chinese lexicon of the Zhou Dynasty: *Tianming*, the "Mandate of Heaven." Some of the early Chinese classics credit the duke of Zhou with this idea. As it came to be understood, the Mandate of Heaven ordered that the ruler governed with divine blessing as long as he was virtuous. On the other hand, if the ruler acted in a wicked manner or was inept, heaven withdrew its mandate and the ruler's reign was no longer morally legitimate. Because the Chinese understanding of the Mandate of Heaven made the ruler's legitimacy dependent not only on his birth but also on his virtue, this concept could be used as a justification for opposing and even deposing the king, which is precisely what the Zhou rulers did.

In spite of its mandate from heaven, the Zhou Empire and its dynasty started to decline a hundred years after its conquest of the central plain. The dynasty *did* retain, nevertheless, a religious and symbolic aura long after the Zhou king had ceased to be important in the political domain. The Chinese people would never forget the early years of the Zhou dynasty. Their Axial Age would be inspired by the search for a ruler who would be worthy of heaven's mandate. The Axial Age in China would not break with the past, but would develop slowly as the Chinese progressively developed a deep understanding of the meaning and value of the traditional religious rites performed by the Zhou kings.

Ninth Century BCE

When these sacred rites were performed by the Zhou king, the vassals and ordinary people were reminded that the king was in fact the *Tianzi*, the son of Heaven (God), who was mandated to rule the Chinese people. They understood that the exterior aim of the religious ceremonies was to preserve the natural order of the universe and thus to ensure that the king and human society conformed to the Way *(Dao)* of Heaven. At all times of his life, the king was obliged to conform to the Way of Heaven. His role was not to create foreign or domestic policies from his own resources of mind and heart, but simply to follow the Way. This ancient ideal would later inspire many of the spiritualities of the Chinese Axial Age.

While the Chinese did come in the ninth century to a certain understanding of their religious system, they had not yet developed self-consciousness, and consequently they had not yet started to reflect on and analyze the deeper inner and spiritual effects of their religious ceremonies. But later, during the third century, Xunzi, one of the most rationalistic sages of the Chinese Axial Age, reflected upon these ancient rites and was able to penetrate their spiritual importance. He saw that the external gestures of the rites had an effect on the performer's inner self. Above all, the rites enabled the participants to transcend themselves. During the Axial Age, people would become aware that going beyond the limitations of selfishness brought deeper satisfaction than mere self-indulgence: "He who curbs his desires in accordance with the Way will be joyful and free from disorder, but he who forgets the Way in the pursuit of desire will fall into delusion and joylessness."[1] During the Chinese Axial Age some of the sages would reject the artifice of religious rites, but others would build a profound spirituality based on the liturgical ceremonies.

By the end of the ninth century, the Zhou Dynasty was in dire straits. While the religious rites were still performed with beauty and grace, and still had a profound effect on the participants, a few tough-minded critics were beginning to lose faith in their magical efficacy. However, the response to this growing critical situation would not be fewer rites, but more.

Eighth Century BCE

The eighth century in China was a time of transition and unsettling changes. The Zhou kings continued the dynasty and performed their ritual tasks, but they had no real political power. Land for hunting and breeding of cattle was no longer abundant, and therefore livestock were scarce. The wealth of the noble families in the cities now depended on agriculture rather than on hunting and raiding. Because there were fewer military and hunting expeditions, the *junzi* ("gentleman") spent more time at court, increasingly occupied with protocol, etiquette, and the minutiae of ritual.[2]

Restraint, control, and moderation were now valued, and life became more and more carefully regulated. Because this was an uncertain time of transition and change, people desired clear directives. Most of the activities of the noble class were transformed into an elaborate system of ceremonies, thus making the principles of aristocratic life accessible and clear to all persons. With this knowledge a *junzi* would know exactly where he should place himself in a feudal gathering, how he should stand, greet people, and comport himself; he would know precisely when to speak and to remain silent; what to wear and how to use the appropriate gestures, and to assume the desired facial expressions for each occasion.

Religion, too, had to be rethought. In this system of ritualized behavior, everything had a religious value. In the early days of the Zhou, the royal ceremonies had been devised to maintain the order of nature.

Now that the monarch was in decline, the rites transformed the whole of life into an elaborate ritual performance so that the order of human civilization would be granted peace and order. These ritual actions were intended to express the humility of the participants; but the chronicles indicate that actually no real humility or unconcern for status were shown in the performance of these rites:

> The ritualized lifestyle of the nobility did instruct aristo-crats to behave with apparent self-surrender, reverence and modesty to one another, but the rites were mostly informed with self-interest. Everything was a matter of prestige. Aristocrats were jealous of their privileges and their honor, and exploited the *li* to enhance their status.[3]

The most authoritative school of ritual was based in the princi-pality of Lu. In the ritual code developed by this school, two important principles were set forth: first, the efficacy of a ceremony was dependent on the precisely correct performance of every one of its constituent actions; second, this required perfection was possible only on the con-dition that each one of the participants be fully aware of the meaning of the rite as a whole, that is, be mindful of the genuine self-surrender and humility to be expressed in the rites. Later on, in the sixth century, one of the ritualists initiated China's Axial Age with these two princi-ples as his starting point. By doing this he revealed the latent spiritual power of the apparently self-serving and tedious ceremonies.

It should be noted, however, that even at this early stage, before the beginning of the Chinese Axial Age, some of the Lu ritualists under-stood the meaning and value of self-surrender.[4] These were the greatly revered Yao and Shun, the sage kings of remote antiquity. Both were truly gentle and modest persons, endowed with an ethical power that brought spiritual benefit to the people. In the eyes of the people, Yao and Shun had become "saints," men of kindness and humanity who had established in the empire a golden age of peace and harmony. Rather than holding on to their own status and prestige, they had both put the good of the people before their own personal interest. They were the models of the self-surrendering virtues that the *li* were supposed to cul-tivate. Later the Axial sages would claim that every single human being had the potential to become like these great men.

Seventh and Sixth Centuries BCE

The seventh century was a period of turbulence in the Yellow River region, but the violence was kept within bounds, due in no small part to the ritual reform initiated by the literati of Lu. By this time, life in the principalities was closely regulated by the rituals, to the degree that the various areas of ordinary life started to resemble the elaborate ritual ceremonies of the Zhou court. In spite of this regularized conformity, some of the rites had considerable spiritual potential. However, this sacred capability went unnoticed by the Chinese.

In the sixth century, several military, social, and economic factors made the time one of change and crisis. When Chu defeated the armies of the league of Chinese states in 597, warfare became increasingly aggressive and violent, much different from the stately ritualized campaigns of the past. There was also a growing scorn for ritual observance in other areas of life: for example, people began to place profane objects in the tombs of their relatives rather than the prescribed ritual vessels. And the old spirit of moderation and restraint was in decline: many of the Chinese developed a new attraction for greed and luxury, and this materialism put a strong strain on the economy. Some of the ordinary gentlemen at the bottom of the feudal hierarchy began to imitate the lifestyle of the great families, with the result that there were now too many aristocrats. Some members of the nobility could no longer own a fief because the land had become limited, and some of them lost their lands and titles and were reduced to the rank of commoners. This turmoil was more than a social and political crisis; it also had specifically religious dimensions. In the Chinese mentality, heaven and earth were so interdependent that many people feared that because of the current scorn for the Way of Heaven, the entire cosmos was endangered. The ritualists of Lu perceived the new greed, aggression, and materialism as a scandalous assault on the sacred rites. Toward the end of the sixth century, Lu was on the verge of total anarchy.

In time, outright chaos ensued when around 475 the Period of Warring States began. By that time there were advanced military technologies; peasants were being drafted as soldiers. As the name implies, this era was exceptionally brutal and violent. However, in philosophical and theological thinking, it was an extremely creative time. The Period of Warring States was, in fact, also known as the Period of One

Hundred Philosophers. That alternative name implies that this age of political disorder moved the intellectuals to address the urgent issues of the day. And clearly, the most pressing concern was the simple and practical matter of creating and preserving human harmony. The question of the day was, What does it take for people to get along with each other? And there was no shortage of responses to this question. There were at least four or five major philosophical schools proposing their particular solutions. Confucianism and Daoism were the most significant.

In this time of disorder and crisis, a young man appeared on the scene. He was drawn to the ritualists and was profoundly dedicated to the Zhou Dynasty, especially to the great duke of Zhou. He was an avid student of traditional ceremony and the classics; he had mastered the traditional ritual culture and understood the deeper meaning of the rites; he was convinced that, properly interpreted, the rites could bring the people of China back to the Way of Heaven. His disciples later called him *Kongfuzi*, "our Master Kong." In the West, he is called Confucius. And with this celebrated sage, China's Axial Age was about to begin.

Confucianism

Confucius was China's most important Axial Age figure and, perhaps, the most influential Chinese figure of all time. The most historically reliable information we have about him is found in a book called the *Analects (Lunyu)*, a collection of his sayings, conversations, and anecdotes compiled after his death by his disciples. Some scholars claim that Confucius was not a historical figure, but a literary creation, a character invented to symbolize certain things for the Chinese elite. But this and other related views are controversial claims in Confucian scholarship, and regarding them no consensus has been reached. So it seems appropriate to present the majority view on the historiographical issues concerning Confucius. Our chief concern, however, is the beliefs and practices set forth in the sage's teaching.

From the *Analects*, and a few other sources, most scholars of Confucius surmise that he was born around 551 BCE and died around 479, during the Spring and Autumn Period in the state of Lu, a small principality that began to compete with others as the eastern Zhou Dynasty declined. He is known in the West as Confucius, but throughout Chinese history he was called *Kongfuzi*, or "Master Kong." The Jesuits missionaries in the seventh century CE gave him the name Confucius. In addition to the date and place of his birth, we can say only a few other things about him. He came from the lower nobility, was relatively poor, and remained poor all his life. In spite of his modest beginnings, or perhaps because of them, he was a student dedicated to learning. In the sayings of and about Confucius in the first half of the *Analects,* the reader comes upon a man of profound humility, more concerned with self-improvement than with judging others. He was passionately dedicated to the arts and was of the opinion that music had a moral impact; listening to appropriate music was able to make the amateur a better person. He respected authority and held that a humane society was dependent on respect for one's superiors. He desired to gain significant political power but never succeeded in doing so. His interest in politics was motivated by the will to do good for society and the well-being of all citizens. Confucius believed that the real way to human harmony was establishing good government and in promoting the moral character of the ruler and other public servants. When the leader is virtuous, so the people will follow suit.

Practical Thrust of Confucius's Teaching

Confucius lived during an especially brutal time in Chinese history. Because hostilities between kingdoms and corruption in government were mounting, it was likely necessary that he think about practical social and political matters. A large portion of his teachings were directed toward the rulers and government officials, and consequently are in the nature of political philosophy about practical matters. For example, In the current state of Chinese civilization, how best do the authorities rule? He also had much to say about the practical aspects of family life. But in matter of both family and politics, his main interest was in ethics or morality.

Confucius does not say much about the gods or spirits or the human soul. While it is true that he is generally considered China's greatest religious figure and was himself later worshiped as divine, he actually said little about the spirit world. He never denied the existence of the gods and spirits, but he did not make them central to his view.

He forcefully urged people to be moral, to practice goodness and kindness, but never did he indicate that a person of compassionate behavior would be rewarded by the gods or enjoy a favorable afterlife for such conduct. Nevertheless, it is appropriate to include Confucianism in the category of religion. This is so because of his emphasis on practicing one's beliefs. Also, although he was reticent about the gods and spirits, he did speak of Tian, or heaven. Once he suggested that heaven itself authorized him to teach, and in so doing, he applied the Mandate of Heaven to his own work. Consequently, Confucius saw heaven as legitimating his teaching. Furthermore, even though he was not concerned with divine beings as such, he was extremely interested in ritual, especially the sacrifices performed on state occasions for the welfare of the state. He valued rituals very highly, not so much because they pleased the gods, but because he considered them as salutary for human life. They helped to mold moral character.

The central thrust of Confucian thought is practical. But his practical concerns are informed by a specific vision of the way human beings and human society ought to be and act. Before turning to the practice of Confucian ethics, we reflect on his ideals for individuals and human relationships. This will facilitate our understanding of his ethics and it will help connect Confucius to the other Axial Age sages.

Human Ideals

Confucius proposed several ideal types, as there are in other religions. The highest type of person for Confucius was the sage, a person who was the complete embodiment of Confucian values. In his later life he stated that he had never encountered a real sage and had given up hope of ever doing so. He also spoke of the ideal types of the good man and the complete man. But the type he stressed above all others was that of the *junzi*, usually translated as "gentleman" or "nobleman." One of the characteristics of the gentleman is being mannerly and gentle. Confucius also intended the word to mean someone who had attained a noble character and superior status. And for Confucius, nobility and superiority are qualities that are earned by hard work and not gained by birthright.

Drawing on his study of earlier Chinese culture, especially the figure of the duke of Zhou and other individuals associated with the early Zhou period, Confucius held that there are certain characteristics that defined the gentleman. The foremost among these was the quality of *ren*. *Ren* is often translated as "humaneness" or "humanity," but "compassion" would also be an appropriate rendering of the word. Confucius was not the first to coin the concept of *ren*; it was an old aristocratic term signifying something like "noblesse oblige," that is, the obligation of the aristocrat to be kind to those of lower station. But Confucius was the first to make *ren* central to his teaching. He did believe that *ren* was the prominent characteristic of the gentleman, but he never fully defined it or specified if it were innate to human nature or acquired. He preferred to treat it by discussing examples of persons possessing it. If it were an inborn quality, it always needed to be cultivated and nurtured to rise to full expression. If it were an acquisition, then it would also require cultivation to be instilled. Whether he viewed it as a natural potential or as a product of education, Confucius believed it to be necessary to dedicate oneself to the difficult discipline of being good.

Enough was said by Confucius about humanness and the gentleman to derive an idea of what he meant by *ren*. In more than one place, he states that humanness involves observing a norm known as the Golden Rule: Do not impose on other what you would not want imposed upon yourself. For Confucius, humanness or *ren* involves another component: *reciprocity*, that is, the method of determining what others may desire or not desire. The guide for making such a judgment is one's own feelings. By being in touch with one's own wishes, one may conceive, on the basis of a common humanity, what others wish. In his emphasis on reciprocity, Confucius also meant that one is to act compassionately on what one knows others may want.

Confucius also speaks of *ren* in the language of loving others, or one's fellow man. He did not hold that the human person would, or should, love everyone equally. He proposed that a person should love others in proportion to the benefit one received from them. Since it is evident that a person benefits most from his or her parents and from other members of the family, that person then is obligated to love and care for them most. Confucius not only believed that filial piety was the most natural expression of human love, but he also was convinced that it was the basis of all forms of loving. But Confucius did not mean that love stops with the family. From learning to fulfill filial responsibilities, a person is to extend his or her love to friends and neighbors, to the village, the common people, and ultimately to all of humanity, but with a love that is less than for those who are nearest.

In his teaching on the ideals of human behavior, Confucius laid out a difficult path. Accordingly, the disciples of Confucius thought his path a hard one to walk. Discussing the Confucian way, one of his disciples stated, "A Gentleman must be strong and resolute, for his burden is heavy and the road is long. He takes benevolence as his burden. Is that not heavy? Only with death does the road come to an end. Is that not long?"[5] The striving for goodness is a lifelong process. Confucius never guaranteed an end to his way. He did not assure reward or success, but he did ensure that those who followed the path of cultivating goodness did so for its own sake and not for any other reason.

The prime qualities of the *junzi,* the gentleman, were humanness, kindness toward others, empathy. He was also wise. According to Confucius, wisdom was knowing what was right and what was wrong, being a good judge of character, possessing self-knowledge. He told his followers, "When you understand something, to recognize that you understand it; but when you do not understand something, to recognize that you do not understand it, that is wisdom." Wisdom also meant that one was able to think for oneself. A gentleman did not blindly follow others, or as Confucius would say, "A gentleman does not behave as an implement."[6]

The quality of equanimity was also a possession of the *junzi.* "In his attitude toward the world the gentleman has no antagonisms and not favoritisms," said Confucius. The gentleman did not permit external circumstances to determine his disposition. Master Confucius said, "A man of quality indeed was Hui! He lived in a squalid alley with a tiny bowlful of rice to eat and a ladleful of water to drink. Others would not have endured such hardships, but Hui did not let his happiness be affected. A man of quality indeed was Hui!"[7] This quality of equanimity applied also to the opinions of others. In the very first passage of the *Analects,* Confucius defines the highest standards of this quality: "Not to be resentful at others' failure to appreciate one, surely that is to be a true gentleman." Somewhat later in the same section he takes this trait to even a higher level: "One does not worry about the fact that other people do not appreciate one. One worries about not appreciating other people."[8] Consequently, peace and serenity characterize the gentleman.

Summary

We have reflected on the basic dimensions of the teachings of Confucius. We have seen how his teaching is mainly focused on human character and the importance of shaping it so that it express humaneness, a quality he believed fulfilled the potential of human beings and made possible a society that thrives in harmony.

Humanness and the other virtues treated by Confucius in the *Analects* comprise an ideal type of what he envisioned for individuals and society. His morality emphasized the development of character rather than the performance of ethical acts. Yet acting ethically is basic in molding virtuous moral character, and to promote such behavior Confucius also stressed the importance of certain disciplines, especially *li* (ritual and propriety), filial piety, and reverence in the realization of *ren*.

We now examine the specific ways of training the person so that the characteristics of the gentleman might be more abundantly expressed. And we also study the ways in which such self-cultivation was a benefit to society.

Self-Cultivation of the Gentleman: The Fostering of Virtue

In the view of Confucius, the social and political disorder of his day was rooted in spiritual defilement: greed, hatred, the love of power, self-centeredness, and insensitivity to human life. These dispositions, he believed, were not aspects of life that could be restrained by mere legislation and extensive policing of the populace. His answer to these deep-rooted problems of his China was cultivating persons of virtue. We have already explored how the virtues Confucius thought most important would be embodied in the one he called the gentleman, his idea of the ideal individual. Now we go on to study how Confucius thought these virtues could be taught and instilled in the populace, and how virtuous individuals could work for greater harmony within and among societies.

Confucius held that self-discipline was the key to the cultivation of virtue, to the bringing forth of what is best in persons. He did not develop as clear-cut a plan as the Buddha's Noble Eightfold Path for his disciples to follow. He did, however, establish some specific norms for guiding them along the path of virtue, which he called the "Way of Dao." We are able to list some of his fundamental guideposts for virtue.

According to the Dao, his followers were to avoid eating too much and becoming too comfortable. Conscious self-restraint helped to subdue the person from lapsing into ego-centered thought. A disciplined life required mindfulness in word and in deed. A type of meditation, called "quiet sitting," prepared a person to be clearly aware of personal thoughts and experiences, and this heightened awareness formed space for critical self-examination. Those following the Dao were dedicated to learning, especially to the study of certain Chinese classics: books on ritual, the *Yi Jing* and the *Book of Odes;* the *Wu Jing* or the *Five Classics,* the first canon of Confucian writings. Also important to the cultivation of virtue was an educated appreciation of music, dance, and poetry, and careful attention to appropriate clothing and food. In spite of Confucius's attentiveness to seemingly mundane aspects of life, he did also encourage detachment from possessions, wealth, recognition, and comfort.

Proper Observances of *Li*

The most important guidepost for the self-cultivation of virtue was, in the view of Confucius, the proper performance of *li.* He extended the ordinal meaning of *li* to refer not only to the public formal ritual sacrifice performed for the gods, ancestors, and spirits, but also to all occasions of human interaction. He believed humans, not only in their relations with the deities, but in all their dealings with others ought to act and comport themselves with all the dignity appropriate to a sacred, explicitly religious rite. He depicts the features of this dignified approach to all relationships with illustrations of social etiquette or manners: "The things which the gentleman values in the Way are three: in demeanor he banishes his violence and rudeness; in composing his expression he keeps close to sincerity; and in the style of his utterances he banishes coarseness and impropriety."[9]

Confucius was not, however, interested in ritual and manners simply for the sake of presenting oneself in a refined way or even for gaining certain personal advantages. His real interest was ritual as a way of responding to the difficulties of his times. Like other sages of the Axial Age, Confucius experienced a profound alienation from his troubled time. In his judgment, the root cause of the current disorder, the violence and vendetta in China, was neglect of the traditional rites that had for so long governed the conduct of the principalities. During the time of the ancient kings, Yao and Shun, and later under the early Zhou, the Way of Heaven had been followed perfectly, and human beings lived together in harmony. The rituals had shaped life activities according to the Dao, the Way of Heaven, and they brought about the self-cultivation of virtue. But these days the princes, preoccupied by warfare and motivated by the pursuit of luxury and their own selfish ambition, never gave a second thought to the Dao. In the view of Confucius, the best solution was to return to the ritual traditions that had worked so well in the past. Observance of rituals was the most important means for the cultivation of virtue, the performance of *li*, and the overcoming of violence and vendetta of China's troubled times.

When performed with the proper intention and disposition, observance of the rules of ritual for correct behavior has the potential to make persons more humane. Confucius, then, connected *li* to moral development. In the Shang and early Zhou dynasties, ritual was understood chiefly as the performance of external acts. Simply going through the prescribed motions was required to make the ritual effective. Closer to the time of Confucius, *li* came to include the inner attitude of reverence and sincerity of the rituals' participants. The sacrifice needed to be performed in the proper spirit so that it would not be ineffective and displeasing to those it was meant to honor. Confucius took this care with the interiority of ritual a step further by relating it with the virtue of humanness. The observance of ritual now becomes an act that not only gratified the divine being but also shapes the moral character of the participant and the observers.

Focus on This World

Confucius venerated the traditions of the past and wanted to restore their observance as a means of resolving some of the problems of the current times. It should be noted, however, that some of his interpretations of them were innovative and radically different in emphasis.

The old religion focused on heaven: people had frequently performed the sacrificial rites simply to gain the favor or the gods and spirits. Confucius's focus, however, was on *this* world. Even though he was not interested in metaphysics or theological speculation, he was not a religious skeptic. He practiced the traditional ancestral liturgical rites punctiliously, and was filled with numinous awe when he thought of heaven. In private belief and public practice he exhibited faith in the transcendent supreme reality of heaven. But he did bring the religion of China down to earth. Rather than concerning themselves about the afterlife, people should concentrate on living an ethical life in this world. The rites comprised a road map that would direct them on the course of such a good and holy life.

He redefined the role of the *junzi*: the true gentleman should be a scholar of ritualized, correct behavior as prescribed by the traditional rites of family, political, military, and social life. In the old days, only an aristocrat had been a *junzi*, but Confucius insisted that anyone who studied the Way with enthusiasm could become a gentleman. Such a man was a mature and profound person who always made efforts to curb his ego and surrender to the dynamics of the rites. He submitted all details of his life to the rituals of consideration and respect for others. "If a ruler could curb his ego and submit to li for a single day, everyone under heaven would respond to his goodness."[10] The observance of ritual shapes the moral character and humanness of the participant gentleman and the observers.

Ego Principle

Like the sages of India, Confucius regarded the "ego principle" as the source of human pettiness and self-interest. If people would lose their ruthless selfishness and surrender to the altruistic demands of performing the rites at all moments of their lives, they would be transformed by holiness and beauty. And he insisted that the performance must be done in full awareness of what the person was doing. Psychological acuity and sensitive appraisal of each circumstance were required, not simply going through the motions.[11] When performed with the right spirit, the rites were a spiritual-ethical education that helped people go beyond the limitations of egotism and social rank and live life with dignity and grace.

Sacred Public Ritual

To explore now how *li* is a means of refining humanness, we focus on *li* as sacred public ritual rather than the manners of everyday life. The dynamics are generally the same in all cases, but they are more evident in the public sacred ritual.

Because they were elaborate events involving many persons, the rituals performed in the time of Confucius required extensive study before they could be enacted correctly. Not only were rituals specialists necessary, but also musicians, dancers, and actors who performed for the pleasure of the audience, consisting of both human and divine beings. The offerings sacrificed were animals, usually oxen, pigs, and sheep. Sometimes the gods and spirits were offered silk and jade, or rice and millet. More important, however, was the reverential and gracious attitude with which the gifts were offered. In the *Book of Odes* the spirits rewarded those who sacrificed in the correct mental attitude with a long life.

In the view of Confucius, many facets of the rituals promoted and refined the sense of humanness. The study necessary to perform the ritual provided a type of discipline and self-restraint as well as supplied knowledge about the meaning of the ritual itself, which Confucius believed embodied the mystery of heaven. In addition to this mystical dimension, the ritual had more mundane aspects that were seen as contributing to moral development. It evoked certain emotions and states of mind such as reverence, gratitude, and humility. It encouraged a spirit of cooperation among people and taught the importance of subordinating personal needs and desires to social concerns. Like meditation, ritual demands concentration and attention to detail. Finally, there is the way that ritual produced a sense of interconnectedness of humanity and divinity; it reminded one that he or she was part of a vast fabric of interdependent relationships involving the gods, other human beings, and the universe.

The relationship between humanness and *li* is dialectical, each one strengthening the other. As persons grow in humanness, the expression of that quality while interacting with others becomes easier and more authentic. The deeper their sentiments of compassion and the greater mindfulness of those movements of the will, the more are they likely to put them into action and to do so with sincerity of heart. In the same way, the more persons act kindly and compassionately and reverentially, the more they become aware of those qualities within their true selves.

Individual Moral Cultivation and a Better Society

Was Confucius of the mind that the solution to the social and political problems of the Zhou period was to place everyone on a program of moral self-cultivation? Since Confucius was strongly a realist, he did not expect such a thing. It is likely that he did not think that the common people had the time or even the mental power to undertake this regimen. But he did believe they were capable growing in moral strength; they only needed another approach.

And this is where government was to exert its greatest influence. It was Confucius's conviction that the chief role of the ruler and the ruling class was not the acquisition of power and wealth—the view that was becoming more and more popular on the eve of the Warring States Period—but to supply for the welfare of the common people. To promote the well-being of the whole of society, he believed it was essential for the ruler and the ruling class to practice the disciplines of moral self-cultivation and act as moral role models for all the citizens. The life of virtue, he thought, must begin at the top and then extend throughout the kingdom. The more virtuous the ruler, the more virtuous the ordinary people.

The theory of the ruler's moral impact in a country is founded on the ancient Chinese understanding of virtue. Here it should be recalled that virtue, or *de*, was considered to be a type of power or force that came to be present in the people of moral and compassionate character. The more kindly a person was, the more this virtuous power resided in him or her. The natural and irresistible response to virtuous acts by those who benefited from them was called *bao*, that is, the sense of gratitude and the wish to reciprocate in kind by acting virtuously oneself. By means of years of practicing virtue, one might gain sufficient virtuous energy to be morally charismatic. An individual with such an accumulation of moral charisma could inspire others to become more virtuous themselves.

Without legislation or proclamation, the virtuous ruler was able to affect the well-being of his state almost without effort, simply by giving a moral example. Confucius said, "Guide them by edicts, keep them in line with punishments and the common people will stay out of trouble but will have no sense of shame. Guide them by virtue, keep them in line with the rites, and they will, besides having a sense of shame, reform themselves." Confucius counseled rulers not to use force. "In administrating your government what need is there for you to kill? Just desire the good yourself and the common people will be good."[12]

But moral charisma does not move only from the top down. Confucius believed that social superiors could be influenced by those who were subordinate to them. For this reason he encouraged his followers to take government positions, where they would be in a place to influence both the lower classes and the ruler and his court. However, even the commoners could contribute to the welfare of society by cultivating virtue. The moral character of all citizens has results throughout a society. The goodness of the individual does make a difference in the world.

Confucius was, therefore, not a timid conservative, simply clinging to traditional ways and preoccupied with liturgical minutiae. He gave a new and innovative interpretation to the old rites. They were not designed to enhance a person's prestige or status; rather, they were intended to transform a person by making the practice of self-surrender and self-forgetfulness a habit. By eliminating egotism from the ritual actions, Confucius brought out their profound spiritual and ethical meanings. He did not encourage servile conformity. Properly performed, the rites that were meant to shape all activities of life demanded imagination and intelligence. He also introduced a new egalitarianism. In past times, only the aristocrat had performed the rites. Now Confucius insisted anybody could practice them, and even a person of humble origin could become a *junzi*.

It is true that he was largely silent about ultimate transcendent reality and the afterlife. Nevertheless, the clue to his profound significance as a religious thinker is found in his assertion that authentic morality is grounded in human nature as well as in its openness to the transcendent, and also in his conviction that when one acts ethically one does the will of heaven. He was committed to the religion of the Lord on High or Heaven, the supreme deity. In fact, he felt he was a prophet with the calling and backing of heaven. He indicated that it was heaven that gave him his message and protected him. "Heaven is the author of the virtue that is in me" (*Analects*, 7, 230). He died in 483 BCE.

The Death of Confucius

After the death of Confucius, his teachings were interpreted by his followers. The two most important of these interpreters were Mengzi and Xunzi, who agreed on much but disagreed about the quality of human nature. The former was convinced of the basic goodness of human beings, while the latter proposed that humans were neither good nor evil. Because Confucius himself was ambiguous about this point, it was much debated and became a central concern for many Axial Age thinkers across cultures.

In the last quarter of the third century BCE, the Qin Dynasty came to power and lasted briefly. The Qin Dynasty brought about the unification of China, but it was not a favorable time for Confucianism or Confucians. The predominant philosophy of the Qin was Legalism, one of the many competing schools of thought of the age. It embraced the use of military and police force as a way to maintain order, and it depended on the centralization of authority. Because the Qin rulers understood Confucianism as a threat to the rule, Confucian texts were burned, but many were preserved by scholars. Even though their regime lasted only fifteen years, the Qin rulers were remarkable enough that the country of China is known by their name.

The Hang Dynasty followed the Qin rule and held power from about 200 BCE to about 200 CE. This was a good era for the Chinese and for Confucianism. The Hang rulers not only reinstated Confucianism, they made it the official state religion. By the first century BCE, people offered sacrifices to Confucius and built temples in his honor. Mahayana Buddhism was introduced to China, and Daoism began to be established, intertwining Confucianism with these religions. The prestige of Confucius has waxed and waned over the centuries, but overall, the Chinese people have overwhelmingly esteemed him. His teachings also made an impact in Korea, Japan, and Vietnam. In 1906 an imperial decree made Confucius "Co-Assessor with the deities of Heaven and Earth." That proclamation was made some decades before the Communist takeover of China under the leadership of Mao Zedong. During Mao's rule, Confucius and Confucianism were labeled as quaint and antirevolutionary. Now, in the post-Mao era, Confucianism appears to be enjoying a renewed interest among Chinese and others around the world.

Daoism

Much of early Daoist thought was a response to the same social and political situation addressed by Confucianism. The Daoists, however, assumed a much different approach to the circumstances. While it is true that Confucianism and Daoism shared much in common, such as the conviction that the problems of the Zhou Dynasty were rooted in greed and an obsession with power, they proposed nearly radically opposed solutions. Consequently, Daoism arose as a counterbalance to the various components of Confucianism.

Historians have distinguished between the elite and folk dimensions of the Chinese traditions. Philosophical Daoism, known by the Chinese word *daojia* ("School of the Way"), was part of the elite form of the tradition, oriented toward the literate and intellectual class; while religious Daoism, known by the word *daojiao* ("Teaching of the Way"), was the folk expression, developed principally for the common people, whose needs and interests differed somewhat from those of a higher social station. Philosophical Daoism is primarily associated with two classic texts, the *Daodejing* and the *Zhuangzi*, which came into existence during the later Axial Age. Religious Daoism, also called the "Daoist Church," was a later development, starting around the second century BCE, when the tradition began to be structured with priests, temples, and hierarchies. Our attention focuses on what is called "Philosophical Daoism," but that terminology does not mean to convey that it had no religious components. It did. What it did lack were rituals, communities, clergy, gods, and similar features often associated with religion in the West. But like any religion, it was a structured response to belief in a comprehensive view of the world that involved the sacred and a concept of the ultimate.

Most scholars date the origins of Philosophical Daoism to around the third or fourth century, the time when its principle text, the *Daodejing,* was composed or at least written down. This would be within or near to the Period of the Warring States. It is clear that the text appeared after the advent of Confucianism, since much of it was clearly intended as a refutation of central Confucian ideas. According to Chinese tradition, the *Daodejing* was composed by a man named Laozi of the sixth century who was several years older than Confucius. As he aged, he became more and more frustrated with society and government, and he departed from the capital city to pass the rest of his days in solitude and quiet contemplation. As he was leaving the city, the gate keeper asked him to leave a remembrance of his wisdom before he departed forever. Laozi hurriedly brushed out a text of five thousand characters; afterward he continued on his journey.

This tradition has no historical basis. In the present time, nearly every scholar of Daoism holds Laozi to be a fiction, a creation of the early Daoists, intended most likely to provide a counterpart to Confucianism and an author for the *Daodejing*. This conclusion has compelling evidence. First, the stylistic and linguistic differences throughout the text make it clear that it was the work of many minds and not a single individual. The same differences also give evidence that the book was written and edited over an extended period of time, maybe even as long as a century. Furthermore, *Laozi* is not actually a name in Chinese; it means "old master" or perhaps "old baby." However, whether or not Laozi was an historical person matters very little. Much more interesting are the ideas expounded in this very intriguing and paradoxical book and the influence they exerted in China's Axial Age. It should be noted that the *Daodejing*, today the text most translated into English next to the Bible, is a mysterious book, composed of eighty-one small chapters of enigmatic verse, difficult to interpret because of its poetic style and elusive subject concerning the obscure and indistinct in life. This text has become a popular devotional classic in the West, even though it was not originally meant for a private individual but for the ruler of a small state. It is something of a mystical manual of statecraft. The ruler is urged to "do nothing," intervening as little as possible in the life of the state. He should be a virtuous man, not however, like a Confucian sage who was constantly making efforts to do things for his people. Rather he should be a ruler who practiced self-effacement and total impartiality and would bring the violence of the Period of the Warring States to an end.

The Daodejing

The title of the book is direct and clear. It is translated as "Classic of the Way and the Virtue," or "Classic of the Way and Its Potency." Difficulties, however, are encountered when one parses the words *Dao* and *de*. *Dao* was a concept employed by all forms of Chinese philosophy. In a formal, philosophical sense it meant the ideal way of things or the manner in which things go well. But it is used in different ways by different thinkers. Confucius intended it to mean the discipline of becoming a sage or the way to social harmony. The *Daodejing* also uses the term in the same manner, but gives it another, more basic meaning. For Daoists, *Dao* meant the way of nature, in a sense that approaches the concept of ultimate reality. In the *Daodejing* it is called the mother of the universe, implying it is source of all things and that which sustains and nourishes them. It is not, of course, to be understood as a personal entity; it is not a god or a goddess. But its jurisdiction is universal. It is the way of everything in the cosmos.

Yet *Dao* is not amenable to precise definition or complete comprehension, and therefore, it is not meant to be understood too clearly or in a manner too concrete. According to the opening lines of the *Daodejing*:

> The way that can be spoken of
> Is not the constant way;
> The name that can be named
> Is not the constant name.
> The nameless was the beginning of heaven and earth;
> The named was the mother of the myriad creatures.
> Hence always rid yourself of desires in order to observe its
>   secrets;
> But allow yourself to have desires in order to observe its
>   manifestations.
> These two are the same
> But diverge in name as they issue forth.[13]

The Twofold Aspects of the Dao

There are two aspects to Dao: that which can be discussed and talked about, and that which cannot; both are part of the same reality. The latter is the deeper, eternal aspect: the ineffable, the inscrutable way. This eternal, stable dimension can be affirmed as the primordial, ineffable Dao. There is also the aspect of the Dao that can be spoken of, the dimension of Dao that is open to name and concept; it is embodied in the appearance of the myriad things that make up the world. This changing Dao can be understood as that which manifests through the myriad things, the items of the cosmos that come into existence and pass out of it. Nevertheless, the ultimately ineffable characteristic of the Dao places restrictions on what and how it may be spoken of. The *Dao* is spoken of through paradox.

This paradox is illuminated, but not explained or resolved, by the Chinese icon *Taijitu*, know as the yin/yang symbol in the West. The black swirl is yin, representing the dark, hidden, passive, receptive, yielding, cool, soft, and feminine. The white swirl is yang, representing the light, open, active, aggressive, controlling, hot, hard, and masculine. This yin/yang symbol represents the Chinese ideal of harmony and wholeness; it suggests that each thing needs its equal and opposite to maintain balance. Like Dao, the concept of yin/yang was shared by Confucianism and Daoism and other Chinese schools of thought, and it most likely antedated all of them. Dao is the force of powers supporting yin and yang.

While yin and yang are truly opposites, they are also complementary and interdependent. One is not able to exist without the other. Essentially, the relationship between yin and yang accounts for the process of change: yin gives rise to yang, yang gives rise to yin. This is an eternal, harmonious pattern.

The icon of the *Taijitu* is spoken of here for two reasons. First, it is a presentation of the coexistence of change and constancy within the Dao. The Dao brings about, or is, the change in the world, as symbolized in the swirling movement of yin and yang. At the same time, the Dao is the source of balance, harmony, and wholeness symbolized by the circle, the representation of eternity and completeness. The pattern of constant change is its unvarying quality. Second, the emblem of *Taijitu* is referred to here because its representation of yin and yang in balance is helpful to understanding the relationship of Daoism and Confucianism. It may be that one of the reasons for the rise of Daoism was to counterbalance the very strong yang elements in Confucianism. Consequently, the *Daodejing* placed value on many things connected with the yin dimension of life: depth, mystery, intuition, the feminine, receptivity, darkness, enigma, passivity. Throughout the book, yin like these are valorized, as if to balance the yang emphasis in Confucianism.

Following the Dao

Like the Confucians, the Daoists who composed the *Daodejing* considered the *Dao* as the appropriate way for human persons to order and live their lives. However, unlike the Confucians, the Daoists understood following the way as conforming to the Dao of nature, the changes and rhythms of the universe and the natural world. The Dao of humanity was, indeed, the Dao of nature. The Confucians, on the other hand, associated the way not with nature but with culture, the correct observances of tradition, ritual, and *li*. The Daoists considered the very neglect of nature was at the root of society's misery. For early Daoism, Confucianism was not the solution to the problem, but indeed its very manifestation. Confucianism furthered the alienation of human beings from the Dao of nature by its human centeredness and by its close regulation of human relationships. To Daoists, Confucianism spoiled the very spontaneity of human life with its minutely thought-out rules and well-rehearsed rituals. Spontaneity, not precise calculation, was nature's way.

The Daoists believed that the solution to human suffering was a return to the way of the cosmos, the way of an older age. At the beginning, this counsel was meant for the rulers and the ruling class, for like the Confucians, the Daoists were of the opinion that the welfare of society was greatly dependent on the quality of the rulers. Therefore, a great portion of the *Daodejing* sets forth a social and political philosophy. But since the book contains elements of both political philosophy and spiritual practices, it is appropriate to examine each aspect. We look first at the Daoist ideal of the sage, the material that concerns most explicitly personal spirituality.

Daoist Personal Spirituality

The ideal of the sage or master or the ruler has a strong element of mysticism. Here *mysticism* means the experience, on the one hand, of losing one's sense of being a separate individual self, and, on the other, achieving a sense of participation in a much greater reality. This mystical enhancement is encouraged by means of the practices and way of being in the *Daodejing.*

The most important of these practices includes decreasing the ego in its craving for recognition and control. True sages and rulers were not to be self-promoters, seeking for advancement and credit for their accomplishments. Their chief concern was the welfare of others. The Daoists held that such self-effacement involved relinquishing the drive of the individual ego and assuming one's place in the great nexus of the universe. This, in effect, was conforming oneself to way of nature.

Blending into the world entailed several actions for the Daoist sage and ruler. One was the taking up of a simple life, close to nature. Chinese literature is filled with many stories of individuals who forsook life in the city to wander the mountains and valleys of China or to settle in simple huts, doing not much more than enjoying the joys of nature. These individuals were the counterparts to India's *samanas,* who lived simply with little or no possessions. The Indian *samanas* were more oriented to asceticism and the interior journey than were the Daoist sage or ruler. The Daoists were not seeking to transcend the harsh cycle of rebirth, nor did they consider the world to be covered with a veil of illusion. For the Daoists, the world was real, and for those making efforts to follow the Dao, it was a service of genuine pleasure and insight. Nevertheless, the *samanas* of India and the sages and rulers of Daoism had certain ideals in common. Each group aspired to minimize and ultimately to abandon all self-centered desires and attachments. The *samanas* were seeking to eliminate the *karma* that kept them in bondage to *samsara.* The Daoists wanted to restore harmony and balance between themselves and the world.

To promote mystical enhancement, the Daoist sage also practiced Buddhist-like equanimity based on the way of nature. Just as the Dao of nature embraces and supports all things, so does the sage. He or she makes efforts to avoid the dualisms of good and bad, right and wrong, beautiful and ugly by accepting everything, even those aspects of life that are unusually shunned or rejected. The ideal of transcending the dualism caused by human judgments had far reaching consequences for Daoist thought and practice.

One final aspect of the life of a Daoist sage or master that needs consideration is the concept and practice of *wu wei*. It is *wu wei* that helps us to understand the connection between the development of personal, individual spirituality and Daoist political philosophy. The *Daodejing* was intended in the first place to offer counsel on how to manage government rather than one's personal life and spirituality. Nevertheless, the ways for governing a political entity effectively and conducting one's life in an appropriate manner coincided. This convergence of political and spiritual excellence is seen most clearly in the Daoist practice of *wu wei*.

Wu wei is often translated as "non-action," but it may also be rendered "actionless action" or "acting by not acting." This does not imply doing nothing, but rather acting in the most simple and effortless way possible in order to accomplish what needs to be done. It may be said, nevertheless, that *wu wei* has the appearance of not acting at all. *Wu wei* is based on the recognition that the world—heaven, Earth, and humanity—follows its own path and rhythms. Living in accordance with *wu wei* is what those in the West call "going with the flow." The practice of *wu wei* is the relinquishment of the desire of human beings to exercise control, which is perhaps the greatest obstacle to living in accord with the Dao.

As a political practice, following *wu wei* is associated with the Daoist analysis of suffering in ancient China. The *Daodejing* considers that widespread suffering is the result of governments' acting in opposition to the Dao of nature. Such governments are characterized by two traits. First is the self-centeredness of the ruling class and its indifference to the well-being of the common people; second is government's tendency to interfere in the lives of individuals. In face of this, the *Daodejing* recommends that rulers practice the natural way of *wu wei* by diminishing their self-absorption and living in a simple manner.

The whole of Daoist political philosophy may be in the belief that government should stay out of people's lives as much as possible. The ancient kings, with the performance of a series of external religious rites, had ruled by the potency that established the Way of Heaven. The *Daodejing* urged rulers to internalize these old liturgical ceremonies and to develop an internal spiritualized conformity to the Way. The Confucians, by imposing their rituals on society, had encouraged people to concentrate on purely external spirituality. Instead of taking an aggressive posture, the ruler, according to Daoist thought, should withdraw and be small. Instead of plotting and scheming, he was encouraged to relinquish thought, calm his mind, relax his body, and liberate himself of ordinary ways of looking at the world. He should allow his problems to resolve themselves by the discipline of *wu wei*. This way of not doing things could be achieved only by filling his heart with stillness and emptiness. Such self-emptying required long mystical training. That is the reason why thirty chapters of the *Daodejing* are devoted to the mystical discipline that was intended to transform the inner life of the ruler and endow him with the power to restore the world, as the kings of old had done. The sage ruler who practices *wu wei* affirms to himself, "I do nothing and the people transform themselves; I prefer stillness and the people correct and regulate themselves; I engage in no activity and the people prosper on their own; I am without desires and the people simplify their own lives." The Daoists had no contemporary examples of virtuous leaders, practitioners of *wu wei*, to support the effectiveness of their claims; they could only appeal to the legendary rulers of bygone eras. But Daoism and Confucianism shared this conviction that for the country's well-being it was essential that ruler diminish his selfish desires and the search for power either by *wu wei* or *li*.

Those who composed the *Daodejing* were some of the great Chinese sages of the Axial Age. Theirs was a vision and ideal that was essentially utopian.

Zhuangzi

In the figure of Zhuangzi, Daoism appears to have transferred its focus from the political arena to an exclusive interest on individual spirituality. His objective was to address not the ruling class but the individual seeking to live in accord with the Dao.

In the opinion of most scholars, Zhuangzi was an actual person whose traditional dates are 369 to 286, making him a contemporary of Mengzi and the Period of the Warring States. He was a master of the spiritual life and one of the most important Daoist sages of the Chinese

Axial Age. It was said that he had an idiosyncratic turn of mind and was completely unconcerned with status or physical appearance or comfort. However, it is clear that he was inspired by the old masters who had written and compiled the *Daodejing*, but without an acceptance of their political philosophy. He is considered to be the principal person who drew out and emphasized the mystical components of Daoism. He is credited with the writing of the "Inner Chapters" of the book that bears his name.

The book began as a defense of private life. Zhuangzi was irritated by Confucians, who, he thought, were bursting with self-importance, erroneously convinced that they had a mission to save the world by means of their ethical principles. According to Zhuangzi, ethical teaching could not change human nature; it is unnatural and perverse to force people to obey human-made ethical norms and laws; when kings and politicians interfered with the lives of their subjects, they always made things worse. So in the book that bears his name, he proposes freedom from governmental intervention. We go on now to reflect on some other of his essential themes.

Acceptance of Change

The early Daoists believed that opposition to change was a basic cause of suffering. Zhuangzi became convinced that everything was always changing and in flux, always in the process of becoming something else. Human beings, however, were constantly resisting change with their efforts to fix and solidify their thoughts into something absolute. This, he thought, was not how the Way of Heaven operated. The *Zhuangzi* not only warns against such resistance to change, it urges a heart acceptance of it and the impermanence of life. This involved seeing all points of view and all value judgments as relative and tentative. As did the Jains, he cautioned against making absolute judgments, not because of the defilements of the soul, but for the reason that things change. That which appears today as the worst of news may turn out tomorrow to be a blessing in disguise. Anything that isolated itself from the constant transformation of life in an effort to become autonomous and self-contained was going against the natural dynamics of the cosmos, against the Way of Heaven. When he personally had fully and deeply realized this, Zhuangzi felt an invigorating freedom. And he no longer was subject to existential fear. Life and death, joy and sorrow followed each other. At death he would remain what he had basically always been, that is, just a fraction of the unending, changing pageant of the cosmos. After discovering these truths, Zhuangzi made serious efforts to communicate them to his friends and disciples. Once they had given up considering themselves as unique individuals whose lives must be preserved at whatever cost, they could be liberated and at peace. Once persons were thus reconciled with the Way of Heaven and had overcome their propensity for quick judgments, they would be at peace because they were attuned to reality.

Emptying the Mind

The practice of overcoming the tendency to rush to judgment is what Zhuangzi called "emptying the mind" or "sitting and forgetting." He was of the opinion that much of people's suffering was caused by their preconceptions, which predisposed them to view the world in particular ways, ways that disrupt individuals' capacities to respond spontaneously to whatever comes up in life. Such preconceptions are what compel people to evaluate things before it is time. He encouraged a discipline quite similar to the practices or meditation of the Buddha and to the form of Buddhism that develops later on in dialogue with Daoism, namely Zen. The habitual practice of sitting and forgetting was meant to allow the practitioner to give up habitual beliefs and patterns of thinking so that he or she would be enabled to see the world afresh, with openness to the present moment, and freedom of preconceived responses.

Conclusion

Zhuangzi and those who composed the *Daodejing* were the great Chinese sages of the Axial Age. Theirs was a vision and ideal that was essentially utopian. It should be noted that it was not the Daoist sages who ended the violence of the Warring States and unified the empire. It was Qin's state, inspired by Legalist thinking, that accomplished this goal. At this time another philosophical school was coming into prominence: "the men of method," the "School of Law."[14] These Legalists wanted to make people obey methods of controlling social behavior and to impose severe penalties on those who refused to conform. While Confucians believed that only a wise king imbued with ethics and love could reform society, the Legalists were not concerned with a prince's morality; they proposed that, when properly formulated, their methods of controlling social conduct would work automatically, if they were backed up by harsh punishments and a strict legal code. In effect, the intellectual or moral stature of the ruler was irrelevant, because the system could function without his personal intervention. He could, and should, sit back and "do nothing" (wu wei).

Notes

1. *The Book of Xunzi* 20. "A Discussion of Music," in *Xunzi: Basic Writings*, ed. and trans. Burton Watson (New York: Columbia University Press, 2003), 120.

2. Remarks of Jacques Gernet, reported in *Myth and Society in Ancient Greece*, 3rd ed., trans. Janet Lloyd (New York: Zone Books, 1996), 80–82; cited in Karen Armstrong, *The Great Transformation: The Beginning of Our Religious Traditions* (New York/Toronto: Knopf, 2006), 116.

3. Marcel Granet, *The Religion of the Chinese People*, trans. and ed. Maurice Freedman (New York: Harper & Row, 1975), 97–99; cited in Armstrong, *Great Transformation*, 118.

4. Fung Yu-Lan, *A Short History of Chinese Philosophy*, ed. Derk Bodde (Princeton, NJ: Princeton University Press), 32–37; cited in Armstrong, *Great Transformation*, 118.

5. Mark W. Muesse, *Religions of the Axial Age: An Approach to the World's Religions* (Chantilly, VA: Teaching Company, 2007), part 2, 103.

6. Ibid.

7. Ibid.

8. Ibid., 103.

9. Ibid., 114.

10. *Analects* 12:1. Translation suggested in Benjamin I. Schwartz, *The World of Thought in Ancient China* (Cambridge, MA, and London: Harvard University Press, 1985), 77; cited in Armstrong, *Great Transformation*, 206.

11. Jacques Gernet, *Ancient China: From the Beginnings to the Empire*, trans. Raymond Rudorff (Berkeley and London: University of California Press, 1968), 116; cited in Armstrong, *Great Transformation*, 206.

12. Muesse, *Religions of the Axial Age*, 118.

13. Philip J. Ivanhoe and Bryan W. Van Norden, *Readings in Classical Chinese Philosophy*, trans. Philip J. Ivanhoe (New York: Seven Bridges, 2001).

14. A. C. Graham, *Disputers of the Tao: Philosophical Argument in Ancient China* (LaSalle, IL: Open Court, 1989), 267–78.

Chapter Seven

SHINTO AND MAHAYANA BUDDHISM

In this chapter we focus on the defining soteriological characteristic—that relating to salvation—of Mahayana Buddhism, the most elaborately developed form of the post-Axial religion founded on the teaching of Siddhattha Gotama. Our plan is to study the Mahayana as it is lived in Japan, because there the contours of its growth from Theravada Buddhism and its differentiating essence can be accounted for and appreciated more clearly than in the land of its origin or in the other areas where it is practiced. Furthermore, the exploration of our Buddhist subject will be made concurrently with Shinto, which is the largest religion of the Land of the Rising Sun. This procedure seems appropriate for several reasons. First, in Japan the growth and practice of the Mahayana and Shinto are closely interrelated and interdependent, and therefore, the Buddhist tradition can be understood more effectively when studied in tandem with Shinto. Second, even though Shinto is almost exclusive to Japan and has the traits of a pre-Axial religion, it is regarded as one of the "classic" eleven or twelve "major world religions"[1] and consequently merits our scrutiny. Finally, we pursue this reflection on the two principle religions of Japan because it will enhance our understanding of the differences and relationship between pre- and post-Axial religion.

Shinto

Shinto has no binding set of dogmas, no deity deemed supreme and most sacred, and no defined set of prayers or devotions. Rather, it is a conglomeration of religious practices that expresses reverent alliance

165

with innumerable supernatural realities encountered in nature, society, and the home. Salvation to a transcendent afterlife is not a primary concern in Shinto. Much more stress is placed on providing for an abundant life in this world rather than preparing for the next. The beliefs and ways of thinking of Shinto are deep in the subconscious fabric of Japanese society. It is one of Japans' largest religions.

Prehistoric Shinto

Shinto originated in prehistoric times as a religion based on awe and respect for the whole of nature and especially for certain sacred sites. These sites may have been originally used to worship the sun, rock formations, trees, and even sounds. Because these phenomena were associated with deities known as *kami*, Shinto became a complex polytheistic religion. The term *Shinto* is derived from the Chinese, *shendao*, meaning "the way of the higher spirits or gods." Its equivalent in Japanese is *kami-no-michi* or "the kami's way"—*kami* generally meaning "gods" or "deities," but in a more inclusive sense, "beings possessing sacred power or superior potency, filled with a numinous or charismatic force." For long it has been part of the myth of Shinto that Japan was at one time populated exclusively with *kami*. The *kami* are believed to be integral to all aspects of life and manifest themselves in various forms. There are nature *kami* that reside in sacred stones, trees, mountains, in the sea, and under the ground. There are clan *kami*, called *ujigami*, which were originally the tutelary deities of specific clans, frequently being the deified ancestor of the clan. There is the *no kami*, or god of the rice paddies, who is worshiped at rice-planting and harvest festivals. And there are *ikigami*, who are living human deities. Shinto conveys a religious faith about Japan and its past. "The customs of prehistoric Japan were the way followed by *kami*, the awe-inspiring beings from whom the Japanese people have descended."[2] The primordial rulers of the Japanese clans especially were revered as the descendents of gods. The Yamato clans adored the sun goddess who was regarded as the rule of the heavens and the ancestress of their chieftains. Probably in the fourth century BCE, these clans won their ascendancy over the other groups by placing their chieftain on a somewhat shaky imperial throne as a descendent of the sun.

The *kami,* however, are not transcendent deities in the usual Western and Indian sense of the word. Although they are divine, they are close to humanity; they inhabit the same world of heaven and Earth as ordinary humans do; they make the same mistakes as humans do and feel and think the same way. Those who died would automatically be inscribed among the *kami* regardless of the moral character of their lives.

Early Chinese Influence

Prehistoric Shinto, then, was principally a haphazard cult of nature worship. It became a clearly worked-out pattern of national culture only when Chinese civilizing influences became operative in Japan in the fifth century CE. By eagerly adapting Chinese ideas and procedures to fit their own needs, the Japanese transformed their lives. Always proficient at improving their methods and skills in the practical arts, once the way is shown, they quickly learned all that the Chinese were able to teach them about metalworking, wood carving, faming, horticulture, gardening, silk-work culture, road and bridge building, and canal dredging.

Almost overnight the people passed from a primitive to a relatively advanced type of material culture. In regard to writing and communication, they adopted without change, except for cursive simplifications, the entire body of Chinese ideograms of characters, pronouncing them with the Japanese words that were the translations of the Chinese. If there were no Japanese equivalents, they adopted the Chinese sounds with characteristic modifications. In the realm of social relations, Confucian ideas produced permanent changes of emphasis in morals. There followed especially a strong reinforcement of the ideal of filial piety.

While prehistoric Shinto had been mainly formless, without a sense of direction, and only loosely tied to ancestor worship, it now took on the characteristics of history's most comprehensive ancestor cult. Not only was the emperor's descent from the sun goddess stressed, but the high officials began to trace their own origins from the deities most closely related to the sun goddess, while the common people were supposed to be descents of the more distantly related deities. In this manner, the mythical foundation was laid for the claim that the whole people were organically related to the emperor by a divine family relationship.

Chinese culture was an early and important influence on the Japanese, but an even greater impact was made on their society and their Shinto religion by Mahayana Buddhism, coming first from Korea and then from China. When this religion came to Japan in the sixth century CE, it brought with it compelling new experiences and interpretations of the sacred as well as new literature, a new art, an emotionally gratifying ritual, and fresh insights into many fields of human thought and action, including logic, medicine, and social service.

We focus now on Mahayana Buddhism: its origins in India and its principle doctrines; its spread first to China, and then to Korea; and then its arrival in Japan, where it exerted a great influence on Shinto, and Shinto had a significant impact on it.

The Origins and Principle Doctrines of Mahayana Buddhism

Divine Authors of Salvation

Sometime between the third century BCE and the first or second century CE, the doctrines later embodied in Mahayana Buddhism began to take shape, especially among the Mahasamghikas, a group of Buddhist monks who broke away from the Theravada tradition of Buddhism in 350 BCE. This faction distinguished itself doctrinally from the Theravada teaching by its belief in the Buddha as a supernatural being who only *appeared* to be embodied in this world, and socially by their acceptance of popular religious beliefs and practices allowing a greater role to the laity. The Mahasamghikas, from which seven subschools arose, may be regarded as the forerunners of the Mahayana movement.

This movement turned out to be a very important new development, effective in producing the most elaborate form of Buddhism and making it into a prominent world religion. It transformed the monastic way of early Buddhism into a popular religion that offered eternal rewards to the faithful. As Mahayana developed, it claimed that the Buddha privately taught that there are divine authors of salvation, so that men and women do not have to save *themselves* but can get help. To the common people, the Mahayana offered the good news of the existence of a whole multitude of saviors whose main desire was to cure the sufferings of human beings. The pure benevolence of these saviors was the best assurance for those devoted to them. With their loving assistance, humans could at least hope to gain heaven after death, if not what could only be self-won: *nirvana.*

In the development of Mahayana, the first step was the glorification of Gotama. He was regarded no longer simply as an extraordinary human being but as an object of religious devotion, adored and worshiped as a divine being who came to Earth out of compassion for suffering humanity. Before his descent to earth he was a *bodhisattva*, that is, a person destined to be enlightened. The next step was the belief that Gotama was not the only Buddha, not the only divine author of salvation; there had been many Buddhas before him. Some had come to Earth, and some remained in the heaven, and some were in the making, the Buddhas of the future. The universe became radiant to its outer limits with compassionate beings who could and wanted to aid suffering humankind. Prayers now were possible. A rich and luxuriant cultus sprang up; the devout were furnished with wall paintings and sculpture as aids to devotion. Salvation was no longer something to be achieved only by self-effort. Divine beings with vast stores of merit were eager to share with the faithful.

In Mahayana the authors of salvation came to be regarded as being of three kinds. First there are the *Manushi Buddhas,* saviors who, like Gotama, appeared on Earth in the past as human beings, achieved enlightenment, taught men and women about the true way of life, and then, after fulfilling their duties, realized nirvana. They are fundamentally teachers; prayers cannot now reach them.

The second type of saviors are the *bodhisattvas,* who are actually more important than the Buddhas and have greater religious reality. In the full form of the Mahayana, the bodhisattvas are a great, and even innumerable, company of supernatural beings who are attentive to prayers and come actively to people's aid. The prevalent popular understanding of bodhisattvas, especially in China and Japan, has been that they are beings who vowed many existences ago to become Buddhas and have lived ever since in such a manner as to acquire almost inexhaustible stores of merit. This merit is of such a great abundance that they could easily achieve the full status of Buddhas and pass into nirvana. But since they are such compassionate beings, out of love they postpone their entrance into nirvana and transfer their merit, as need arises, to those who call upon them in devotional reflection and prayer. They sit enthroned in the heavens, gazing down on the needy world, and sometimes, in redemptive pity, they descend in the guise of ministering angels to do deeds of mercy.

The third kind of savior is the *Dhyani Buddhas*. These "contemplative Buddhas" differ from the bodhisattvas in having fully achieved their Buddhahood; but they are in a different category also from the Manushi Buddhas in having achieved their Buddhahood in human form. They live in the heavens, and in the indefinite interval between the present time and the compassionately postponed final entrance into nirvana they minister to human needs, as did Gotama between his enlightenment and death. Their name indicates that they are Buddhas of contemplation (*Dhyani*), and their images shown them in deep meditation and calm. In Japan one of the greatest of the Dhyani Buddhas is Amida Buddha of the Pure Land.

Amida Buddha

Amida is one of the great gods of Asia. He once was a monk, took the vow countless ages ago to become a bodhisattva, rose to his rank as a Dhyani Buddha, and now presides over the Western Paradise, known as the "Pure Land." Because he is the compassionate, loving, self-sacrificing Lord of this happy heaven and generously admits all who beseech him in faith, he has even surpassed Siddhattha Gotama, the deified Buddha, in the estimation of the masses in China and Japan. Whereas the bodhisattvas serve present need, Amida promises future bliss in the afterlife. His aspiring devotee, who is unable to imitate Gotama in helpfulness or to acquire the merit acquired by the monk and bodhisattvas, turns to Amida in faith and has merit transferred to him from the store of the Lord of the Pure Land. In this conception of the divine authors of salvation, original Theravada Buddhism is completely transcended.

But this is true for the whole of the Mahayana scheme of salvation. Gotama surely taught and practiced compassion and goodwill for all, but his expressions of love were to a certain degree impersonalized, as his philosophy of life required. However, in its conception of the character of the bodhisattvas and Dhyani Buddhas, Mahayana raises pure altruistic love to supremacy in the moral sphere, and by insisting on its expression in supernatural beings who respond to prayers of the faithful, has moved counter to Gotama's teaching that a person should not pray but should devote one's efforts to saving oneself.

Those who adhere to the Mahayana tradition believe that Gotama taught several kinds of doctrine, depending on the nature of his disciples. To some he taught the Theravada Noble Eightfold Path of Salvation; to others he imparted the Mahayana ideal of the compassionate, altruistic, self-sacrificing bodhisattva.

The Vow of the Bodhisattva

The ideal of altruism, exemplified in Amida, led to perhaps the most inspiring of all Buddhist doctrines. This teaching may be formulated as such: Just as the bodhisattvas, who are now divine but at one time were human, vowed in a distant past to become Buddhas and then from pure altruistic, self-sacrificing love for suffering human beings postponed their entrance into nirvana by transferring their merit to others, so too any human being of the present, whether a man or a woman, may, if he or she wishes, make a similar vow with regard to the future.

Everyone is potentially a Buddha and may now take the vow to be a bodhisattva. The length of time required to fulfill the destiny thus undertaken may be practically beyond reckoning, but authentic benevolence needs no urging and waits for nothing. As the Mahayana doctrines developed into their fuller forms, this ideal was more fully articulated. Various stages in the career of a bodhisattva were delineated, and a body of writings arose to convey instruction on how to enter into the beginning stages. According to a seventh-century scripture, the *Bodhicaryavatara*, the initial stages can be entered by those who experience joy in the good actions of all living beings and who wish to spend themselves in the increase of such good persons endowed with this temperament may then pray to the Buddhas to help them in acquiring enlightenment—not that they may pass into nirvana, but rather that they may secure the good of all living beings. For this purpose they make their solemn vow to postpone their entrance into nirvana until they have assisted all living beings within range.

Doctrine of the Triple Body

This is a doctrine that came to prominence in Mahayana concerning the essential nature of the Buddha. Several centuries after his death, the three facets of the Buddha's nature were articulated in the form of a doctrine developed initially by the Sarvastivada school but quickly taken up and elaborated by the Mahayana.

According to this development, Buddha Gotama, and all Buddhas, are in their essential nature, or unmanifest form, identical with *Dharmakaya* ("dharma body"), that is, ultimate truth, absolute reality, reality itself, Buddha Nature in pure essence, ultimate eternal Buddha reality, *Tathata* ("Absolute Suchness or Thusness"), *Sunyata* ("Emptiness"), the "Void" in which subsists nirvana. This is their *first body:* their "dharma body," or the "Body of the Cosmic or Absolute Buddha." This first body indicates the eternal Buddha reality that is the ground and source of the world known by and present to an enlightened Buddhist consciousness. It is undifferentiated and impersonal. The eternal Buddha reality ranges throughout the vast celestial realms and reaches down in manifestations in the earthly regions.

At the same time, Buddhas have the power to manifest themselves in sublime celestial forms, in splendid paradises where they teach doctrines and are surrounded by hosts of bodhisattvas and supernatural beings. This is their *second body:* their "enjoyment body" or "body of spiritual bliss." This second body is the heavenly manifestation of its source, the *Dharmakaya*, particularly in the celestial Buddhas and bodhisattvas, and capable of taking name and form and of offering help along the path to nirvana to earthly beings. The second body is differentiated and personal.

Furthermore, motivated by boundless compassion, the Buddhas project themselves into the human world, disguised appropriately so as not to frighten and alarm, but instead to provide suffering human beings with what is necessary and useful. This is their *third body:* the this-worldly manifestation of the Body of Spiritual Bliss in earthly appearance, differentiated, personal, and limited in time and space. The prime example here is the historical Buddha, Siddhattha Gotama; he was the passing manifestation on Earth of a triple body.

Derived originally from an analysis of the significance of Gotama Buddha, this doctrine in its application became a faith considering him:

the *Dharmakaya* or the Void is the ground of being from which emanates the Body of Spiritual Bliss manifested in such heavenly powers as Amida and the bodhisattva who once dwelt in the Tushita heaven and who compassionately came down to Earth to be the historical Gotama. When Gotama Buddha's earthly mission was accomplished, he returned to the source of all being, the *Dharmakaya* (nirvana).

In these doctrines there is quite apparently a similarity with Hindu Vedantic speculation. These doctrines of Mahayana point to an Absolute (Void) that resembles in many respects the *Brahman-atman* of Hindu monism. But there is a difference that must ultimately be ascribed to the influence of the career and personality of the historical founder, Gotama. Whereas in Vedantic thought Brahman-atman is understood as the inconceivable Absolute of strictly neutral being, in Mahayana the Absolute Essence or Suchness is identified with a sort of "love behind things" that produced and is the ground of particular Buddhas—a Buddha essence at the heart of the universe. "The importance of this conclusion for religion is surely evident. For here the Buddhas, as expressions or projections of Being Itself, are not merely indifferent or unfeeling expressions of It, but rather a manifestation of compassionate love *(karuna)* drawing ignorance-clouded minds along the bodhisattva way of love back to Itself."[3]

In relation to the common people, these positions of the Mahayana led to the belief that, because Absolute Suchness or Buddha essence (the *Dharmakaya*) is manifest in all things, there is a Buddha potential in every person. "Anyone may take up the career of a Buddha-to-be without having to be reborn. The stimulus of this great hope penetrated throughout East Asia, and its optimistic implications thrilled the aspiring natures of the devout with a new zeal."[4]

Conclusion

From the development of the doctrines and practices of Mahayana much was to come. Not only was the entire aspect of Buddhism changed for the believer, but its fortunes outside of India improved at once. Countries that responded slowly to the appeal of Theravada doctrines now adopted the Mahayana with eagerness. And because the Mahayana was by its very nature expansive, it changed as it moved: the peoples among whom it made its way contributed to its development.

The Spread of Mahayana Buddhism in Northern Lands

China

At a very early period, perhaps as early as the third century BCE, China and India were in contact. Ming Di, in 65 CE, permitted a statue of the Buddha to be erected and the Buddhist cult to spread, without himself being a disciple of the Buddha. Buddhism initially made little progress in China. However, for a number of reasons the attitude of coolness eventually broke down. During the three centuries that followed the dissolving of the Han Dynasty (206 BCE–220 CE) into turmoil, the nomad tribes of central Asia entered China in great numbers, causing disunity and misery. The scholars and intellectuals looked in vain for signs of a public return to the old Chinese will to make this world a happy dwelling place for an orderly and harmonious human family. In great discouragement, many of them turned from the optimistic humanism of the Confucians to the mystic consolation of back-to-nature quietism of Daoism. As an un-Chinese contempt for the world possessed them, they became restive and ripe for Buddhism.

This rather negative reason for the eventual success of Buddhism in China was more than matched by a positive one. This was the great brilliance of the highly developed thinking discovered in the Buddhist texts, an intellectual subtlety and logical precision that was unparalled in Chinese thought up to that time. The intellectuals were strongly drawn to it.

The ordinary people also were being prepared for Buddhism. Among the infiltrating itinerants from beyond the Great Wall of China were adherents of the Mahayana beliefs and practices, who brought with them a gospel message for the masses. From the south, too, the Mahayanist missionaries came directly from India. With their flexible beliefs and way of thinking, they were able to be sensitive to the valid needs and modes of Chinese thought. The stress on filial piety essential in Buddhism itself enabled them to place this virtue alongside the preservation of the holiness of animal life, abstinence from intoxicants, and the other elements of the Five Precepts of the Buddhist community. They began to teach that to practice the virtue of filial piety, sons should add to the traditional Confucians funeral rites the Buddhist ceremonies for the dead as a means of making the destiny of their ancestors happier. The Buddhist monks' vivid imagery of the afterlife was compelling. China had lacked a genuinely satisfying idea of the afterlife. Confucianism had had little to provide in the way of comforts, except the stark faith that one would join one's ancestors at death and be dependent thereafter forever on the filial piety and remembrance of one's descendents. As Mahayana Buddhism developed, it far surpassed both Daoism and Confucianism in presenting appealing pictures of the afterlife. This was one of the reasons it began in the fourth century CE to make a wider popular appeal. Confucianism and Daoism were not, of course, entirely displaced, but Buddhism won a place alongside them. At one at the same, a person was able to be a Confucian seeking the internal welfare and harmony of the family, a Daoist bearing up with the processes of nature, and a Buddhist aiming at security after death. The three religions appeared to complement each other. Eventually in all of China, monasteries were established, large temples filled with images of the various Buddhas and bodhisattvas were multiplied, and the intellectuals were attracted to the many schools of Buddhist thought.

Japan

After its introduction into China and then Korea, Buddhism arrived in Japan, in 552 CE, as a gift from a beleaguered kingdom in China. Threatened by the power of Sila, one of the three independent Chinese states, and hoping for Japanese assistance, the king of the Chinese state of Paekche sent, as tribute, to the Emperor Kimmei of Japan a gold-plated image of the Buddha, some sacred writings, and a letter concerning the excellent and yet difficult Buddhist doctrine. The letter stated that this doctrine could produce immeasurable good fortune or a painful retribution; it also included a statement that from farthest India and through all of China the Mahayana doctrine had found reverent acceptance. Surely the emperor, eager to emulate whatever had made China great, must have been impressed by that statement. When he took up the matter with his counselors, some were cautiously receptive; others were in outright opposition to the new religion. Those who opposed believed that the native gods of Japan, the *kami*, would be angered. In an effort to be prudent, the emperor passed on the golden Buddha image to the head of the Soga clan to try it out on his family, to see whether or not the *kami* would object. When a pestilence broke out among the people, it was believed that the kami *did* object, so the golden image was heaved into a canal, and Buddhism fell out of the emperor's favor.

When the emperor died, the monarch sent another embassy to Japan, which included priests, two hundred sacred texts, a nun, an image maker, and a temple architect. The embassy was received with courtesy and allowed to construct a temple for its own use, and once more the Soga clan urged that the new religion be given a fair trial. But a pestilence once more broke out, and again the Buddha images were hurled into the canal.

But presently a perplexity presented itself. Because the pestilence continued, the head of the Soga clan suggested that it was not the *kami* who were angered, but the *Buddhas,* who resented the coldness of their reception. The cautious Japanese authorities decided to let the matter rest.

The Attractions of Buddhism in Japan

For the Japanese clan leaders and the court aristocracy, and eventually for the common people, Buddhism was attractive, and after a while, it became a great success in Japan. What was the secret of Mahayana's extraordinary success? The answer is quite simple: the Mahayanists claimed that the Buddha privately taught that there were divine authors of salvation and that one does not have to save oneself but can get help from a savior or saviors. Also, it had a great quantity of intriguing scriptures, written in the Chinese characters then being adopted entirely by the Japanese. These scriptures, which needed interpretation but no translation, stimulated the imagination by their universal scope, their rich symbolic imagery, their provocative ideas, and their applications in ritual, magic, and art. The private needs of individual were also provided for by emotionally gratifying Buddhist consolations: texts that comforted the sick with explicit understanding that they had magical curative effects, solemn and beautiful funeral rites, memorial services for the dead, cremation and preservation of the ashes, and prayers for the repose of the dead chanted by a priest at the "Buddha-altar" in the home, graced by a wooden memorial tablet inscribed with the name of the deceased.

By the time that the next emperor ascended to the throne, Buddhism had made substantial progress. Even though the provincial military and the Shinto priests were opposed to the new religion, the emperor viewed it favorably. As new Buddhist missionaries continued to arrive, the tide began to turn. In 588 CE, when the Empress Suiko ascended the throne, her nephew Shotoku Taishi, a devout Buddhist, became regent. He sent groups of scholars to China with the commission to bring back a complete knowledge of Buddhism and of the Chinese system of government. Shotoku is considered to be the true founder of Buddhism in Japan. Under his orders, the first Buddhist temple in Japan was built and the first monastic school was organized. Subsequently six schools of academic Buddhism—Saron, Hosso, Jojutsu, Kusha, Ritsu, and Kego—flourished at Nara, the capital, and the Great Statue of Buddha at Nara was constructed to symbolize the authority of the imperial government. These were not exclusive schools, and temples were apt to have scholars trained in several of the schools. To demonstrate the humanitarianism of the Mahayana, Shotoku erected a hospital, a dispensary, and a house of refuge. Other leaders devoted to Buddhism donated almshouse, irrigation canals, orchards, harbors, ferries, reservoirs, and good roads. The new religion turned out to be good not only for the individual, but also for society as a whole. Since Buddhism had won the adherence of the court, it began slowly to reach down to ordinary people.

Native Beliefs and Traditions Systematized as Shinto

The new ferment of ideas stirred by the introduction of Buddhism brought several important results, one of which was the attempt, under imperial sanction, to use the Chinese characters to put into writing the native myths and traditions still current among the local clans. Partly in response to the arrival of highly structured Buddhist doctrines in Japan in the sixth century CE, pervasive but previously unorganized native beliefs and rituals were progressively systematized as Shinto. The desire to put the legitimacy of the imperial lineage on a firm mythological and religious basis led to the compilation of *Kojiki*

(Record of Ancient Matters) and *Nihon Shoki (Chronicles of Japan)*, in 712 and 720 CE respectively. The *Kojiki* was written and intended as a history of Japan from the creation of the world to the middle of the seventh century CE. Paralleling it, with additions that gave it great historical accuracy, was the *Nihon*. In tracing the imperial line back to the mythical age of the gods, these texts explain how the *kami* Izanagi and Izanami created the Japanese islands and the central gods Amaterasu-o-Mikami (sun goddess), Tsuki-yomi (moon god), and Susa-no-wo (god of storms). The great-great-grandson of Amaterasu is said to be Emperor Jimmu, the legendary first sovereign of Japan.

Almost a century later (about 806 CE), during the first decade of the Heian Era, appeared the *Kogoshui,* or *Gleaning from Ancient Stories,* a defense of the practices of ancient priestly families connected with Shinto. Still later, in the first quarter of the tenth century, came the *Engishiki,* an important compendium of Shinto traditions in fifty parts, the first ten of which contain lists of ritual prayers or litanies for various ceremonial occasions, called *norito.* The *norito* served then and for centuries afterward as the models of prayers in all Shinto shrines, whether in the country at large or in the court. All of these treatises showed the influence of Chinese and Buddhist ideas.

More undilutedly Japanese were two outstanding works of the Heian period reflecting Japanese life, love, and religion. They were produced when Japanese minds were stirred to creativity by the opportunity presented by the Chinese characters to put old and new thoughts into writing. One was the *Manyoshu,* a collection of four thousand poems, compiled toward the end of the eighth century. The other was a work of brilliance, Lady Murasaki's long novel, *The Tale of Genji,* dealing with beauty-oriented court at Kyoto in its early years (around the tenth century CE).

The absence of official sacred scriptures in Shinto illustrates the religion's lack of moral commandments. Instead, Shinto stresses ritual purity and cleanliness in one's dealings with the *kami.*

The Shinto Myth

The imperial court had been profoundly concerned that an official version of the Shinto folk traditions be formulated. Japanese national pride and Chinese standards of rationality and order required that the native myths about the early history of Japan and its people be woven into a more or less unified narrative. The result was what may be called the "Shinto myth." There are slightly variant forms of the officially approved versions of this myth. According to one of them, the previously mentioned *Kojiki,* the story runs as follows:

> Japan is a special creation of the gods. Two deities produced the Japanese islands and their inhabitants. These were the primal male, Izanagi, and the primal female, Izanami. They came together and Izanami bore from her womb the eight great islands of Japan. Then they brought into being a populace of thirty-five deities. When Izanami finally died and went to the underworld (the Land of Yomi), in due time Izanagi followed after her, hoping to persuade her to return to the upper world with him. But she had begun to decompose. When he neared her in the darkness, he saw she was swarming with maggots. She screamed, "Thou hast put me to shame," and sent after him eight thunder deities, generated in the decay of her own body, and fifteen hundred warriors or *Yomi.* When he fought these off, she herself began to chase him. As he fled into the upper world, he picked up an enormous rock and blocked the pass of the underworld with it. The two formerly loving deities, standing on opposite sides of the rock, made their farewells. Finally, Izanagi, who was now covered with pollution, went down to the ocean to bathe. When he stepped into the water and, in a typically Japanese act of purification, washed away the filth out of his left eye, he produced the most highly revered of the Japanese deities, Amaterasu, the goddess of the sun. After this important creation, he produced the moon-god, Tsuki-yomi, from the washing of his right eye, and the storm god, Susa-no-wo, from his nostrils. [Shinto's preoccupation with pollution and ablution is clearly foreshowed in these myths.]

Years later, the sun goddess Amaterasu looks down from her seat in heaven and becomes concerned about the disorder in the islands. The storm god's son was ruling there, but she was not satisfied. Finally she commissioned her grandson Ni-ni-gi to descend to the island and rule for her. He first reigned from the southernmost island of Kyushu. Later, his great-grandson, Jimmu Tenno, the first human emperor, took off from Kyushu on a conquest of the province of Yamato, on the central Japanese island of Honshu and established his capital there, in the year set by tradition at 660 BCE. In the meantime the leading families of Japan and the whole Japanese people descended from the minor deities, or lesser *kami*, residing on the islands.

Thus according to the myth, one is to understand that the emperor of Japan is a descendent in an unbroken line from the sun goddess Amaterasu, and the islands of Japan have a divine origin, and so also the Japanese people. Moreover, Japan is regarded as full of gods and goddesses. The polytheism is practically unlimited. It was characteristic of the earlier Japanese to discover gods everywhere, to see a god or godling in every kind of force or natural object. Therefore, they called their country "The Land of the Gods" and in later times estimated that their deities must number some "eighty myriads" or even some "eight hundred myriads." We may observe further that the chief place in the pantheon was given to the sun goddess Amaterasu, whose temple at Ise is the holiest shrine in Japan, but she has never been regarded as more than the first among her peers. Associated with her were not only those born from her, Tsuki-yomi, the moon god, and Susa-no-wo, the amoral and capricious storm god, but also a vast number of deities.

Buddhism and Shinto in Medieval and More Recent Times

Heian Period: Tendai, Shingon

Early in the Heian Period (701–756 CE), the Tendai sect was introduced into Japan by the priest Saicho, and the Shingon sect was introduced by Kukai, also known as Kobo Daishi. The arrival of Tendai and Shingon Buddhism was the opening of a new age, the Rationalist and Esoteric schools. These Mahayana sects were the most important Buddhist sects at the imperial court; they served the court aristocrats and contributed to the development of the fine arts. They also helped to foster the fusion of Buddhism and Shinto.

Tendai

This sect was founded by Saicho. In 804 CE the emperor sent him to China to study *Tian-tai* and then to gain recognition for it in Japan. Saicho saw in *Tian-tai* an interpretation of Buddhism that stressed the basic oneness of all beings and the promise of universal salvation. Buddhism was for all the Japanese, not only for monks. Therefore, he gave Buddhism a nationalist emphasis by placing his religious movement at the service of court and country. He was successful in spreading Buddhism among the common people by making it a Japanese religion open to all. Moreover, he and his followers, and eventually the common people, were persuaded that the gods or *kami* of Shinto were forms taken by the one Buddha reality. Consequently, he proposed that Shinto be called "One Reality Shinto." Buddhism and Shinto thus appeared as two aspects of one Truth. Many important monasteries, with their related temples, have flourished under the intellectual influence of the Tendai sect. Its impact in Japan is pervasive and powerful until this day, although its membership is not as great as that of some of the other Buddhist sects.

Shingon

In all religions the power of the saving name or mystic rite has at some time been emphasized. Esoteric beneficial effects are sought by a sort of holy magic, performed against a background of rational belief— a pantheon or a cosmology of impressive character. The tendency to make use of wonder-working formulas and gestures arose in China during the eighth century in the *Zhen-yan* or "True Word" school. Its overall outlook was mystical. It placed its main reliance on a large pantheon of Buddhist savior beings with whom identification was sought on the higher religious levels, and whose good offices were solicited through formulas, the use of picture charts or mandalas, gestures, invocations, and liturgies that were believed infallibly to bring good results: obtaining the help of the Buddhas in curing sickness, rescuing the dead from hell, controlling the weather, ensuring health and good fortune, and the like.

The Zhen-yan school was imported into Japan, where the name was pronounced "Shingon." The Japanese adherents enlarged its outlook and subdued its magical features by assimilating to it the rational and eclectic interests of the Tendai sect. Consequently, the Shingon has turned out to be as comprehensive and many sided as the Tendai. Its popular appeal has been very significant. It was founded in the ninth century by one of Japan's great men, Kukai.

After studying Zhen-yan in China, Kukai returned to Japan to teach the "true word" that all the phenomena of the universe, including human beings, are manifestations of the "body, voice, and mind" of a single, all-inclusive, and ultimate Buddha being, manifested in the form of Mahavairocana, the Great Sun (known in Japan as *Dainichi*). The other Buddhas and the bodhisattvas are his emanations, phases of his indestructible energy at work in the universe. Gotama Buddha was his historical earthly manifestation. Mahavairocana is therefore identical with the *Dharmakaya* of the philosophers; however, he is more personal than impersonal because he possesses body, mind, and speech, differentiated into Buddhas, bodhisattvas, gods, demons, men, animals, plants, inanimate things, and substances. Kukai taught that by meditation, repetition of magic formulas, and the performance of gestures with hands and fingers one can identify oneself with powerful Buddhas and bodhisattvas. The implications here in this tradition are elitist. The ordinary person can comprehend only something of this because it is but partially conveyed in the allegory and symbol of ritual and ceremony. For esoteric knowledge of this kind, a person must be tutored by a Shingon master. Any person should, however, be encouraged in the love of temples and worship, for one can ascend from any level of spirituality to attain enlightenment through realization of the mystery of the world as seen from inside, that is, the Buddha in the heart.

Kamakura Period: Nichiren, Zen, and Pure Land

During the Kamakura Period (1185–1333 CE), an age of austerity and martial arts, three major developments occurred in Japanese Buddhism that had perhaps the greatest impact on Japan.

Nichiren

The first development, Nichiren Buddhism, is an entirely Japanese phenomenon, a unique form of Buddhism in its emphasis on nationalism and sociopolitical activism. It was founded during the Kamakura Period (1192–1333 CE) in the tumultuous thirteenth century, when the emperor was vainly struggling with the lords of the provinces for the control of the nation and needed more religious support than he was receiving. Help came from an unexpected quarter. A young monk, Nichiren, the son of a fisherman, after studying the doctrines taught in a Tendai monastery, found himself deeply impressed by the comparative simplicity and truth of the scripture that was the Tendai favorite, the *Lotus Sutra*. On a mountaintop, while watching the rising sun he experienced a sense of identity between the Buddha reality in the sun (Mahavairocana) and the Buddha reality revealed in the *Lotus Sutra*. To be sure of this, he went from one Buddhist study center to another—Amida, Zen, Shingon, and Tendai—and emerged from his search with the firm conviction that all the prevalent schools confused the basic Buddhist truths by following false paths. So he made it his aim to restore original Buddhism by launching a crusade to call the nation back to the *Lotus Sutra*.

Zen

The second development is the Zen meditative schools established by Eisai, founder of the Rinzai sect, and later modified by Dogen, founder of the Soto sect. These schools were rapidly adopted by the upper classes and had a profound influence on Japanese culture. Zen was also favored by the warrior elite of the time because of its directness and its stress on self-discipline and meditation. The main aim of the meditative schools is immediate insight *(satori)*, the kind of enlightenment the Buddha Siddhattha Gotama achieved. The way to enlightenment is sitting meditation, called *zazen*, and riddles, called *koans*. Salvation, however, is ultimately attained not by meditation but by insight following meditation, an awakening to the unitary character of all reality. The main difference between the two sects is that in the search for insight, Rinzai Zen places considerably more importance on koan practice than does Soto Zen.

Pure Land

The third important development was the rapid rise of popular Buddhist sects among the common people: the Amida Pure Land Schools promulgated by evangelists such as Genshnin and articulated by monks such as Honen. In the Pure Land schools, the largest Buddhist tradition in Japan and throughout Asia, the motive is an appealing one to the common people. Its main concern and proximate goal is to receive entrance into the Western Paradise of Amida Buddha by committing oneself in faith to him. Pure Land teaches that chanting Amida's name as an expression of faith in him is the best way to achieve rebirth in his Western Pure Land Paradise. By concentration solely on this aspect of Buddhist belief, an extraordinary simplification is reached. The entire emphasis is unquestioning faith in the Celestial Buddha Amida and the devout repetition of his name. This faith, together with humility, is believed to be sufficient for salvation, eternal life in Amida's heaven. Unlike the founders of the sects of the past, the founders of the Kamakura sects put more stress on experience than on learning. These men and their followers introduced Buddhism to farmers, fishermen, warriors, merchants, and artisans.

As to the continuing growth of the Mahayana, this in general is the picture: what the Buddhist speculative theologians of India set forth by means of suggestion and outreach, the Chinese took up and developed as the logical foundation of their differentiations, and the Japanese, eager to learn, came forward to complete the Chinese developments, always adding something of their own.

Mixed Shinto

The Rise of Mixed Shinto

By the middle of the seventeenth century CE, Buddhism had obtained a dominant influence in court circles. Years later, in thousands of villages, the common people were expanding their belief and practices (their "folk religion") by adopting congenial elements not only from Buddhism but also from other types of Chinese religion, particularly religious Daoism and yin/yang magic. The result was the so-called mixed Shinto. Scholars have called mixed Shinto, with its architectural modifications and altered rituals, *Ryobu* ("Two-Sided") *Shinto* or *Shinbutsu Konko* (Mixed Shinto and Buddhism). According to Ichiro Hori, when Buddhism appeared in the villages, the priests had to compromise with local people and their community gods. As a result of these compromises, a special Buddhist temple, called a *Jingu-ji*, was built within the precincts of almost every Shinto shrine and dedicated to the Shinto *kami* of that shrine. The *Jingu-ji* were built so that the Buddhist priests could serve the *kami* with Buddhist rituals by special permission of the *kami*. In reverse, the local or tutelary *kami* was enshrined in each Buddhist temple and served by Buddhist priests and Buddhist formulas.

When Shinto shrines began to give a place to Buddhist (and Daoist) rituals, there were certain doctrinal consequences. "At first the *kami*," says Joseph Kitagawa, "were considered to be the 'protectors of Buddha's Law.'...Soon, however, this belief was reversed so that the *kami* were considered to be in need of salvation through the help of Buddha....Some of the honored *kami* also received the Buddhist title of *bosatsu (bodhisattva)*."[5] In the ninth century, Kobo Daishi, founder of the Shingon school, taught that the Buddhas and bodhisattvas appeared as various gods in different nations and had so appeared in Japan. Dengyo Diashi, founder of the Tendai school, made a suggestion that was similar. Priests of Buddhist sects reported having visions and intuitions that were accepted as proof that the gods of Japan were in reality Buddhas and bodhisattvas who "appeared" as gods of the Japanese islands. Amaterasu was identified as a manifestation of the Buddha Mahavairocana. In this synthesis, the deities of the Buddhist pantheon were given the honored position of the "Originals," whereas the deities of the Shinto pantheon were thought to be their Japanese appearances or manifestations.

Mixed Shinto: Family Model and Guest Hospitality

This amplified or mixed Shinto was made natural and possible by two central orientations that have had a pronounced role in Japanese religious history: (1) the extension of the "family" concept and (2) hospitality to guests.

The Family Model

Japanese society has always retained a basic family or clan system, in and through which individuals have acquired their sense of selfhood or identity, religiously as well as socially. Although many young people in Japan are breaking away from it, this pattern of behavior has carried over into education, politics, and industry. Each family and clan has had its own shrine where the "family (tutelary) deity"—usually a long-honored ancestor, associated with later ancestral spirits and often with locally important gods—has been honored and asked for aid and protection. Roadside stone pillars and images called "road ancestor beings" or "ancestral way persons" blended protective and fertility themes.

Even after welcoming into its structure elements of Buddhism, Daoism, and Confucianism, rural Shinto retained this primary clan and family pattern and remained a vital and independent force. Members of families and clans continued to recognize deep ties with the *kami* who had done so much for them in the past. Aristocratic families residing in the capital continued to send subsidies to their home shrines.

The Guest Mode

The villages and their clans were receptive to deities that may be called divine guests from the outside, who visited occasionally or came to stay, such as the emperor's ancestress Amaterasu, Inari the grain goddess, and overseas powers like the Buddhist and Daoist deities.

The Decline of Mixed Shinto

It is not surprising that Shinto nearly succumbed. Certainly Two-Sided Shinto had an immense influence on the people of Japan. It won the majority to its interpretations. In ensuing years, not only did most of the Shinto shrines make room for Buddhist worship and Buddhist priests, but the latter introduced into the old Shinto rites images, incense, sermons, and elaborate ceremonies. The simple primitive appearance of the Shinto shines was greatly altered by the exterior application of the intricate ornaments of Buddhist temples and by the addition to the shrine property of pagodas, drum towers, large bells, assembly hall for preaching services, and the like. Even the unadorned Shinto gateway, or *torii*, was supplied with curves and ornate decoration.

Japanese appropriation and adaptation of Buddhism continued to the fourteenth century CE, when public order dissolved in three hundred years of feudal strife, during which the emperor, his headship of the nation thoroughly obscured, was condemned to impotence while dictators *(shoguns)* vainly stove to control the powerful noble and the *samurai*, or military class. At the end of the sixteenth century, a shogun arose who brought an end to the centuries of feudal warfare. This marked the beginning of the period of the Tokugawa regime (1603–1867 CE). It was a period of some importance to Shinto, for its own revival or renaissance occurred during this period.

The Revival of Shinto as a Separate Religion

The revival of Shinto was a slow and gradual process. During the disorders that attended the end of the Kamakura Period in the first half of the fourteenth century CE, those who supported Emperor Go-Daigo in his successful effort to gain control of the nation could not have failed to raise the question of whether the descendent of the sun goddess should have been rejected. That Shinto and its central themes should be so nearly submerged in Buddhism also worried many.

As the fourteenth century wore on, several of the hereditary priests of the Watara family, who took care of the outer shrine at Ise, sought without great success to free Shinto (their Ise Shinto) from Buddhist and Chinese infusions, and a century later one of the Urabe priests at the Kasuga shrine at Nara wrote a treatise that tried to distinguish the ancient Shinto elements within the current Buddhized (Ryobu) Shinto. Then suggestions were made by the Watari priests and others that the thesis of Ryobu Shinto should be reversed, that is, that the Japanese *kami* be declared the "Originals" and the Buddhist deities their appearances. This was not with great success.

But a purer Shinto had friends in other quarters. Support for its independence from Buddhism was unwittingly evoked by the Tokugawa shogunate. By the end of the seventeenth century, Christianity was being suppressed, and the ports of Japan had been closed to all but a few

Dutch and Chinese traders. After a desperate uprising of Christians during the period 1637–1638 CE, the government attempted to smoke out all remaining Christians by ordering every Japanese to secure a certificate from a Buddhist temple to prove that he or she was not an adherent of the proscribed religion. This greatly upset some Shinto priests, who, obliged to have recourse to Buddhist temples, asked recognition as representatives of an independent religion. They received immediate support from a number of Japanese Confucian scholars, who also desired the disengagement of Shinto from its Buddhist entanglements. Confucianism had been influential among the literary classes ever since the first introduction of Chinese learning into Japan in the fifth century. In medieval Japan, it took a new turn with the introduction of neo-Confucianism and the philosophical views of Zhu Xi and Wang Yangming. The latter was generally frowned upon as being too theoretical and subjective, but Zhu Xi was widely received as a major guide to the nature of the world and its history. During the Tokugawa Period, Japanese scholars from the seventeenth century on became his interpreters, and they took an anti-Buddhist "rationalist" position; this ultimately meant that they desired to see Shinto purged of its Buddhist accretions and restored to its "ancient Way." There was even a proposal of a Confucian-Shinto amalgamation, to be called Suika Shinto, to displace Ryobu Shinto.

It was clear that the Japanese masses still loved the "purer" Shinto rites, especially those performed at the grand shrine of the sun goddess Amaterasu at Ise, to which in times of plentiful harvests they flocked in great numbers to express their thanks for the sunshine that had favored the crops. Encouraged, the Ise priests toured the countryside promising the practice of visiting Ise at least once in a lifetime.

Shinto Classical Scholars: Motoori

All of this inspired scholars of the Shinto classics to a nationalistic concentration on "native ancient learning." During the eighteenth and early nineteenth centuries, three outstanding scholars took advantage of the anti-foreign atmosphere to revive what came to be called "Pure Shinto" or "True Ancient Way": Kamo Mabuchi, Motoori Noringa, and Hirata Atsutane. The second person of this group was perhaps the greatest scholar in Japanese history. His commentary on the *Kojiki* is still regarded as authoritative. However, his conclusions were as subjective as his scholarship in other respects was factual. He scorned the position of his contemporaries, who unhesitatingly acknowledged the dependence of Japanese learning on Chinese sources, and strongly upheld the superiority of the ancient way of Japan and insisted on the divine origin of the emperor. He rejected the opinion that because the Japanese had no native system of ethics, they were obliged to borrow from Confucianism. He claimed that only a depraved people need a moral system; by reason of their divine motivation, the Japanese were so naturally upright in the lives that they were in no need of an ethical code and therefore never had one. Motoori concluded that the Japanese consequently should relinquish all foreign modes of thought and action and walk in simplicity the ancient way of Shinto.

But these were scholarly opinions. Not until the nineteenth century did Shinto triumph from a political point of view.

The Restoration of 1868

The vindication of the Shinto myth came in the second half of the nineteenth century, when the second great transformation of Japan took place (the first being the influx of Buddhism). The necessity for this transformation was borne in on the Japanese rather suddenly. Though they strove to remain a "hermit nation," they could not prevent American whaling ships from appearing off their coasts and from time to time suffering shipwreck. The sailors who reached shore were either killed or repatriated through the Dutch traders who were the only foreigners permitted in Japanese waters. The whalers had other problems, including the need of water and provisions by the time they reached Japan, and they naturally wanted to be able to put into port to stock up. The shogun finally concluded a treaty that provided for kind treatment of shipwrecked sailors, permission for freeing ships to obtain provisions and water ashore, and the opening to trade of three unimportant ports. In concluding this treaty, the shogun did not obtain the approval of the emperor. After the death of the emperor, the antishogunate forces of the imperial court began a struggle to unseat the shogun. In the course of this struggle, the shogun was finally led to abolish his own office, retire to the background, and leave the way open for the restoration of the emperor, in 1869, to full authority over the nation. It should be noted, however, that the shogun had permitted a process of Westernization to begin that could not be stopped.

The Constitution of 1889 and the State Cult

The Japanese conservatives soon realized that the adoption of Western economic and industrial methods, even when they were modified to Japanese requirements, involved very significant changes in culture and outlook. This moved them to be even more resolved somehow to preserve the ancient military ideals and values in the modern setting. They arranged that in the Constitution of 1889 the army and navy were not placed under civilian control but were made responsible to the emperor alone. And what is of main importance here, they raised the old Shinto myth of the emperor's descent from the sun goddess to high place in the national life by incorporating it in the constitution itself.

Buddhism Disestablished

The conservatives went about developing a state cult that could be expected to give Shinto a continuing influence in the nation's life. To this end they felt that the Shinto myth should be isolated from its Buddhist involvements and made to stand clear. Accordingly, one of the first acts of the Emperor Meijii, after the restoration, was to disestablish Buddhism, make Shinto the state religion, and order the elimination of all Buddhist elements, including priests, from the Shinto shrines. Adopted by the leaders of the Meijii Restoration as a "pure" Japanese religion, it received the support of the state, was isolated from Buddhism, and was fundamentally transformed to support patriotic and nationalist feelings in the building up of World War I. But so closely were Shinto and Buddhism interdependent that the national return to a "pure" Shinto turned out to be impracticable. The common people continued to support both religions. In 1877, Buddhism was allowed to exist by being granted autonomy. In the Constitution of 1889, absolute religious liberty of all citizens was guaranteed, though the government showed where its official heart lay by retaining a department, called the Bureau of Shrines, to convey its attitude of special regard and care for the refurbished and redefined national faith. This department was ultimately divided into a Bureau of Shinto Shrines, under the Department of Home Affairs, and a Bureau of Religions, under the Department of Education. The division was made appropriate by the official distinction drawn by the government between "State" Shinto and "Sectarian" Shinto, a matter that requires our further attention.

State Shinto to 1945

State Shinto was the government-sponsored program of patriotic rites that was conducted until 1945 in shrines taken away from sectarian control and made national property. (The American occupation authority caused its compulsory features to be abolished in that year. Worship at the former state shrines is now voluntary—although for public officials it is virtually obligatory.) The purpose of the state cult was the cultivation of patriotic feeling with the Japanese. It arose initially from the need to keep the people faithful to the "spirit of ancient Japan" through all the changes brought about in the life of the nation by the adoption of Western technology.

Agnosticism and Efforts to Revise the Myth

Shinto at first was aversely affected by the upheaval of Japanese life and culture that accompanied the wholesale importation of Western ideas in the post-restoration era. Thousands were estranged and turned away for a time from the officially sanctioned state shrines. The simultaneous resurgence of Buddhism, and the reentrance of Christianity, helped produce a religious attitude among the people that threatened the end of the old native Shinto faith. But in truth all religions suffered. Disbelief and agnosticism became pervasive.

Shortly after its early contacts with Western culture and science in the eighteenth century, the Japanese government began to take measures to restore and promote Shinto as a national faith. It urged a reinterpretation of the Shinto myth that would make it acceptable to the critical intelligence of the nation. Semi-official approval was given to the view that the deities of the national myth were originally human beings with superior gifts. Japanese scholars humanized the whole of Japanese mythology and thus tried to reconcile themselves with historical science as understood in the Western world.

Shinto as National Ethics

In another direction, the Japanese government made efforts to save Shinto by making it over into a positive force, a national institution of a moral and a historical character. The official government view was that Shinto was not really a religion but a system of national ethics and a cult of loyalty to national institutions. To make this clear, the restoration, or Meijii, government in 1882 officially separated what is known as Jinja-Shinto, or State Shinto, from Kyoha-Shinto, or Sectarian Shinto. The latter was stated to be ineligible for government financial support and was accorded the status of an independent religion with the same status as Buddhism and Christianity. State Shinto was declared to be solely a system of state ceremonials whose patriotic object was to unify the popular mind in accordance with the national morality.

Religious Practice Today in Japan

The concept of religious practice in modern Japan is complex. Urbanization has separated many Japanese from the family ties to a specific Buddhist temple and Shinto shrine. While most Japanese are not adherents of any one particular religion, many, however, still consider themselves both Shintoists and Buddhists. Shinto and Mahayana teaching are deeply embodied in everyday Japanese life, though the people may not be keenly mindful of it. Most Japanese people do not often give the distinction much thought. The Agency for Cultural Affairs statistics for 1996 show the combined membership of both Shinto and Buddhism as approximately 19 million, which is about 54 percent more than the total population of Japan. In the religious sentiments of most Japanese, Shinto and Buddhism peacefully coexist rather than conflict. For the average person, however, religious affiliation does not mean regular worship or attendance. Most people visit shrines and temples as part of annual events and special rituals marking life passages. The same Japanese person may have a wedding at a Shinto shrine or Christian church and have a funeral at a Buddhist temple. Life cycle events are often commemorated visits to a Shinto shrine. The birth of a child is celebrated with a formal shrine visit at the age of approximately one month, as are the third, fifth, and seventh birthdays and the official beginning of adulthood at the age of twenty.

Shrine Shinto Today

In 1945, the 110,000 shrines formerly under the control of the government's Home Ministry were cut off from state supervision and subsidies. The first effect of this disestablishment and return of the shrines to local control was confusion and paralysis. Attendance at the shrines fell off sharply, and the priests, used to rituals and prayers that had formerly been supplied by the Home Ministry, were thrown on their own resources. But after a period of readjustment, a religious atmosphere more genuine than before was developed, and the shrines began to regain their popularity. Eighty-six thousand shrines are maintained by a nationwide Shrine Association financed by private funds and voluntary gifts. Most of the shrines are therefore functioning and enjoy genuine popular support.

The typical village shrine is situated on a low knoll, where it reposes among cryptomerias and pines. As the worshipers approach the *haiden*, the sanctuary for worship, they step aside to wash both hands and cleanse out the mouth at the "water-purification place." They draw near the outer shrine, bow before it, clap both hands politely (the distinctive Japanese way of obtaining the gods' attention), bow, ring the bell, bow again, leave an offering on a cloth or drop it in the treasury box provided for the purpose, pray, bow again in mediation and reverence, and then retire quietly, pausing to turn around and bow low.

A little beyond the outer shrine stands the inner sanctuary, or *honden*. Here the worshipers do not enter, but they know that the chief treasure of the shrine is housed within it, an object called the *shintai*, or "god-body," a precious object that is generally never permitted to be seen. The meaning of the *shintai* has varied according to the faith and sophistication of the worshipers. The more devout among the common people have associated the sacred object with one of the old gods of the land or with a deified ancestor and have even offered prayers to it as if it had ears to hear. Perhaps the majority, however, no longer identify it as having a distinctly religious value; instead it signifies the place of a magical power of some sort or the seat of a good luck agency to be persuaded into friendliness. Those who are sophisticated look upon it as an object symbolic solely of the continuing virtue and spirit of deified ancestors and heroic persons of the past.

Shrine and Temple Festivals

At the beginning of the year, the major annual event, the New Year Festival, takes place, beginning at midnight on December 31 and lasting three days. These are national holidays, the occasion for millions of people to worship at both Buddhist temples and Shinto shrines, which are sometimes found in the same compound. Some shrines and temples record an attendance of more than one million visitors each during these three days. There are also Shinto rites of the agricultural year. All the various phases of the cultivation of rice are solemnized, starting with the emperor's prayer in February that farmers may have success when the rice is sown and later transplanted in the paddy fields.

It is usual to observe the Buddhist festivals as if they and the distinctively Shinto ones are of the same general character and interest. They are very popular and promote community-wide participation. Among them is the observance of the Buddha's birthday on April 8, and from July 13 to 15 the major Buddhist festival, the *Obon*, which celebrates the return of the spirits of the dead, in whose honor jubilant dances are performed.

This is hardly a complete list of the festivals of the year, for there are many local and regional festivals, 450 by one count, all arousing great interest and enthusiasm. In the great cities, these events of the ritual year are being infiltrated by such new festivals as Christmas.

Shinto in the Home

The ambiguity that once obscured the government's position has been absent in domestic Shinto. Most private homes have a *kami-dana*, or god shelf, which has been the heart and center of domestic Shinto. On it are placed memorial tablets made of wood or paper, each inscribed with the name of an ancestor or a patron god of the household or locality. Sometimes Amaterasu, sometimes Inari the goddess of rice, or both, is given respect by the presence of their symbols. In the majority of cases, a miniature shrine containing a sacred mirror, a strip of paper with sacred texts written on them, or talismans obtained at Amaterasu's shrine at Ise or elsewhere occupies the center of the god shelf. Thus the god shelf itself becomes a temple area in miniature. It may be the repository of any object surcharged with family history and significance.

Domestic rites are still performed daily in many homes. They may involve no more than the placing of a small offering of food and the murmuring of a prayer. However, exceptional occasions or crises in family life compel more elaborate rites, such as the lighting of tapers and the offering of rice brandy. Usually, religious life in the home is not exclusively Shinto in character. Buddhist priests often are summoned to perform rites connected with important aspects of family life. This is particularly true after a death; then the Buddhist priest, being a "funeral specialist" whose services are indispensable, is called to minister in the home.

The family also may maintain in addition to the *kami-dana*, but usually in another room, a Buddhist altar, in which are placed wooden tablets bearing the "heavenly names" of the departed, made known by the Buddhist priest. Here the priest may chant sutras at specific intervals. This is another instance of how Buddhism interacts with Shinto in meeting the needs of a family. It has been estimated that more than 60 percent of households own a Buddhist altar.

Sectarian Shinto

The ambiguity that once obscured the government's position has been absent also in Sectarian Shinto. Although among the sects there have been ethical culture groups that renounce religious interests, the motives of the majority of those that sustain the sects have been forthrightly and unconsciously religious. During the years that the government sponsored the so-called nonreligious ceremonies of State Shinto, a sphere for Sectarian, that is to say religious, Shinto was permitted. Under the provision of the Constitution of 1889, which granted religious liberty to all citizens, Shinto sects were allowed to formulate their own beliefs and ceremonies but were required to find their own means of support, as were the various branches of Buddhism and Christianity. Of the thirteen sects recognized by the Bureau of Religions before World War II, about half came into existence after the restoration of 1868. Any attempt to classify these self-propagating religious sects discloses their generally eclectic character. In D. C. Holtom's classification, only three can be called pure Shinto sects. Of the others, two have sought unification with Confucianism. Since World War II and the withdrawal of the government from the sphere of religion, hundreds of Shinto sects have formed, and some sixty have registered with the government as Sectarian Shinto denominations.

Confucianism and Daoism

Although not practiced as a religion, Confucianism has profoundly influenced Japanese thought. While introduced somewhat earlier than Buddhism, it has functioned mainly in the sphere of moral precepts rather than as an organized religion. It has an impact on the practice of proper forms of conduct, especially in social and family relationships. Confucian teachings about filial piety and life in society continue to form the foundation for much of social life and ideas about family and nation. Neo-Confucianism, introduced in Japan in the twelfth century, is an interpretation of nature and society founded on metaphysical principles and is influenced by Buddhist and Daoist ideas. In Japan, where it is known as Shushi school, after the Chinese neo-Confucian scholar, Zhu-XI (*Shushi* in Japanese), it stressed the concept that family stability and social duty are human obligations. Daoism from China has had an influence on Japanese thought and has a special affinity to Zen Buddhism. Zen's stress on emptiness, exhortation to act in harmony with nature, and admonitions to avoid discrimination duality are parallel to Daoist beliefs.

Notes

1. *Major Religions of the World Ranked by Number of Adherents.* Available at: http://www.adherents.com/Religions_By_Adherents.html.

2. David S. Noss, *A History of the World's Religions,* 12th ed. (Upper Saddle River, NJ: Prentice Hall, 2007), 328.

3. Ibid., 212.

4. Ibid.

5. Joseph M. Kitagawa, *Japanese Society* (New York: Columbia University Press, 1966), 3ff; cited in Noss, *History,* 338.

Chapter Eight

JUDAISM, CHRISTIANITY, AND ISLAM

The creative period of the Axial Age, as we have seen, did not arise as a decisive, clean break with the past. Rather, it was prepared for and anticipated by earlier movements. We continue, therefore, in this chapter to consider how the soteriological structure and its related traits came historically to characterize Judaism, Christianity, and Islam.

Judaism

In the Jewish tradition, there is a conviction that the human drama is a manifestation of God's powerful presence and activity. This view of history, as we shall see, emerged from the vision of the great prophets whose insights sharpened and intensified the ancient Jews' consciousness of life as a continuous interaction with their God. The great men of prophetic calling gave the succession of Israel's historical events a coherent meaning as the working out of God's purpose. This understanding of history as a divine theophany was prevalent among the Jews most clearly in their sixth-century Axial Period. We go on now to trace the successive stepping stones to Judaism's Axial transformation, beginning with the ninth century.

Ninth Century BCE

Near the end of the ninth century BCE, the northern kingdom of Israel had become a major power in the eastern Mediterranean. It had expanded into several ancient Canaanite strongholds, absorbed their inhabitants, and exploited their skills. In Samaria, King Omri (885–874) built a superb new capital, and his son, Ahab (874–853), built an impressive ivory palace there and established trade links with Phoenicia, Cyprus, and Greece. He also married Jezebel, a Phoenician princess, whose name has become linked with wickedness.

Jezebel imported the cult of the Phoenician god, Baal, into Israel. Ahab, who was not an apostate and frequently consulted the prophets of Yahweh, saw nothing objectionable in his wife's devotion to Baal. For centuries, Yahweh's worship had been nourished by the hymns and rites of Baal. As archaeologists have found, most of the Israelite population worshiped other local gods besides Yahweh, and worship of Baal flourished in Israel until the sixth century BCE. Devotion to a sacred assembly of gods was very important to the people of Israel and Judah. However, in the ninth century some Israelites were beginning to reduce the number of gods they worshiped. Rather than presiding over a large divine household, Yahweh presided alone over a host of lesser divine beings. They were his "heavenly hosts" and the warriors in his sacred army.

As the national God, Yahweh was without peers or rivals or superiors. He was at the center of an assembly of holy ones who all acclaimed Yahweh's fidelity to his people. While the Israelites did not deny the existence of other gods, they did declare that their patronal god was more effective than the national gods of their neighbors. But since Yahweh was experienced as a warrior god, with no expertise in agriculture or fertility, many Israelites, to ensure a good harvest, carried out the ancient rites of Baal, for he was believed to have the power that gave fertility to the land.

Elijah and Elisha

Objection to the worship of a foreign god was voiced by a small group of prophets who were convinced that Yahweh was able to provide for all the needs of his people. In the ancient Middle East, prophecy was an established spiritual practice. From Canaan to Mari in the middle Euphrates, prophets spoke ecstatically for their gods. In Israel and Judah, prophets were regularly associated with the royal court. They often criticized the monarch and were dedicated to preserving the purity of devotion to Yahweh. In the First and Second Books of Kings, we have accounts of the ninth-century prophets Elijah and his disciple, Elisha.

Elijah is the first prophet on record to insist on the exclusive worship of Yahweh. He did not doubt the existence of Baal, but he asserted that this deity was not the god of Israel and should stay in Phoenicia (modern-day Carthage). When Israel was afflicted by a severe drought, even after Baal's patronage had been sought, Elijah saw his opportunity and challenged more than 450 of Jezebel's priests, who were devoted to the service of Baal, to a contest on Mount Carmel.[1] First, he proclaimed to the people that it was time that they made a choice, once and for all, between Yahweh and Baal. Then he called for two bulls—one for Yahweh and the other for Baal—to be placed on two altars. He and the Baal priests would call upon their respective gods and see which one sent down fire to consume the victim. For a whole morning, the priests of Baal invoked him to descend, but nothing happened. But when Elijah called on Yahweh, immediately fire fell from heaven and devoured both bull and altar. The people fell prostrate in awe before Yahweh. Elijah then commanded that all the prophets of Baal be slaughtered. He climbed up Mount Carmel and sat with his head between his knees, deep in prayer, supplicating Yahweh to end the drought. The rain fell in torrents, and Elijah ran in ecstasy beside Ahab's chariot. Yahweh had shown that he successfully assumed the function of Baal, proving that he was as effective at preserving the fertility of the land as at waging war.

When the storm ended, Elijah left Israel and found sanctuary in Yahweh's shrine on Mount Sinai. He went there in hope of receiving a revelation.[2] In the past, the divine warrior Yahweh, like Baal, had frequently disclosed himself in the disruptions of nature. But now here at Sinai it was different; Yahweh did not reveal himself in the violent forces of nature but in the mystery of a voiced silence. "And after the fire a sound of sheer silence. When Elijah heard it, he wrapped his face in his mantle and went out and stood at the entrance of the cave."[3] This was a moment when Yahweh's transcendence was made manifest. Rather than disclosing his divine self as imminent in the natural world, Yahweh had become separated from and other than the world. Historians often speak of the "transcendental breakthrough" of the Axial Age. Clearly this was such an occurrence. However, like the ancient pre-Axial religion of Israel, it was also deeply aggressive. It came after a massacre and preceded a new round of violence. Standing in a cave on Mount Sinai, covered in his cloak, Elijah heard Yahweh sentence Ahab's successor to death. All would die except those who had not knelt before Baal.

When people concentrated on defining the god to which they were transcending, instead of focusing on the greed, hatred, and egotism from which they were transcending, there was a danger of stridency and aggressive chauvinism. Freedom was an essential value of the Axial Age, and Elijah's strong-arm tactics were what some later Axial sages would call "unskillful." It was counterproductive to force people into a spirituality for which they were not ready. It was unhelpful to be dogmatic about a transcendence that was essentially indefinable.[4]

Elijah's contest with the prophets of Baal marked the start of a new conflict in Israel and Judah. From this time on, a strident battle with rival deities would inform the spirituality of the prophets. Through them Yahweh accused the other deities of neglecting the fundamental obligation of social justice; he was moved by the plight of the needy and rewarded practical compassion as much as cultic purity. Concern for social justice was not a new development, nor was it peculiar to Israel and Judah. The protection of the weak had long been common policy throughout the ancient Near East.[5] Throughout the Middle East, justice was a basic requirement of religion. So Elijah's insistence on these virtues does not indicate the beginning of a new Axial Age spirituality; social justice was already deeply rooted in the ancient traditions of the Middle East.

While Israel had become a major power in the ninth century, to its east a completely different sort of a mighty political entity was slowly coming into being. In 876 BCE, the Assyrian king had subdued the Phoenician towns on the Mediterranean coast, and when Shalmaneser III came to the throne in 859, a strong confederation of local kings, led by Hadadezer of Damascus, tried to obstruct Assyria's western advance. In 841, Assyria defeated Damascus and became master of the region. The kingdom of Israel became its favored vassal and enjoyed a new period of peace and prosperity.

In the late ninth century, the Israelites still found the gods of their foreign neighbors alluring, but they were committed to Yahweh, whom they chose as their god. This was *not* monotheism. If no other gods existed, such a choice would not be necessary. Monolatry—the worship of a single god—was a liturgical arrangement. Those who were devoted to Yahweh alone urged Israelites to sacrifice only to Yahweh and to ignore the worship of other deities. This posture, however, required courage, a narrowing of resources provided by sacred entities, and a loss of familiar and beloved sacred beings. Israel was about to embark on a long, painful journey of severance from the cultic consensus of the Middle East, on its way to the Axial Age.

Eighth Century BCE

In this stage of its history, we see the first stirring of Judaism's Axial spirituality, which comes to fruition some two hundred years later. During the eighth century, the art of literacy spread throughout the Semitic world. Writing developed, so now scribes of Israel and Judah began to develop a royal archive to preserve the ancient stories and customs. Toward the end of the century, the earliest part of the Pentateuch was probably committed to writing. But even more important, we find the seeds of the self-abandonment that would be crucial to all the religious traditions of the Axial Age. Here too, the catalyst of change was the eruption of violence in the region.

During the first half of the eighth century, while the northern kingdom of Israel was flourishing, Assyria was growing stronger and stronger, and would soon dominate the entire region. And as Assyria's loyal vassal, Israel enjoyed an economic boom under King Jeroboam II (786–746). But, as in any agrarian state, wealth was restricted to the upper classes, and the rift between the rich and poor became obvious. Peasants were heavily taxed and subject to forced labor, and the artisans in the cities fared little better. This systemic injustice was both a religious and economic problem. In the Middle East, a king who abused his duties to the needy violated the decrees of the gods and put the legitimacy of his reign into question. Therefore, it was not surprising that prophets rose up in the name of Yahweh to attack the injustice of the government. Amos and Hosea were the first literary Hebrew prophets, and it is clear that they were disturbed by the social crisis of their time. Their teachings were transmitted orally by their disciples, and at the end of the eighth century, they were written down and compiled in anthologies of prophetic oracles.

Amos

Amos's message was shocking. He predicted that Jeroboam, who had neglected his duties to the poor, would be killed, Israel destroyed, and its people taken into exile. Yahweh had always been experienced as a divine warrior coming to Israel's aid. But now Yahweh was no longer on the side of Israel, as he had been at the time of the exodus. He would use the king of Assyria to punish Jeroboam for his lack of concern for the poor.

The spirituality of the Axial Age could frequently be iconoclastic. In addition to turning the ancient devotion to Yahweh, the divine warrior, upside down, Amos also cast a scornful eye on Israel's beloved liturgical rites. Yahweh was sick of listening to his people's noisy chanting and strumming of harps. Instead he wanted justice and integrity to flow like water. Finally, Amos undermined the Israelites' pride in their unique relationship with Yahweh. Other peoples had also been liberated by Yahweh. Now he was preparing to bring violence to the kingdom of Israel.

Amos's message was in line with the spirituality of the Axial Age, which could frequently be iconoclastic. Religion was not about holding on to cherished practices and beliefs; it often demanded that people critically question their traditions and their own behavior. The Axial spirituality also required modesty and self-surrender to the divine. In his communication Amos delivered a stinging blow to Israel's ego and self-esteem, calling them to humility and submission to Yahweh. He was not speaking his own words, but Yahweh's. "This was one of the earliest expressions in Israel of the spirituality of self-surrender, which was at the heart of the axial idea. Rather than using religion to build up their sense of self worth, the Israelites had to learn to transcend their self-interest and rule their nation with justice and equity."[6]

Hosea

Hosea was active in the northern kingdom at about the same time as Amos. His wife, Gomer, became a sacred prostitute in the fertility cult of Baal.[7] He saw his longing to win Gomer back as a sign that Yahweh also yearned after unfaithful Israel, and that the Lord was prepared to give her another chance.[8] Like Elijah, he was trying to eliminate

Baal and persuade Israelites to worship Yahweh alone. But where Elijah had concentrated on purifying the cult, Hosea's concern was ethical. Baal worship had led to the moral decline of the Israelites: "Swearing, lying, and murder, and stealing and adultery break out; bloodshed follows bloodshed."[9] There was sexual laxity because so many people were frequenting the sacred prostitutes and lying around drunkenly after sacrificial banquets. Instead of giving spiritual and moral guidance, priests consulted wooden idols.[10]

All of this was rooted in a lack of inwardness in Israel's religion.[11] The people worshiped other gods only because they did not truly know Yahweh at a profound level. Their understanding of the divine and religion was superficial. Hosea demanded greater awareness and interior devotion. Religious practices must no longer be performed by rote and without interior devotion. People must become more conscious of what they were doing. Hosea was not talking about purely rational, notional knowledge; the very verb *yada* ("to know") implied an emotional attachment to Yahweh and an interior appropriation of the divine. It was not enough merely to attend a sacrifice or a festival. "For I desire steadfast love," Yahweh demanded, "and not sacrifice; the knowledge of God, rather than burnt offerings."[12] Hosea tried to make the Israelites mindful of God's true devotion to them. The exodus, for example, had not simply been an exercise of power on Yahweh's part. And when Yahweh lived with the Israelites for forty years in the wilderness, he was committed to the Israelites like a parent teaching his children to walk, carrying them in his arms, and leading them like a child "with cords of human kindness, with bands of love." Yahweh had been like one "who lifts infants to their cheeks"; he had "bent down" when he gave the people their food.[13] Hosea was attempting to help the people appreciate the pathos of God and to relate to him with the inner devotion of love.

Amos and Hosea had both introduced an important new dimension to Israelite religion. Without *good ethical behavior*, they insisted, ritual worship alone was worthless. And religion should be used to urge the abandonment of egotism. Hosea, in particular, urged the Israelites to examine their inner lives, reflect on their feelings, and develop a deeper vision based on introspection and a loving heart. Some of these qualities also were manifest in the early portions of the Pentateuch, which were being produced in Israel and Judah about this time.

J and E Documents

Scholars have long recognized that there are different layers in the Pentateuch, the first five books of the Hebrew scriptures (Genesis, Exodus, Leviticus, Numbers, Deuteronomy). It seems that two early texts were first combined, and then, later, in about the sixth century, edited by a priestly writer who added his own traditions. One of these early sources is called "J" because the author called his god "Yahweh," and the second is called "E" because the author used the more formal divine title of *elohim*. J and E were not original compositions; they only recorded and brought together into a coherent narrative the ancient stories that had been recited by the bards of early Israel and had been transmitted orally from one generation to another. It seems likely that while they both contain older material, they represent two different strands of tradition—one southern, one northern—-that were combined and written down in the late eighth century and included in the royal archive in Jerusalem.[14] They present a sustained chronicle of the history of early Israel.[15]

In both J and E we see early indications of the Axial spirituality of *kenosis* or self-surrender. It is clearly present in J's story of Abraham's vision of Yahweh at the oak of Mamre, near Hebron.[16] Abraham had looked up and saw three men standing near his tent. Immediately, he ran to them "and bowed down to the ground."[17] Strangers were potentially dangerous persons; they were not bound by the laws of local vendetta; with impunity they could kill and be killed. But rather than attacking them so as to defend his family, Abraham prostrated himself as though they were *gods*. He then treated his visitors with an elaborate meal so they would be refreshed on their journey. The act of personal surrender along with practical compassion to the three total strangers led to a sacred encounter: during the course of the following conversation, it happened very naturally that one of these strangers was no other than Yahweh himself.

Even more compelling is E's story of the sacrifice of Isaac.[18] Abraham had been assured that he would become the father of a mighty nation, but he had only one remaining son. Then, E relates, "After these things God tested Abraham." He called him by name, and Abraham exclaimed, "Here I am." Patriarchs and prophets often responded to God with this cry (Exod 3:4; I Sam 3:4; Jer 1:4), which indicated their total readiness and presence. But God then issued a terrifying command:

"Take your son, your only son Isaac, whom you love, and go to the land of Moriah, and offer him there as a burnt offering on one of the mountains that I shall show you."[19] This story presents a new understanding of the divine. In the ancient world, a firstborn child was often regarded as the property of God, and it was required that he be returned to him in sacrifice. The rationale was that the blood of the young child restored the deity's depleted energies and assured the circulation of power in the cosmos. But here there was no such rationale. Elohim was making a purely arbitrary demand, to which Abraham could only respond in faith.[20] Furthermore, this god was completely different from the other deities of the region; he did not share in the human condition, he did not need an input of energy from men and women, but could make whatever demands he chose.

Abraham did not hesitate. Immediately he saddled his donkey and set out for the land of Moriah with Isaac and two servants, carrying in his own hands the knife that would kill his son and the wood for the holocaust. After binding Isaac, he laid him on the altar and seized the knife. It was an act of unconditional obedience that threatened to drain his life of meaning and value. The God he had served so long had shown that he was a breaker of promises and, worse, a slayer of children. Only in the last moment did elohim send his "angel" to stop the killing, demanding Abraham sacrifice a ram instead. This dramatic narrative marks an important cultic transition, when animal sacrifice was substituted for human sacrifice; it also shows that elohim was a friendly, benevolent presence. The narrative, therefore, foreshadows Axial religious ideals. However, in the fact that it shows that elohim also was experienced as terrifying and cruel, leading his devotee to the brink of meaninglessness and the destructive potential of an experience of the divine, it casts both Abraham *and* his God in dubious light.

Isaiah I

In the book of the prophet Isaiah, who was active in the kingdom of Judah to the south of the kingdom of Israel, we find that God begins to be experienced as a transcendent reality. In 740 Isaiah had a vision of Yahweh in the Jerusalem temple.[21] In this encounter Yahweh was no longer known as a genial deity in human form with whom it was possible to share a friendly meal. In the cult hall Isaiah saw the terrifying reality that lay behind the temple rites. Yahweh sat on his heavenly throne, surrounded by his assembly of holy ones. On either side, two angels covered their faces: "Holy, holy, holy is the lord of hosts; the whole earth is full of his glory...." The foundations of the temple shook. God was no longer merely the holy one of Israel but the ruler of the whole world. And even more important, he was totally "other" and "separate" from humanity. Isaiah was filled with terror: "Woe is me! I am lost, for I am a man of unclean lips." One of the seraphs purified his lips with a burning coal and Yahweh asked, "Whom shall I send and who will go for us?" Isaiah immediately replied, "Send me!" The divine message Isaiah was to transmit was bleak: it contained a description of a desolate, depopulated land.[22] When Isaiah delivered the message, the fearful description was becoming a daily reality in the Middle East due to the invasions of the Assyrians.

When Tiglath-pileser III had become king of Assyria in 745 BCE, he began the violent process of establishing a completely new type of empire, progressively taking apart the old system of vassalage and incorporating each subject people into the massive Assyrian state. When a subject king showed the first sign of rebellion, the country was invaded by the imperial army and the monarch was replaced by an Assyrian governor. When the kingdom of Israel in the north, the once-powerful state, fell into disarray after the death of Jeroboam II, the Assyrian army in 738 marched in and reduced it to a tiny state with a puppet-king on the throne.

The rise of Assyria posed a serious theological problem. Each of the subject peoples worshiped a national god—a holy one like Yahweh, who was the custodian of its territory. When the god of one country encroached upon another, a problem could arise. The god of Assyria was Asshur, and once Assyria had begun to absorb one nation after another, the balance of power between the gods had also changed. If the vicar of Asshur, Tiglath-pileser, had conquered the kingdom of Israel, did it follow that Asshur was more powerful than Yahweh?

When the people of Judah learned of what had occurred to Israel, they were horrified and felt deeply threatened. Isaiah, however, was not worried. He had seen Yahweh enthroned as king of the whole world, and he knew that Judah was safe. He belonged to a religious world different from Amos and Hosea, who had worked in the northern kingdom of Israel. The people of Judah must trust only in Yahweh; the northern kingdom of Israel had fallen because it had taken pride in its weapons and diplomacy.[23] Jerusalem was a refuse for the "poor," so its people must depend on Yahweh rather than putting their trust in wealth and military power.[24] Isaiah told the people that the divine warrior was once again on the march, fighting for his people. He spoke of Yahweh not just as the national god but the god of history, forcibly bringing peace to the region by destroying the destructive power of his enemies. To achieve the final triumph, Ahaz, king of Judah, should not engage in worldly politics but put his faith in Yahweh alone. It was idolatry to depend arrogantly upon mere human armies and fortifications. This reliance on Yahweh alone was a Judean version of the northern cultic movement to worship Yahweh exclusively, and Isaiah's insistence on humility and surrender seems at first sight similar to the Axial spirituality of *kenosis,* self-surrender (also translated "self-emptying").

> Yet it also inflated the national ego of Judah at a perilous juncture of history. Isaiah's revolutionary idea that Yahweh was not simply the patronal god of Israel, but could control the gods other nations, was based upon a defiant patriotism. In many ways, Isaiah belonged to the old cultic world. He preached a violent, agonistic, vision, which absorbed and endorsed the aggressive politics of the time.[25]

The little kingdom of Judah was one of a handful of nations to retain a degree of independence after the Assyrian campaigns. At the end of the eighth century, Jerusalem flourished and expanded extensively. And Hezekiah, who succeeded his father in 715, engaged in a religious reform to centralize the cult, permitting worship only in the Jerusalem temple and abolishing the rural shrines. The reform was of short duration; the general public still continued to worship other gods. But because of his religious reform, the biblical historians remember Hezekiah as one of the greatest kings of Judah. His foreign policy, however, was not successful. When in 705 Sennacherib became the Assyrian king, Hezekiah entered an anti-Assyrian coalition and began to prepare Jerusalem for war. In 701, Sennacherib invaded Judah and began to devastate the countryside. Finally his soldiers surrounded Jerusalem itself. But according to the biblical author, the "angel of the Lord set out and struck down one hundred eighty-five thousand in the camp of the camp of the Assyrians; when morning dawned, they were all dead bodies. Then King Sennacherib of Assyria left, went home, and lived at Nineveh."[26] The foreign policy of Hezekiah left him with only the small city-state of Jerusalem. "Patriotic pride and chauvinistic theology had almost annihilated the nation."[27]

Seventh Century BCE

In Israel, the seventh century was a watershed that saw the beginnings of the religion of Judaism. Manasseh (687–642), son of Hezekiah, remained a loyal vassal of Assyria, and Judah prospered during his long reign. Manasseh was not interested in the worship of Yahweh alone. He set up altars to Baal, brought an effigy of Asherah into the Jerusalem temple, and instituted child sacrifices outside Jerusalem. After the death of Manasseh, his son Amon reigned for only two years before he was assassinated and his eight-year-old son, Josiah, was placed on the throne. By this time, Assyria was in decline and Egypt was in the ascendancy. In 656, Pharaoh Psammetichus I forced the Assyrian troops to withdraw from the Levant, and Josiah became the vassal of Egypt.

When Josiah was about sixteen years old, he underwent a religious conversion. In 622 he began extensive building work on Solomon's temple, the great memorial of Judah's golden age. During this construction, the high priest Hilkiah discovered the book of the law (*sefer torah*). He proclaimed that this was the authentic Law that Yahweh had given to Moses on Mount Sinai. Most scholars believe that the scroll contained an early version of the Book of Deuteronomy, which describes Moses gathering the people together on Mount Nebo in Transjordan, shortly before his death, and delivering a "second law" (Greek, *deuteronomion*). It was almost certainly an entirely new scripture. The Deuteronomist writers added to the JE narrative, explaining that Moses "wrote down all the words of the Lord" and "took the book of the covenant and read it in the hearing of the people."[28] Now it was claimed that this was the very scroll that Hilkiah had found in the temple. For centuries this precious document had been lost, and its teaching had never been but into action. Now that the *sefer torah* had been found, Yahweh's people could make a new start.

As soon as Josiah heard the words of the scroll, he ripped his garment in great distress: "Great is the wrath of the Lord that is kindled against us, because our ancestors did not obey the words of this book, to do according to all that is written concerning us."[29] Reform was surely required, and Josiah summoned the whole people to listen to and obey the clear directives of the scroll. Immediately Josiah inaugurated a program that followed Yahweh's laws by the book. He eradicated the cultic traditions that Manasseh had reintroduced, burning the effigies of Baal and Asherah. He pulled down the house of sacred male prostitutes in the temple and the furnace where Israelites had sacrificed their children to Moloch.

In the light of the *sefer torah*, it became clear that for centuries the kings of Israel and Judah had allowed practices that Yahweh had expressly forbidden from the very beginning. It was clearly seen that Yahweh had sternly demanded exclusive allegiance. His people must love him with all their heart and soul and not worship other gods of the people around them. They must have no dealings with the native inhabitants of Canaan. In his reform, Josiah followed the unambiguous instructions of Yahweh to the letter.

Even though the Deuteronomists claimed to be conservative, basing their message on the original faith of Israel, they were, in fact, patently innovative. They were learned men, and their contribution to Judaism was a remarkable achievement. They drew on earlier material, old royal archives, law codes, sagas, and liturgical texts to create a new vision, making the ancient traditions pertinent to the new circumstances of Israel under Josiah. Their vision of a secular sphere, an independent judiciary, a constitutional monarchy, and a centralized state looks forward to modern times.

They also developed a more rational theology. It was essential that the Israelites behave with justice and kindness to one another. The passionate insistence of the Deuteronomists on the importance of justice, equity, and compassion went even further than the teaching of Amos and Hosea. In fact, if their reform had been fully implemented, the Deuteronomists would have altered significantly the political, social, religious, and judicial life of Israel. They pioneered the idea of scriptural orthodoxy in an effort to make Judaism a religion of the book.

Josiah's attempt to reform the nation was a great experiment, but it ended in tears. The map of the Middle East was changing. The

Assyrian Empire was in the final stage of its decline, and Babylon was in the ascendant. In 610, Pharaoh Psammetichus died and was succeeded by Necho III, who the following year marched through Palestine to come to the aid of the beleaguered Assyrian king. Josiah intercepted the Egyptian army at Megiddo and was killed at the first encounter. None of the reforms survived his death. The dream of political independence had been shattered, and Judah was now a minor player in the struggle between Egypt and the new Babylonian Empire, which threatened its very survival.

Sixth Century BCE

In the sixth century, during a time of unbridled and shocking violence, Israel entered upon *its* Axial Age. Each time Judah rebelled against Babylonia, King Nebuchadnezzar came down on the little Jewish kingdom with his powerful army and subjugated the region in harsh military campaigns. In 597, Judah submitted to Babylon, and eight thousand exiles were deported. In 587, when Zedekia, a Babylonian appointee on the throne of Judah, rebelled, Nebuchadnezzar and his army fell upon Jerusalem, destroyed its temple, and razed the city to the ground. In 581, a third group was taken into exile. For Israel, exile was a period of intense suffering and humiliation.

A New, Deeper Religious Vision

Jeremiah, who had not been deported, believed that the exiles of 597 would save Israel. If they were able to survive the time of trial in exile, they would be able to transcend themselves and develop a deeper, more interior and heartfelt devotion to Yahweh, who would make a new covenant with them. Having lost everything, some of the people of Israel *did* turn within and started to acquire a more interior and direct knowledge of the divine, a characteristic of the Axial Age. Those who are to be saved from punishment of sins are called to "seek the Lord their God."[30] And this means a deepening of what true religion demands and coming into union with the transcendent reality of God by a life of observing God's commandments, pursuing what is right, and practicing humility. God seeks for a religion of the heart, which is to be a condition of the covenant that is to come.[31]

The development of a new religious vision can be seen in the prophetic career of Ezekiel, who was deported to Babylon in 597. He experienced a series of visions that marked his painful passage from terror to a more serene interior spirituality. In delivering God's message to the Jews, he was to proclaim that their job was to repent, to experience the full weight of the sorrow; to realize that Israel had only itself to blame for disaster; and to build a rightly ordered life in Babylon. In stating that their crimes of lawlessness and injustice were just as serious as idolatry, Ezekiel interpreted ritualistic sacrifices in light of the ethical imperatives of the Axial Age.

While Ezekiel's vision and message to the Jews was condemnation, it was also a communication of new life. One day, when they had fully repented, Yahweh would bring the exiles home. But this would be more than a simple restoration. The sufferings of exile must result in a deeper vision. Yahweh promised, "I will give them one heart and put a new spirit in them; I will remove the heart of stone from their flesh and give them a heart of flesh, so that they may follow my statutes and keep my ordinances and obey them."[32]

Monotheism

In 559 a new power appeared in the Middle East: Cyrus succeeded to the throne of Persia, in what is now southern Iran. In 539, he invaded Babylonia and was greeted by the conquered Jews as a liberating hero. Second Isaiah had watched Cyrus's progress and became convinced that the suffering of exiles was coming to an end. He called Cyrus the messiah: "My shepherd and he shall carry out all my purpose."[33] The prophet believed that the historic reversals of his time would enable both Israel and the foreign nations "to know that it is I, the Lord."[34] This new exercise of divine, liberating power would show all parties who Yahweh was and what he could do. Moved entirely by the desire to help his people, Yahweh had inspired the career of Cyrus to cast down the mighty empire of Babylon. When Israel would be liberated from exile, Yahweh would transform the wilderness into a lake, and plant cedars, acacias, myrtles, and olives to the delight of its people on their homeward journey. Could any other deity do such things? No, Yahweh declared scornfully to the gods of the goyim, "You indeed are nothing and your work is nothing at all." No sane person would worship them.[35] Yahweh had annihilated the other deities and in effect had become the only God. "I am the Lord," he announced, "and there is no other."[36]

This is the first unequivocal assertion of monotheism in the Bible, the belief that only one God exists and that there are no others. Often this doctrine is seen as the great triumph of the Jewish Axial Age. It took Israel many centuries to reach a clear definition of monotheism. During many centuries, the Jews accepted that other nations had their own gods who were to be of no concern to them. Now Israel acknowledged only Yahweh, who was the most powerful of all gods and demanded exclusive devotion. The transition from this conception and practice to a clear-cut definition was effected by the preaching of the prophets. Jeremiah had insisted that by the side of Yahweh, Lord of all the earth, there is no room for any other gods. And when foreign cults threaten Israel's faith, he asserts the impotence of false gods and worthlessness of idols.[37]

When the hopes of the nation collapsed during the exile, and the power of Yahweh may have appeared to be defeated, the indictment of idols becomes more severe and better reasoned in Second Isaiah 40:19–20; 41:6–7, 21–24; 44:9–20; 46:17. And finally the assertion of unqualified monotheism becomes absolute in Second Isaiah 44:6–8; 46:1–7, 9. He was the earliest monotheist. He preached that Yahweh was not merely more righteous and more powerful than the gods of other nations, but that Yahweh was indeed the *only* God, and that other gods were nonexistent.

The one and only God is the absolute and transcendent reality, for which the favorite expression of the prophets is "holy." The holy transcendence of God is a recurrent theme in the teaching of the prophets. He is wrapped in mystery and is infinitely above humankind. At the same time his kindness and compassion make him near.

Self-Transcendence and Future Salvation

Running parallel with this emerging understanding of a single, holy, and transcendent God is the deepening appreciation of what true religion demands. Those who are to be saved from punishment for sins are called to "seek the Lord their God."[38] And this means coming into union with the transcendent reality of God by a life of observing God's commandments, pursuing what is right, and practicing humility. God asks for a religion of the heart, which is to be a condition of the covenant that is to come.[39]

To those who seek him, the transcendent God promises final salvation. A "remnant" will be allowed to survive.[40] This idea makes its appearance in Amos 5:15, and in the subsequent prophets it is further developed and defined. The "remnant" is at one and the same time those who survive the immediate peril and those who are to win final salvation. What ever the crisis experienced, the surviving Jews are always considered as the promising shoot, the nucleus of a sacred nation, assured by God of its great future.[41]

In this future age the Israelites will return to the Land of Promise.[42] There in the kingdom of God they will enjoy salvation. There will be such happiness as the chosen people have never known. Material prosperity and power do not, however, lie at the heart of the prophetic hope of future salvation; they are only concomitants of the establishment of God's kingship. For God's future kingdom implies a profoundly spiritual outlook: virtue and holiness,[43] a new mode of life and divine forgiveness,[44] true knowledge of God,[45] peace and joy.[46]

To bring about this final salvation and to establish and govern this ideal kingdom, King Yahweh would send his earthly representative. He would be known as Yahweh's "Anointed One," the messiah. The hopes of the prophets Isaiah, Micah, and Jeremiah are still centered on an individual king, in the near or distant future. This hope survived the collapse of pretensions to political domination and the severe lesson of the exile. Although this royal messianism went into eclipse, just before the beginning of the Christian era a hope for a king messiah reappeared and became widespread. Others, however, hoped for a priestly messiah, while yet others set their hope on a supernatural one. An eventual messianic salvation has been affirmed by many Jewish thinkers, for example, Hermann Cohen, Franz Rosenzweig, Martin Buber, Abraham Hershel, Joseph Dov Soloveitchick. It has also been questioned today by some—for example, David Hartman.

But the hope that arose in the Axial Period for a new age, on a socially and ethically transformed Earth, has ever since been part of the traditional Jewish outlook. It is the expectation of the kingdom of God, affecting the future of Israel and the world. This hope began with the great prophets, Amos, Hosea, Jeremiah. Second Isaiah spoke of a cosmic dimension, a universal transfiguration to be established by God's power. The expectation of the coming of the kingdom of God has been integral to the Jewish religious perspective, sometime vividly and centrally, and sometimes lying in the background of awareness.

Christianity

As a tradition closely related to Judaism, Christianity began as a first-century CE movement, grounded on the life and death of a Jewish preacher, Jesus of Nazareth, who was crucified at the behest of the Jewish authorities about 30 CE. Jesus was deeply Jewish, and he himself did *not* found a new religion; many of his sayings had parallels to the teachings of the Pharisees. His followers claimed that he had risen from the dead. They believed that he was the Son of God who enjoyed a privileged intimacy with God and was assigned by him with a special task: to be the long-expected Jewish messiah, who would shortly after his death return in glory to bring the kingdom of God on Earth to its fulfillment. Jesus was associated with the suffering servant in Second Isaiah, who suffered humiliation for his fellow humans and had been raised by God to an exceptionally high status.

Paul of Tarsus

The horizons of Christianity were expanded by Paul of Tarsus, the first Christian writer. He believed that Jesus had given him a mission to go beyond the Jewish world to evangelize the gentiles: for Jesus had been a messiah not only for the Jews, but for *all* human persons. Paul was convinced that the death and resurrection of Christ had created a new Israel that was open to the whole of humanity. The apostle from Tarsus, then, had the universal vision of the Axial Age. God had concern for everybody.

In a letter to his converts in Philippi in Macedonia, written about twenty-five years after Jesus' death, Paul cited a hymn that speaks of other elements of the Axial vision he shared with early Christians. This letter reveals that from the very beginning, Christians experienced the mission of Jesus as a kenosis, an act of his self-surrender to God. The hymn states that Jesus, like all human beings, had been in the image of God; however, he did not cling to this high status, "but emptied himself to assume the condition of a slave....And was humbler, yet, even to accepting death, death on a cross." Christians came to see Jesus as having made a painful and humiliating descent out of love in order to save the human race. Paul taught the great Axial Age principle of humble self-surrender: to be authentic followers of Jesus, Christians must also empty their hearts of egotism, selfishness, and pride. They must be united in love with a common purpose and a common mind. In the baptismal rituals that initiated them into the new church, they made a symbolic descent with Christ into the tomb where they identified with his death and then lived a different kind of life. They left their profane selves behind and transcended to a share in the enhanced humanity of the Lord. Paul himself, in the spirit of the Axial Age, claimed that he had transcended his limited, individual self: "And it is no longer I who live, but it is Christ who lives in me."[47]

The religion that Paul experienced and taught was a religion in a new, unique Axial configuration, shaped by the virtue of humility, self-surrender, and love. You could have faith that moved mountains, but it was worthless without love, which required constant self-surrender and the transcendence of egotism: love never preened with self-importance, clinging to an inflated ideal of the self; it was empty, self-forgetful, and always respectful of others.

Salvation

In the Zoroastrian, Hindu, Jain, and Buddhist traditions, the Axial Age characteristics of transcendence and salvation, as we have seen, are explicitly thought of as radical change or self-surrender or conversion from the egotistical self to the Sacred, to ultimate transcendent reality. Both in the teaching of Jesus and in the practical consciousness of Christians, salvation is a like transformation from ego-centeredness to a radically God-centered life. It consists in surrender of the self in faith to God's limitless sovereignty and grace, which gives rise to a new spirit of trust and joy. This surrender, in turn, frees the believer from anxious self-concern and transforms him or her into an instrument of divine love to the world.

However, in traditional Christian doctrine this transformation is presented as the *result* of salvation rather than as constituting salvation itself. In Christian theology a distinction is generally drawn between *justification* and *sanctification*. The former is identified as a change of juridical status before God, and the latter as the resulting transformation of a person's moral and ritual condition. Christ's sacrificial life, death, and resurrection on humanity's behalf frees sinful men and women from guilt so that they are counted as innocent in God's sight. As a consequence of this purification, they are opened to the recreative impact of the Holy Spirit and enter into a process of sanctification. The sanctifying fruits of the Spirit are "love, joy, peace, patience, kindness, goodness, faithfulness, gentleness, self-control" (Gal 5:22).

The sanctifying transformation of human existence and the juridical change bring about a new reconciled relationship to God and a new quality of holy life arising within that relationship. This new relationship and enhanced life are facts of experience and observation. And this reality of persons transformed, or in the process of transformation, from self-centeredness to God-centeredness constitutes the substance of Christian salvation.

In the teaching of Jesus concerning salvation, as reflected in the Synoptic Gospels, the emphasis is on the sanctifying transformation of human existence. Most of Jesus' message was the summons to his hearers to open their minds and hearts now to God's kingdom or rule, and to live consciously in the presence of God as his instruments of divine purpose on Earth. But the teaching of Jesus was at the same time a challenging call to a radical conversion to turn away from ordinary, sinful, self-centered existence to become parts of the present and future kingdom of God. The summons was away from a life centered in the self and its desire for possessions, wealth, status, and power to a new life centered in God and lived out as an agent of divine love.

> Such a challenge cut through the normal web of self-concern, requiring a choice between the true quality and style of life, found in a free and perhaps costly response to God, and spiritual death within a stifling shell of self-concern. "For

whoever would save his life will lose it" and whoever loses his life for my sake and the gospel's will save it (Mark 8:35).[48]

Both in the teaching of Jesus, then, and in the practical consciousness of Christians the reality of salvation is the transition from ego-centeredness to a radically God-oriented life. While there is in traditional theology of salvation a juridical component, according to which Jesus' death constituted atonement for human sin, the reality of Christian salvation is no juridical abstraction but an actual and concrete change from sinful self-centeredness to self-giving love in response to the grace of God. "The experience of salvation is the experience of being an object of God's gratuitous forgiveness and love, freeing the believer to love his and her neighbor."[49]

Islam

Muhammad is part of the charismatic company of prophets who brought about momentous changes in the lives of countless persons. His strong influence on people was due in part to a complex of personal traits and qualities, especially vitality, intelligence, articulateness, and dedication. Neither his genius nor his prophetic power is open to a facile explanation.

The date of his birth was perhaps 571 CE. According to tradition, his father, a Quraysh of the Hashimite clad, died before his birth, and his mother died when he was six years old. He became the ward of his paternal grandfather, and then of his uncle. The Qur'an states that Muhammad grew up in poverty. Like all the great Axial sages, Muhammad lived in a violent society. Arabia was torn by a vicious cycle of tribal warfare. It was also a time of economic progress. The city of Mecca established a flourishing market economy, and its merchants took their caravans into the more developed areas of Persia, Syria, and Byzantium. Muhammad himself was a merchant and delivered his message to the Meccans in an atmosphere of rugged finance and neglect of old tribal values that required the community care for the poorer, weaker members of the clan. There was a widespread malaise, and the old pagan faith that had influenced the Arabs in their nomadic days in the desert no longer met their changed circumstances.

Muhammad's Critical Thinking

Muhammad in his youth shared the religious beliefs of his community: the worship of Hubal and al-'Uzza, their belief in Satan, good and evil omens. But as he entered into maturity his view began to change. He looked more and more on the Meccan polytheistic religious practices with questioning and distaste. He was critical of the constant quarrelling about religion and honor among the Quraysh chiefs. He was even more dissatisfied with the primitive survivals in Arabian religions, the idolatrous polytheism and animism, the immorality of religious convocations and fairs, the drinking, gambling, and dancing that were fashionable, and the burial alive of unwanted infant daughters practiced not only in Mecca but throughout Arabia.

Why were his views changing? And more precisely, how did he become receptive to ideas of one God, the last judgment, and the religious life that were parallel to those of the Jewish and Christian religions? No evidence exists that he had direct knowledge of the Hebrew scriptures and the New Testament, even though he always highly regarded written scriptures and the people who venerated and used them: "the peoples of the book." Perhaps he learned about Judaism and Christianity due to the influence of Christians and Jews in caravans passing through Mecca, or foreign merchants trading in Mecca, and Jews and Christians at the commercial fairs, where representatives of these faiths had the practice of addressing the crowds. What he learned he acquired progressively and from a variety of sources.

When indicating the influences that possibly helped Muhammad, the future prophet, form his opinions, Muslims stress the interior force that led him ultimately to transcend what he learned from persons in his environment. Muslims contend that he was not molded and put in motion by his surroundings, but reacted to and upon them. They also reject any implication that Muhammad took the information he learned from other persons and incorporated it later in the Qur'an. The Qur'an was not the work of Muhammad, Muslims insist; rather, it was revealed to him in its entirety by God or by an angelic messenger sent down from God. The most they acknowledge is that in the days before the revelations, he received from others certain "foreknowledge," that is, truths and moral prescriptions that were made known through prophets such as Abraham, Moses, and Jesus. By this means he was enabled to understand and interpret what was eventually revealed to him.

Spiritual Anxiety and Prophetic Call

Muhammad's need to resolve his religious difficulties eventually became urgent. He seemed to have entered a period of spiritual anxiety. Apparently he had been strongly impressed by the belief common to both Jews and Christians that there would be a last judgment and punishment by everlasting fire of those who were not true believers. The one true God could not, they attested, be represented by any image, but only by prophetic messengers. Such messengers or spokespersons had in the past appeared in Palestine and Persia. Muhammad asked himself, Would no one come to Arabia and give a warning? Certainly God would send a prophet there. The thought that the last day and last judgment might be at hand began to upset him. He went off into the hills around Mecca to reflect privately. He was then about forty years old.

According to Muslim tradition, Muhammad entered a cave near the base of Mount Hira, a few miles north of Mecca, and remained there for days at a time. Suddenly on one night—"the Night of Power and Excellence"—he perceived a vision before him of the angel Gabriel, Allah's messenger, exclaiming, "Read: In the name of the Lord who createth, createth man from a clot. Read: And thy Lord is the Most Bounteous, who teacheth by the pen, teacheth man that which he knew not."[50] When the vision came to an end, Muhammad was able to reproduce the whole revelation. According to the early tradition, he quickly returned home to his wife, Khadija, half-doubting, and half-believing. He said to Khadija,

"I am worried about myself." Then I told her the whole story. She said, "Rejoice, for by Allah, Allah will never put thee to shame, By Allah, thou art mindful of they kinsfolk, speakest truthfully, renderest what is given thee in trust, bearest burdens, art ever hospitable to the guest, and dost always uphold the right against any wrong." Then she took me to Waraqa, (to whom) she said, "Give ear to (him)." So he questioned me, and I told him (the whole) story. He said, "This is the namus [the Greek word *nomos*, Law] which was sent down upon Moses."[51]

But Muhammad was not immediately comforted. He seems to have doubted whether the voice he heard had really come from an angelic messenger or from a mere spirit. If the latter were the case, he would perhaps be possessed or even insane.

After a period of self-questioning, lasting perhaps many months, Muhammad came to look upon himself as being miraculously a true prophet and apostle of Allah, a messenger of the one and only God already known to the Jews and Christians and worshiped by the people of Arabia as the chief of the more powerful of the many gods. As it began to appear that the experiences of encounter with God would continue to occur spontaneously, without his willing them, he came to believe that Allah was using him as a mouthpiece; the verses he uttered were real revelations. His first doubts about them disappeared. At last Arabia was being given a scripture, of later date and greater authority than the scriptures of the Jews and Christians. He became certain that through him, Allah would establish a religion with greater authority than Judaism and Christianity; this would be a universal religion meant to surpass and replace other religions.

The Meccan Ministry: The Message

We now focus on the shape and content of Muhammad's first preaching in Mecca. Muhammad's mission was to convert the Meccans from their cultic polytheism to the worship of Allah, the One God, and to reform their corrupt morality.

It was not necessary for Muhammad to introduce the Meccans to Allah, for they already worshiped him, and in moments of great need, they even acknowledged that he was in fact *the* God. And they were mindful of the fact that Allah was identical with the God of the Jews and Christians. It was well known that Christian Arabs, alongside the pagan Meccans, frequently made the *hajj* pilgrimage to the Kaaba, commonly regarded as Allah's shrine in Mecca. One of the very first things Muhammad required his converts to do was to pray facing Jerusalem, the city of the Jews and Christians whose God they were now going to worship.

However, the Meccans worshiped other gods as well, and that is one of the central aims of the Meccan preaching: to convince the people to surrender their attachment to the other deities and their idols. Muhammad therefore preached that there was indeed only One True God, Allah; that God was working in history for humankind from creation to the last days; that thanksgiving and obedience were due to God; that there would be a final judgment and an afterlife, for the good in a true paradise of peace and pleasurable repose, for the evil in a fiery hell.

It should be noted that from the beginning, the religion Muhammad preached was much more than an acceptance of monotheism. The Qur'an required the Meccans to change their immoral ways. The emphasis of the earliest chapters of the Qur'an was overwhelmingly on social-economic justice: it is good to feed the poor and take care of the needy; it is evil to accumulate wealth solely for one's own behalf. Muhammad condemned the powerful rich for the oppression of the enfeebled poor and insisted that charitable service for one's fellow human beings was the identifying characteristic of all faithful Muslims.

Regarding his prophetic ministry and preaching, Muhammad understood himself as the successor of the other prophets, notably Moses and Jesus. However, in the message he gave the Meccans he was not simply adding to Judaism or Christianity; rather his mission was for something far more radical. Muhammad was convinced that his message was not a completely new revelation but rather the restatement of the revelation first made to the father of humanity, Adam, and then to a series of other Prophets. Muhammad's religion was a renewal of the pristine, and pre-Jewish, religion of Abraham. Abraham came before both the Torah and the gospel. In fact, according to Muhammad, Abraham was the first Muslim, the first person to submit to God in absolute monotheism. Abraham and his son Ishmael had build the Kaaba in Mecca and instituted the rite of the pilgrimage in Mecca and its environs.

Meccan Opposition and Migration to Medina

During a period of more than a decade (610–622 CE), Muhammad experienced disheartening, and even threatening, community opposition to his ministry in Mecca. His following was destined, it seemed, to be small. So Muhammad began to call for help and search for another, safer region for his preaching. His call for help fell on responsive ears. Pilgrims from Medina (originally Yathrib) heard Muhammad preaching at one of the market fairs connected with the annual pilgrimages in and around Mecca. His word compelled them, and they interested him. They agreed to prepare their city for Muhammad's coming. Twelve of the group from Medina concluded a type of agreement in principle to cease their polytheism, not to steal or commit fornication, not to kill their female offspring, not to plunder their neighbors, and not to disobey Muhammad. Eventually Muhammad began to send his followers quietly and secretly in small groups to Medina. Muhammad himself followed in September 622. His migration or *hegira* to Medina was looked upon by Muslims as a turning point in the fortunes of Muhammad and his movement. They regard this migration as the birth of Islam, the "year one" of their calendar.

Within a short time, Muhammad succeeded in subduing the longstanding feuds among the Arabs of Medina and in establishing a brotherly unity between his Meccan fellow immigrants and the native Medinese Arabs. He built a house that was both his home and a place of worship, the first mosque. And he created a new cult. The following practices were soon established: weekly services on Fridays, prostration during prayer (at first in the direction of Jerusalem, but after the Jews in Medina conspired against him, toward Mecca), a call to prayer from the mosque's roof (at first only for the Friday services, and then every day at the time for private prayer), the taking up of alms for the poor and the support of the cause.

In January 630 CE, Muhammad marched into Mecca and with ten thousand men subdued the city. The Prophet of Allah reached the stature of the greatest chief of Arabia. And with magnanimity toward his former fellow townspeople, he excluded only a handful of them from the general amnesty he proclaimed. He then made sure of his political and prophetic ascendancy in Arabia. His opponents were conquered by the sword, and faraway tribes were invited to send delegations offering their allegiance. Before his sudden death in 632, he was confident that he was well on the way to unifying the Arab tribes under a theocracy governed by the will of God. Because he was no longer so mindful of an imminent divine judgment on the world, he was absorbed with the task of the moral elevation and unification of the Arab tribes.

On his last visit to Mecca, just before his death, tradition sees him preaching a memorable sermon in which he proclaimed a central truth of the Muslim movement in these words: "O ye men! Harken unto my words and take ye to heart! Know ye that every Muslim is a brother unto every other Muslim, and that ye are now one brotherhood."

Existential Surrender

Eventually Muhammad's religion would be called *Islam* ("surrender leading to peace with God"). Muslims are men and women who have made an existential surrender of their lives to God. This takes us immediately to an essential principle or characteristic of the Axial Age. When Muhammad asked that his converts prostrate themselves in prayer several times a day, this was hard for the Arabs, who did not approve of monarchy and found it degrading to grovel on the ground like slaves. But the posture of their bodies was designed to teach them at a deep level what Islam required: transcendence of the ego that postures and constantly draws attention to itself.

In Islam there is no concept of "salvation," nor is there any thinking about the human condition in terms of "fall" or guilt for an alienation from God that can be healed by a divine act of atonement. The Qur'an does make a distinction between the spiritual condition of self-surrender to God and the contrary condition of those who have not yielded themselves to the Creator and who therefore are in the last resort enemies of God. The Qur'anic summons is a call to turn to God, to give oneself in complete self-surrender to Allah, who is merciful and gracious. It is the Muslim form of the Axial Age ideal of the transformation of human existence to transcendent centeredness. The spiritual condition of Islam, then, is the Muslim parallel to Judaic and Christ salvation and to Hindu and Buddhist liberation.

Compassion for the Poor and Alms

Another ideal of the Axial Age deeply rooted in Islam is practical compassion and alms for the poor. Muslims were also required to give a regular proportion of their income to the poor. This *zakat* ("purification") would purge their hearts of habitual selfishness. Muslims are to cloak themselves in the virtues of compassion and generosity. The basic message of the Qur'an is a command to practical compassion. It is wrong to build a private fortune selfishly, at the expense of others, and good to share your wealth fairly and create a just and decent society where poor and vulnerable people are treated with respect.

In regard to the state of Islam, the Muslim sees no distinction between the religious and the secular. The whole of life is to be lived in the sphere of God's absolute claim, his boundless compassion and mercy, and in obedience to God's commands as revealed in the Qur'an and expounded in the Sharia (Islamic law). In the traditional Islamic conception, the secular spheres of politics, government, law, commerce, science, and the arts all come within the scope of religious obedience. The entire culture and organization of society is, in principle, included in the Islamic way of life, a theocracy.

Sufism

The total surrender of the self to God that is basic to orthodox Islam is further highlighted in Sufism, the Islamic form of mysticism. The central Sufi concepts are *dhir*, God-consciousness, and *fana*, total recentering in God leading to *baqa*, a human life merged into the divine life. The latter is a radical transformation from self-centeredness or self-rule to God-centeredness or divine rule.

Thus while the Hindu saint attains to unity with the eternal Brahman or to a complete self-giving to the divine personal reality of the Transcendent by a path of detachment from the false self and its concerns; and while the Buddhist saint attains to the egoless state of *nirvana* or to oneness with the eternal Buddha nature by overcoming all thought of "I" and "mine"; and while the Christian saint is able to say, "It is not I, but Christ who lives in me"; the Sufi saint likewise gives himself or herself to God so completely that "al-Hallaj could even utter *ana 'l-haqq*, 'I am the Real.'" This was the all too easily misunderstood affirmation that he had given himself to God in perfect Islam so that God had taken over his life. He was saying in effect, "It is not I, but Allah now lives in me."[52]

Islam, then, is human surrender to God expressed outwardly in conformity with the Qur'an, Hadith (a record of Muhammad's sayings and customs), and Sharia and inwardly in an individual self-giving that reaches its ultimate point in *fana* and *baqa*, where the life of God is lived through a human life. Islam therefore is a form of the transformation of human existence from self-centeredness to God-centeredness.

The Spread of Islam

Muhammad's death checked the rapid expansion of Islamic movement only momentarily. The prophet did not neglect to teach his followers their missionary duty.

> Neither the devout Muslim view that it was a purely religious movement engaged in a farsighted effort to save the world from error and corruption, nor the medieval Christian view that it was the outgrowth first of pure imposture and then of rapacity, will bear scrutiny. Both religion and rapacity maybe granted to have played their part as motivating impulses, but it is far closer to the mark to say that Muhammad unified the Bedouins for the first time in their history and thus made it possible for them, as a potentially powerful military group, to yoke together their economic need and their religious faith in an overwhelming drive out of the desert into the land where destiny beckoned and God's will could be fulfilled. Furthermore, the weakness of the Byzantine and Persian empires, exhausted by years of strife with each other, made a permanent conquest of the Middle East possible.[53]

Muhammad's followers made great, successful efforts to spread Islam. In the seventh and eighth centuries CE, Islam achieved a consolidated grip on the Middle East and then spread to western and central Asia, northern Africa, Spain, Portugal, Morocco, Libya, Egypt, Yemen, Saudi Arabia, Oman, Kuwait, Israel, Jordan, Syria, Lebanon, Iraq, Iran, Afghanistan, Bangladesh. In the fourteenth century it expanded into India, Indonesia, China, the Balkans. In the nineteenth century it advanced into Africa. The heart of Islam is the Middle East. It is estimated that as of 2007 there are 1.3 billion Muslims worldwide.[54]

Conclusion: Soteriological Structure

In this and the preceding chapters we have seen how the great post-Axial world faiths came historically to be characterized, in various ways, by the multidimensional "salvation" structure that (1) recognizes human moral weakness and failure or the pervasive insecurity and liability-to-suffering of all life; (2) affirms an ultimate unity of human persons with the Sacred in which or in relation to which a limitlessly better quality of existence arising from union with another sacred reality transcendent to our present selves; (3) teaches the way to realize that radically better possibility, whether by "own-power" spiritual discipline or the "other-power" of divine grace. The salvations offered by the world's post-Axial religions are variations within different conceptual schemes on a single fundamental theme: the sudden or gradual change of the individual from an absorbing self-concern to a new centering in the supposed unity-of-reality-and-value that is thought of as God, Brahman, the Dharma, Sunyata, or the Dao. Thus the general concept of salvation/liberation, which takes a different specific form in each of the great traditions, is that of the transformation of human existence from self-centeredness to Reality [Sacred]-centeredness.[55] This holds for the religions that either have their origins in the Axial Period, such as Judaism, Zoroastrianism, Hinduism, Buddhism, Jainism, Confucianism, and Daoism, and for those that are directly dependent upon them, such as Christianity, Islam, and Sikhism.

And the post-Axial religions provide paths toward the achievement of salvation. Their spiritual practices teach human beings how to cope with the misery of life, transcend their weakness, and live in peace in the midst of this flawed world. They may have had a very small impact on their immediate environment. But they brought about several new movements in history, and up until today they exert, either directly or indirectly, significant influence.

Since the Axial Period is a structure of universal history, it provides us, Karl Jaspers proposes, with an understanding of "something common to all mankind, beyond all differences of creed." This "something" common to all men and women is the aspiration to self-transcendence and salvation. This strong desire is embodied in the mind and hearts of those who practice the world's great religions. It is found, it would seem, in the depths of all human beings. Our knowledge of this common human yearning should be for us, Professor Jaspers suggests, a "challenge to boundless communication" with our fellow human beings no matter what be their difference of religious creed.[56]

Notes

1. I Kings 18:20–46.

2. Exodus 33:17–23; 34:6–8.

3. I Kings 19:11–13.

4. Karen Armstrong, *The Great Transformation: The Beginning of Our Religious Traditions* (New York/Toronto: Knopf, 2006), 66.

5. F. Charles Fenshm, "Widow, Orphan and the Poor in Ancient Near Eastern Legal and Wisdom Literature," in Frederick E. Greenspahn, ed., *Essential Papers on Israel and the Ancient Near East* (New York and London: New York University Press, 1991), 176–82.

6. Ibid., 89.

7. Hosea 1:2; Abraham J. Heschel, *The Prophets* (New York: Jewish Publication Society of America, 1962), 52–57.

8. Hosea 3:1–5.

9. Hosea 4:2.

10. Hosea 4:4–6, 12–14, 17; 5:13–14; 10: 4–11; 14:4.

11. Heschel, *Prophets,* 57–59.

12. Hosea 6:6.

13. Hosea 11:3–4.

14. William G. Dever, *What Did the Biblical Writers Know and When Did They Know It? What Archaeology Can Tell Us about the Reality of Ancient Israel* (Grand Rapids, MI, and Cambridge, UK: Eerdmans, 2001), 280.

15. Frank Moore Cross, *From Epic to Canon: History and Literature in Ancient Israel* (Baltimore and London: Johns Hopkins University Press, 1998), 41–42.

16. Genesis 18:1–15.

17. Genesis 18:2.

18. Genesis 22:1–10.

19. Genesis 22:2.

20. Mircea Eliade, *The Myth of the Eternal Return, or Cosmos and History*, trans. Willard R. Trask (London: Routledge & Kegan Paul, 1955), 108–10.

21. Isaiah 6:1–13.

22. Isaiah 6:3–13.

23. Isaiah 9:8; 10:12; 14:12; 16:6; 23:9.

24. Isaiah 14:30–32.

25. Armstrong, *The Great Transformation,* 99.

26. 2 Kings 19:35–36.

27. Armstrong, *The Great Transformation,* 101.

28. Exodus 24:4–7.

29. 2 Kings 22:11–13.

30. Jeremiah 50:4; Amos 5:4; Zephaniah 2:3.

31. Jeremiah 31:31–34.

32. Ezekiel, 11:19–20.

33. Isaiah 44:28.

34. Isaiah 45:3.

35. Isaiah 41:24.

36. Isaiah 45:6.

37. Jeremiah 2:5–13, 27–28; 5:7; 16:20; Hosea 2:7–15.

38. Jeremiah 50:4; Amos 5:4.

39. Jeremiah 31:31–34.

40. Isaiah 4:2–4.

41. Isaiah 11:10; 37:31; Ezekiel 37:12–14; Micah 4:7; 5:6–7; Zechariah 8:11–13.

42. Isaiah 11:12–13; Jeremiah 30–31.

43. Isaiah 29:19–24.

44. Jeremiah 31:31–34.

45. Isaiah 2:3; 11:9; Jeremiah 31:34.

46. Isaiah 2:4; 9:6; 11:6–8; 29:19.

47. Galatians 2:20.

48. John Hick, *An Interpretation of Religion: Human Responses to the Transcendent* (New Haven and London: Yale University Press, 1989), 45.

49. Ibid., 47.

50. Sura 96. Trans. Mohammad Marmaduke Pickthall, *The Meaning of the Glorious Qur'an* (New York: New American Library of World Literature, 1953).

51. Arthur Jeffery, ed., *Islam: Muhammad and His Religion* (New York: Liberal Arts Press, 1958), 16; cited in David S. Noss, *A History of the World's Religions,* 11th ed. (Upper Saddle River, NJ: Prentice Hall, 2002), 539.

52. A. J. Arberry, *Sufism* (London: George Allen & Unwin, 1979), 59–60; R. A. Nicholson, *The Mystics of Islam* (London and Boston: Routledge & Kegan Paul, 149–50); cited in Hick, *Interpretation of Religion,* 50.

53. Noss, *History,* 552.

54. *Major Religions of the World Ranked by Number of Adherents.* Available at: http://www.adherents.com/Religions_By_Adherents.html.

55. Hick, *Interpretation of Religion,* 36.

56. Karl Jaspers, *The Origin and Goal of History,* trans. Michael Bullock (New Haven: Yale University Press, 1953), 19.

Chapter Nine

ESCHATOLOGICAL DIMENSION

Each of the world religions is characterized by a soteriological structure—a focus on salvation—and consequently each embodies a cosmic optimism, an affirmation of the ultimate goodness of human existence and the universe. However, the post-Axial religions do *not* affirm the graciousness of humankind's life in its present, actual state. The affirmation is about the ultimately benign character of the universe as it impacts human persons and the expectation in faith that the limitlessly good possibilities of life will finally be actualized. Therefore, there is an eschatological dimension—a belief in the ultimate destiny of humankind—to the cosmic optimism of the world religions. That is, it is assurance now, in the present, that ultimately the limitlessly better human existence will be realized. It is the present confidence of an ultimate state that is no longer a waiting period and that endows the present human condition with a trait of a movement toward a limitlessly good end.

The world religions, then, embody the conviction that human existence is a journey toward a final fulfillment that gives value and purpose to the arduous pilgrimage of existence. They are grounded in the faith that the Sacred, the eternal and encompassing reality, is benign, and the outcome of human life will be good. This is the assurance of universal fulfillment.

However pervaded by suffering the lives of hundreds of millions have been and are, and however unrealized their human potential, those lives as seen by the post-axial faiths nevertheless have their place in soteriologically structured uni-

231

verse. The gospels declare that the project of human existence is not meaningless and in vain.[1]

We go on now to examine the eschatological character of the world religions of Semitic and then of Indian origin.

Religions of Semitic Origin: Judaism, Christianity, and Islam

In these religions, the eschatological outlook is of the communal-
historical type. Here the expectation is that history will come to an end
and human persons will be judged and incorporated either into a sacred,
divine kingdom on Earth or ultimately sent to an outer darkness. This
form of eschatological outlook views history, the story of humankind,
as a process, from a beginning through a linear sequence to an end; as a
drama of successive stages, each having its own special character.
"Religiously, the world is an arena in which God is purposefully at work
and in which human volitions are significant as serving or opposing the
divine intention in each new day and year and century."[2] Consequently,
in these religions traditions of Middle Eastern Semitic origin, soteriol-
ogy and eschatology coincide. However, there is also the ever-present
and religiously all-important possibility of realized eschatology, that is,
of anticipating the final end and living now within the pattern of the
ultimate end. The eschatological reality is not only a future state that
occurs beyond death but also a limitlessly better existence that can and
should be entered upon now, in the midst of this present life, thus giving the teaching of the world religions an immediate appeal, excitement,
and challenge.

In Christianity, this is an eternal quality of life, which is to know
"the only true God and Jesus Christ whom you have sent" (John 17:3).
A trait of this eternal kind of existence is joy. In the early church, filled
with the Spirit, "the disciples were filled with joy and with the Holy
Sprit" (Acts 13:52). For they boast "in God through our Lord Jesus
Christ, through whom we have now received reconciliation" (Rom
5:11). "And in its more authentic moments Christianity has always produced a profound sense of release and joy at being forgiven and accepted

by God, and a love of neighbour empowered by the conviction of the divine love for all human beings."[3]

In Judaism, no matter what the dangers and challenges of history may be, the joy of living in obedience to the Torah and receiving God's favor may be experienced now in the present. This joy in the Lord is communicated in Psalm 119: "Happy are those whose way is blameless, who walk in the law of the Lord." Also in Psalm 16:11: "You show me the path of life. In your presence there is fullness of joy." And in the Qur'an, the revelation of Allah, the compassionate and merciful one, is received as good news for all who are open to it. Allah's disclosures provide a new life at peace with God: "Surely God's friends—no fear shall be on them neither shall they sorrow. Those who believe, and are god-fearing—For them is good tidings in the present life and in the world to come" (10:64–65).

Religions of Indian Origin: Hinduism and Buddhism

The eschatological outlook in these traditions is of a more individual and ahistorical type. Here the belief is that the self, at the climax of its long spiritual development, will finally escape from its egoism, come into awareness of its true nature, and consequently transcend the trammels of earthly existence.

This individual-ahistorical outlook is bound up with a certain understanding of history. In the religions of Indian origin, time is seen as a vast cyclical movement that endlessly repeats itself or as a beginningless and endless stream of interdependent change.

> As each point on the rim of a wheel is equidistant from the center, so each moment of revolving time is equidistant from the eternal quality of Brahman, or each moment of the world's incessant flux from the "further shore" of Nirvana; so that the transforming moment of enlightenment can occur whenever the individual is inwardly ready for it.[4]

In Hindu thought the cyclical movement of time is a beginningless and endless dynamic, a constant revolution of extremely long periods in which the universe is shaped out of chaos, goes through its enormous cycle, is consumed by fire, then proceeds again into another round of eternal recurrence. As a consequence of the lack of any final resolution, the sequence of time has no overall purpose. Buddhists generally consider the cosmos

> as a beginningless and endless flux of interdependent insub-
> stantiality (*pratitya samutpada*) within which streams of con-
> scious life, falsely positing their own autonomous existence,
> are subject to the self-centered craving in virtue of which life
> is to them suffering anxiety, unsatisfactoriness. This craving
> binds them to the wheel of samsara so that they are contin-
> ually reborn as part of the whirling cosmic process which
> does not come from anywhere and is not going anywhere.[5]

Such then is how the religions of Indian origin look upon the realm of finite existence. This is in sharp contrast to the way the religions of Semitic origin view the same realm, which for them begins in an act of divine creation, is progressively fulfilled by its history of a divine intention, and is eventually superseded by an eternal heavenly state. But from the human perspective, in the midst of the world's progressive movement and its temporal flow, both the Indian and the Semitic outlooks are eschatological in that they point to the end of the present state of human suffering and to a limitless better quality of existence which the transcendent, sacred reality makes possible. The Hindu expects to reach liberation from *samsara* into the infinite ecstasy of union with Brahman. The Buddhist aspires to attain enlightenment and thus reach *nirvana*. "These are variant concepts of an ineffable state beyond the suffering generated by egoity."[6] A contemporary Hindu philosopher speaking of the samsaric wheel of birth and death says: "The purpose of transmigration is to enable the soul to gain the transcendental experience. Life in the world is a schooling which disciplines the soul and makes it perfect. Viewed in this light, life is a blessing and not a curse."[7] And in regard to Buddhism, Wilfred Cantwell Smith writes:

It has sometimes been said that early Buddhist preaching is pessimistic. This is simply wrong: it is a gospel, good news, a joyous proclamation of a discovery of a truth without which life is bleak, is suffering, but with which there is not merely serenity but triumph. It is indeed fortunate for man that he has been born into a universe where evanescence is not the last word. Because there is Dharma, he can be saved....That we live in the kind of universe where such a truth obtains, firm, reliable and permanent, is the "good news" that the Buddha preached, and that his movement carried half across the world.[8]

For the religions of Indian origin, then, liberation into union with Brahman as well as entry into nirvana are the sacred eschaton for which the Hindu and Buddhist hope and strive for just as devotedly as those of the Semitic religions aspire for the promised eternal life of heaven, paradise, the kingdom.

And in the Indian tradition, as in Semitic spiritual lives, the eschatological reality is not only a future reality reserved for life after death, but also a boundlessly better existence that can and should be entered into now, in the present historical situation. In the Hindu tradition, to attain salvation or liberation in this life is to attain a deep inner peace and happiness, a share in the unimaginable bliss of Brahman. It is to overcome the illusion of being separate from Brahman and experience "the happiness (sukham) of a mind whose stains are washed away by concentration (samadhi), and who has entered the self, it cannot be here described by words."[9]

In the teaching of the Buddha, nirvana may be attained now as the joy that lies beyond ego-centeredness. "Thinking of there being no self, he wins to the state wherein the conceit 'I am' has been uprooted, to the cool [that is, to nirvana], even to this life."[10] In the experience of the Zen practitioner, who experiences the world without self-centeredness, Nirvana is the inner peace and joy of the awakened mind.[11]

Notes

1. John Hick, *An Interpretation of Religion: Human Responses to the Transcendent* (New Haven and London: Yale University Press, 1989), 61.

2. Ibid., 62.

3. Ibid., 65.

4. Ibid., 62.

5. Ibid., 64.

6. Ibid.

7. T. M. P. Mahadevan, *Outlines of Hinduism*, 2nd ed. (Bombay: Chetana Limited, 1960), 256; cited in Hick, *Interpretation of Religion*, 65.

8. Wilfred Cantwell Smith, *Faith and Belief* (Princeton, NJ: Princeton University Press, 1979), 28–29.

9. *Maitri Upanishad* VI: 34. trans. S. Radhakrishnan, *The Principle Upanishads* (London: George Allen & Unwin and New York: Humanities Press, 1969), 845; cited in Hick, *Interpretation of Religion*, 66.

10. *Anguttara-Nikaya* IV: 353. trans. R. M. Hare, *The Book of Gradual Sayings* (London: Luzac, 1965), 233; cited in Hick, *Interpretation of Religion*, 66–67.

11. The post-Axial religions also have the following distinguishing characteristics: individual, identifiable, and international. In the post-Axial religions, in contrast to those of pre-Axial times, there is a change of attention from the social group to the individual. Religion is more of an individual, personal affair, requiring choices and active decisions on the part of the adherents. While social responsibilities and communitarian unity are not neglected and result from sharing of the common faith, they are secondary to the fundamental movement toward individual salvation. And the fact that there is a commonly shared faith, a faith that can be embraced or rejected by a willful act of the individual, means that post-Axial religion is not exclusively a dimension of the particular group's culture and total way of life, but also is expressed and embodied as an identifiable entity with a specified name.

The fact that post-Axial religions are identifiable bodies of beliefs, attitudes, rituals, and codes of behavior, all grounded in permanent centers, means that they are separate from the ethnic contexts in which they originated. The spiritual tradition embodied in each can be passed on from person to person, crossing over ethnic and national borders, and practiced in international contexts. Persons are not obliged to embrace a post-Axial religion simply because they may be born to it. Post-Axial religions are not tied to any race. They are for *all* humanity and not exclusively for particular ethnic societies. They are the "world religions."

It should be noted that the post-Axial religions do not display the above characteristics to the same degree. For example, for some the break with pre-

Eschatological Dimension

Axial religion has never been complete. Aspects of the earlier religions have lived on as folk religion, either beneath the surface or synthesized with the later traditions. Where reference is made to these aspects, they are usually claimed by authoritative exponents of the religion in question not to belong to the essential character of the faith. At times they are strongly disowned. Some post-Axial religions, such as Confucianism, have remained less centered on the transmundane world, and some, such as Judaism, Hinduism, and Confucianism, have remained more ethnic in character.

CONCLUSION TO PART TWO

Ever since humanity passed through the Axial Period, there has come to be in the religious traditions founded during that "hinge period"—the world religions—a "new" understanding of the Sacred. The Sacred is now experienced as the absolute reality that transcends the confusions of this world. In all the forms of the world religions, the Sacred "is that which makes possible a transformation of our present existence, whether by being drawn into fellowship with the transcendent Thou, or by realizing our deeper self as one with the Real, or by unlearning our habitual ego-centeredness and by becoming a conscious and accepting part of the endlessly interacting flow of life...."[1]

New View of Human Needs and the Function of Religion

There is also a new conviction about ultimate human needs. Men and women no longer are required solely to take care of the continuation of the natural material order of the cosmos, but to ensure, finally, in another world that transcends time and space, the ultimate salvation of the true self. Since the end of the Axial Period, the ultimate concern of religions has been centered on the transmundane world and the fulfillment of primordial spiritual needs. Their adherents seek to unite the conditions of daily life with the Transcendent, and thus transform present life into something radically and limitlessly better. All of this holds for the religions that either have their origins in the Axial Period, such as Judaism, Zoroastrianism, Buddhism, Jainism, Confucianism, and

238

Daoism, and for those that are directly dependent on them, such as Christianity, Islam, and Sikhism.

The Axial Age, finally, marks a significant change in the very function of religion in human life. During this era, religion changed from the role it had in pre-Axial times and civilizations—that is, a ritual means for human beings to collaborate with the divine powers to assist in keeping the world in good working order and to obtain from the powers the goods necessary for an abundant life in the world. The gods and goddesses relied on human beings to help them provide the means to ensure reproduction, to maintain the sun on its course, to keep the seasons following in proper order; human beings relied on the deities to provide them with the necessities of life. The men and women of ancient times believed that they had to sacrifice food and other pleasantries to the divinities to encourage the gods to promote the processes of the cosmos and of their own lives. Both divine and human beings cooperated to maintain the well-being of the universe and human existence.

During the Axial Age, however, religion takes on an unprecedented new role in human life: self-transcendence and salvation, providing to human beings the means to undergo whatever transformation is necessary to achieve immortality or happiness or whatever the religions deemed to be the highest good in life. The achievements of these goals were linked to transforming the self from its ordinary state to some other. This might mean taking on a new vision of the way the world works, or accepting the will of a particular god with the power to bestow immortality or paradise, or disciplining the self to a way of life that shapes it in more wholesome and virtuous ways. "However, it is imagined, the rise of the self in the Axial Age means that religions have a new problematic on their hands. Religions responded to this problematic by helping people understand the nature and cause of their problems and by providing ways—innovative ways—to solve them."[2]

Striking Parallels among the World Religions

There is then a striking unity among the world religions. During the relatively short age known as the Axial Period, the Sacred, the Transcendent (the same divine reality Christians call the God of

Abraham, Isaac, Jacob, the Father of Jesus) appears to have become operative in human history: in the founders, the adherents, and the concrete forms of what are known as the world religions.

In response to the impact of the Absolute, those who adhere to and practice the world religions engage in activities by which they transcend themselves and the visible world. As a result, they appear to gain access to salvation, that is, experiential union with the Sacred, which union represents for them an infinitely, limitlessly better life in human history and in the world to come.

It should be noted here that the activities of the non-Christian religions are not without reflections of what is commonly accepted as objective truth, beauty, and goodness (for example, compassionate love for and dedicated service to one's neighbor). It should also be noted, once again, that the salvation experienced in the non-Christian religions appears to be union with the same sacred reality Christians call God, the Father of Jesus.

Historical Development— Scriptural Structure

As a result of our historical and phenomenological analysis of the principal world religious traditions, we have seen that, on the one hand, they are characterized by salient differences. On the other hand, we have also remarked that because they have undergone a profound integral *historical development* or transformation from pre-Axial to post-Axial religions, they consequently are embodied with striking parallels: that is, they all appear to be impacted by the Absolute, and they respond to, and experience union with, the Absolute in ways that seem not to be without similarities. These parallels constitute a common *spiritual structure*, or "type," that each world religion shares in varying degrees. These results of our historical and phenomenological study lead us to pose several questions for our further study.

Questions for Further Study

- How do we make comprehensible the almost simultaneous appearance of the extraordinarily talented Axial sages in separate areas that were geographically isolated from each other?
- How is it that during the millennium before Christ, separate regions of the world brought forth remarkable religious creations upon which the entire history of the human spirit has rested ever since?...Creations that for the first time in history appeared to enable men and women to transcend the material world and have access to a limitlessly better life in union with what appears to be the authentic Sacred, the true Transcendent?
- Do we regard the events of the Axial Period as pure random coincidence? Or do we interpret them as evidence of some underlying, intentional spiritual force, of some plan of divine providence?
- Did the Sacred, the Transcendent, only *appear* to become operative in the adherents of the post-Axial religions, or did this truly happen? Might it be true that the one true God is operative not only in Christianity, but also in the other world religions?

These questions are about the *truth* of the world religions and therefore pertain to their theological status. That is, they refer to the meaning and value they have in light of Christian revelation and faith. And with these theological questions we deal in part 3 of this book.

Notes

I. John Hick, *An Interpretation of Religion: Human Responses to the Transcendent* (New Haven and London: Yale University Press, 1989), 33.

2. Mark W. Muesse, *Religions of the Axial Age: An Approach to the World's Religions* (Chantilly, VA: Teaching Company, 2007), part I, 15.

PART THREE

THE THEOLOGICAL STATUS OF THE NON-CHRISTIAN RELIGIONS

In a reflection on the sources of Christian faith—scriptures, and for Catholics, the Magisterium—we clarify the theological status of the non-Christian world religions by identifying the elements that unite them with and differentiate them from Christianity. In this way we respond to the questions that arose in part 2 as the result of our historical and phenomenological study.

Chapter Ten

A COMMON HUMAN EXISTENCE

One of the important elements that unify the other religions and Christianity is the common "human existence" shared by all their adherents. Before the world religions are corporate convictions about diverse experiences of the Absolute, they are each an understanding, affirmation, and expression of a common "human nature." This "structure of human existence" is common to all human beings, whether they are Hindus, Buddhists, Jews, Christians, or Muslims. As we reflect on this structure, we limit our consideration to those human traits that are the immediate foundation of, and are directly pertinent to, religious existence.[1]

Relationship with Self, Others, History

The existence we focus on is that of beings created in the image of God—besouled bodies. As such, humans are related to, and mindful of, themselves; they are self-reflective, self-aware; that is, they not only know, they *know* that they know. The human person is not simply a part of a large cosmic mosaic. On the contrary, the human person is the most active, self-reflective agent under God.

As free subjects and responsible agents of their lives, human beings experience the need to create relationships with other human persons. The individual person is a social being. According to the Old and the New Testaments, human existence is to be a loving coexistence with other persons. We are commanded to love our neighbor. "You shall not take vengeance or bear a grudge against any of your people, but you shall love your neighbor as your self: I am the Lord" (Lev 19:18). And just as Jesus' existence is one in the service of others (Mark 10:45), so must every person's life be a coexistence of service.

The humanity of men and women is constituted not only by the relationships they have with themselves as subjects or agents, not only by their relationships with the wider community of human persons. Their human nature is also constituted by their relationship to history and the world in which they live. Indeed, inherent to their humanity is their status as co-creators with God of both history and the world (*Pastoral Constitution on the Church in the Modern World*, number 39; see also Pope John Paul II's 1982* encyclical, *Laborem Exercens (On Human Work)*:

> The human person is the image of God partly through the mandate received from the Creator to subdue, to dominate, the earth. In carrying out this mandate, the human person reflects the very action of the Creator of the universe [II, no. 4, para. 2]). Humans are charged with the task to be creative in the redirection of history and the shaping of the world. They are called to be agents of the forward movement of history itself, personal subjects upon whose subjectivity and freedom the fate of history and the world depends.

Anxiety, Sin, and Guilt

As free, responsible, historical subjects existing in the world, human persons experience anxiety. Anxiety is intrinsic to human existence and has several causes. It comes, for one, in the face of meaninglessness. When humans are hindered in the search for a satisfactory meaning for their lives, the power of self-integration and self-affirmation is lost, and anxiety is experienced. Anxiety also arises from the recognition of limitations and the contingencies of existence, and from imagining a life infinitely better than this one.

As a consequence of such anxiety, sin is generated. This is because humans seek to bring anxiety under control by pretending to have power or knowledge of virtues or special favors from a transcendent, sacred source, and this pretense leads in turn to pride, cruelty, and injustice. Or

---

*Unless specified otherwise all dates in part 3 of this book are CE.

else humans seek to escape their anxieties by turning inward and pursuing a life of sensuality. The human race, then, is seen as sinners whose hearts are filled with pride and thereby closed to the will of the Sacred, the Transcendent, and the cry of their neighbors (for example, Gen 8:21; Ps 143; Ps 2). Sin is found in the world and harms not only individuals but history itself (Gen 3–11).

And it follows that, in the face of sin and guilt, anxiety is more deeply experienced, whether from specific actions or as a vague, general backdrop. Without some means to deal with guilt, humans are led to moral confusion and aimlessness. Finally there is the anxiety in the face of the inevitability of death, which is the greatest threat of all to the self. Only in coming to terms with the world can humans deal with the fear of death.

Consequently, the human existence of those who practice the world religions—indeed, of all human persons—is characterized by a split. They experience themselves as limited creatures, plagued by weakness and sin. All men and women are sinners, in need of conversion, that is, in need of a fundamental change of heart: "The time is fulfilled, and the kingdom of God has come near; repent, and believe in the good news" (Mark 1:15).

Relationship with God

The relationship of the adherents of the world religions to history and to the world, as well as their fundamental dignity as human beings, is founded on, or grounded in, their primary relationship with God. Their fundamental relationship with God has several dimensions. He is their creator and recreator. And while it is true that the Creator and Master of the universe is the sacred Absolute and Transcendent to creation, with no one having power over him, he is not a being or abstract power separate from the being of the human person. God is Being Itself, and as such permeates all human persons. Our being is a participation in the very being of God himself. He is the divine principle by which all of us are alive and by which our existence is sustained.

Furthermore, God is inherent to the existence of all persons as the specifically human in them. He is always present to us at the very core of our being, in our true selves, making it possible for us to transcend ourselves in the experience of his absolute, transcendent being, and to be with him the co-creators of history and the world. He is the final perfection to which we are summoned. All human persons stand alone in creation as beings who are absolutely oriented to God and whose very definition and essence are determined by this orientation. In fact, the God of Abraham, Isaac, and Jacob, the Father of Jesus, is a constitutive dimension of all those who practice the world religions and of all persons. In their transcendent and everlasting relationship with the Absolute, they have a way to deal with anxiety, guilt, fear, and death.

God's Self-Communication in Christ

When the Christian tradition states that God permeates all reality and is inherent to human existence, it must be understood, more specifically, that the incarnate Son of God, Jesus Christ in the Holy Spirit and along with the Father, permeate all reality and are inherent to the human existence of those who practice the world religions. From the very beginning, all reality is oriented to Christ. In all created reality is found the presence of God and the self-communication of God in Jesus Christ. The entire universe is Christocentric.

The Christian theological tradition highlights the New Testament's perspective of a Christocentric universe (I Cor 8:6; 15:24–28; 44–49; Rom 8:19–23, 29, 30; Eph I:9–10, 19–23; 3:11; Col I: 15–20; 3:4 Phil– 3:21; Heb I:2–32; John I:3; 12:32). From the very beginning of creation, Christ is already present in the world. There is no creation without Christ. The entire universe is Christocentric and oriented toward the covenant between God and the people of God, and the covenant in turn toward the new covenant grounded in the incarnation of the Son of God in Christ. There is no covenant except in view of Christ. There is no human existence, therefore, except in view of Christ and of our new covenant in Christ. The entire human community and the entire world in which the human community exists are oriented toward Christ. God in Jesus Christ is, in fact, a constitutive element of our human existence.

The inherent presence of Jesus Christ in all reality and the orientation of all reality to Christ are found expressed in the writings of Saint Paul and expanded considerably in the theology of recapitulation by the early Christian writer, Irenaeus *(Adversus Haereses)*. Recapitulation, for Irenaeus, is the taking up in Christ of all that is or has been from the very beginning. God gathers up everything that has been sidetracked by the fall of Adam and Eve and renews, restores, and reorganizes it all in Jesus Christ who is the Savior and the Second Adam. Since the whole human race was lost through the sin of the First Adam, the Son of God had to become a human being in order to bring about the recreation of humankind. "Jesus Christ, the Son of God, who was enfleshed for our salvation'" and came "to recapitulate all things, and to raise up all flesh of the human race…and clothe them with everlasting glory."[2]

Natural Desire for God and the Supernatural Existential

As a consequence of the gift of self-communication of God in Christ to all reality, there is in human nature a twofold effect. There is first the "natural desire for God." Christian theology, from Augustine through Thomas Aquinas, has acknowledged the existence of humankind's desire, inherent in human nature itself, for direct union with God. Only in the vision of God can the human person satisfy fully and definitively its desire to know. No finite reality can satisfy that desire. Only in the encounter with God, with the Absolute, the Transcendent, are its deepest spiritual aspirations fulfilled. The Second Vatican Council makes reference to our desire for a higher life, a desire that is "inescapably lodged in the human heart" and that makes it possible for us to transcend our anxiety about death *(Pastoral Constitution on the Church in the Modern World* 16–18).

The second effect of the self-communication of God in Christ to human nature is what Karl Rahner and other modern theologians identify as the "supernatural existential." This is not grace itself, but God's *offer* of grace to all human persons. This offer, made to the adherents of the world religions, and to all of humankind, is a supernatural gift that gives us in our very human existence, in our actual condition, in our very nature, the radical capacity to transcend the limited and created. It permanently modifies the human spirit, transforming it within, orienting it toward the Absolute, toward God, and thus enabling it freely to accept or to reject grace. It is our basic orientation and the sustenance of our very existence antecedent to our free decision. It is the radical capacity for and openness to knowing God, receiving and accepting God's call for repentance of sins, for conversion, for a change of mind and heart, for receiving God's forgiveness and a share in God's own life, for finding the authentic meaning of life, for pursuing a life of faith, hope, and love, and overcoming existential anxiety and the fear of death.

God's self-offer in Christ—the supernatural existential—stamps the being of every single person. Therefore, everyone comes into this world, even before the actual birth of Jesus Christ, already redeemed objectively, that is, graced by the Spirit of Jesus Christ. No time or place ever existed in which people were not offered Christ's Spirit. Even those born before Jesus are predestined in Christ, a predestination that must freely be accepted or rejected.

The mainstream of Catholic tradition has always been insistent that the twofold reality of the natural desire and the supernatural existential is given to human persons, not to make up for something lacking to them as human persons but as the free gift that elevates us to a new and unmerited level of existence. This gift of Christ sustains us in our actual existence and orients us toward a supernatural end: eternal union with God. By this gift of Christ, we enter into a new relationship of communion with God, and we are transformed interiorly by the spirit of Christ.

Universality of God's Self-Communication in Christ

It must be emphasized that the presence of God and the self-communication of God in Christ, along with the twofold gift in human nature, are universally present and available. They are antecedent to our free decision or any evidence of our worthiness and our qualities, and they condition our moral lives. And since human existence is social as well as individual, these gifts have a social as well as an individual dimension. Therefore, they have an impact on communities, institutions, and social structures in every sphere of human life. The real historical order is already permeated with these gifts, so that a state of "pure" nature does not exist.

Our human existence—and the human existence we share with all other human persons, no matter what their religion, no matter if they have no religion—is qualified from the beginning by the God-given radical capacity—the "supernatural existential," the *potentia obedientialis*—to get beyond ourselves and to reach out toward that which transcends us, the Absolute, toward God who raises us to a new level of existence, a sharing in his own divine life. The question of God, in other words, is implied in the question of human existence. And the opposite holds true as well.

Consequently, *all* human persons, from the very beginning of their existence, are capable of transcending themselves in the experience and knowledge of the Sacred, of the Absolute, of God to whom they are oriented. They are open to the grace of divinization and salvation from the very first moment of their existence and antecedent to their free choice to accept and cooperate with that grace. This is so because God is already present in them as the transcendent force or condition that makes such knowledge possible. God is always present within us, even before we begin the process, however tentatively and hesitantly, of trying to come to terms with God's sacred reality and our knowledge of God. Human beings, then, are transcendent beings.

Primordial Sin

Human persons are also sinful beings. The Christian tradition maintains that all persons, from the first moment of their existence and antecedent to their free choice, are subject to original sin. This is the lack of holiness that qualifies and conditions our moral lives. It is the state or condition in which, because of the sin of Adam and Eve, all human persons are born.

It has the character of sin in an analogous way: it is against God's will; it is a lack of grace that ought not to be. But it is *unlike* sin in that it does not involve a free decision against God's will; rather, it is a given, inherited reality that is integral to the fallen condition of human beings. Related to this unholy state, and as a consequence of it, is a fundamental weakness—"concupiscence"—that makes human beings prone freely to commit personal sins.

While human beings are, indeed, subject to sin and death, God's presence in human beings is, nevertheless, not destroyed by sin. The sinner remains radically open to the offer of grace—the supernatural existential—the call to repentance, reconciliation with God and a loving relationship with him in this world, and after death, in the world to come. All human beings are called by God to salvation.

God's Universal Salvific Will

The distinctive Catholic conviction of faith that all human persons are called by God to salvation is based on the following theological reasoning.

God is characterized by a universal saving will—that is, the one true God: Jesus, Father, and the Spirit—that works in human history for the salvation of all humankind. God works so that all persons might, during their lifetime, share in Jesus' victory over evil, sin, anxiety, and death and, at the end of history, share in the final phase of the kingdom of God (1 Tim 2:1–6).

But salvation is impossible without faith. Salvation depends on having (explicit or implicit) faith in truth revealed by God and responding to that faith in (explicit or implicit) religious activity (Mark 16:16; John 12:32; 18:37; Council of Trent, *Decree on Justification* [*DS*] 1532).

Therefore, since God wills the salvation of all, he reveals himself and his truth to all; he gives to all the grace freely to accept that revelation in faith and to respond to it in religious activity (Council of Orange, 529). God then makes it possible for all human persons to be saved.

It is important to see the Catholic doctrine on God's salvific will for all human persons in the context of the theology of the Reformers. Martin Luther (d. 1546) was unable to accept the Catholic principle that God is essentially a gracious God who desires the salvation of all and who wills humans to cooperate freely with divine grace in the working out of salvation. On the contrary, for Luther, we are unable to do anything on our own. God's mercy is bestowed on whomever God wills (Rom 9:18). God "wills that [God's] power should be magnified in [our] perdition."[3] But Luther also asserts that the true God says, "I have no pleasure in the death of the wicked, but that the wicked turn from their ways and live" (see Ezek 33:11). "Let all men sing...with David and acknowledge that they are sinners but that God is righteous, that is, merciful."[4]

But in *Bondage of the Will*, Luther stresses God's foreknowledge and omnipotence so much that practically no room remains for our human free response. In Christ, humankind has access to the Father's will and heart. "If God is for us, who can be against us?" (Rom 8:31).[5]

The other great Reformer, John Calvin (d. 1564), carries the doctrine of predestination even further. Understanding Romans 9:13 literally, he concludes that God loves some and hates others: "It is just as Scripture says, 'I have loved Jacob, but I have hated Esau.'" In his *Institutes of the Christian Religion*, however, Calvin acknowledges that "God has destined all things for our good and salvation....Nothing that is needful for our welfare will ever be lacking to us" (ch. 14).

But nevertheless, "By God's bidding...salvation is freely offered to some while others are barred from access to it....He does not indiscriminately adopt all into the hope of salvation but gives to some what he denies to others" (bk. III, ch. 21). To no one is salvation owed; God, therefore, does no one an injustice by denying it to anyone. Furthermore, if God cannot punish, how is it possible that his mercy be manifested (ch. 23)?[6]

The Reformer's position in regards to God's salvific will underscores one of the historic differences between Protestant and Catholic theology. The former tradition has tended to place emphasis on the radical unworthiness of the person, even after the redemptive activity of God on our behalf. On the other hand, the Catholic tradition insists that God not only makes a declaration of humankind's worthiness for salvation, but actually transforms men and women, making them new creatures in the Holy Spirit. God offers this interior transformation to each and every person without exception. He excludes no one beforehand. Only a free act of the human will that rejects the divine offer of grace is able to impede God's saving intentions.

The Council of Trent's *Decree on Justification* asserts that "all people" have been called to the status of adopted sons and daughters of God in Christ (ch. 5), but nevertheless they can freely reject the grace of adoption (ch. 5). Insofar as persons open themselves to the divine presence, it is because their hearts have been touched through the illumination of the Holy Spirit.[7]

The transition from the condition of sin as a child of the first Adam to a condition of adopted sonship and daughtership in Christ is called "justification." Justification "is not only a remission of sins but also the sanctification and renewal of the inward person through the voluntary reception of the grace and the gifts whereby an unjust person becomes just" (ch. 7). God's will is that all be saved, and God will achieve that salvation "unless human beings themselves fail in [God's] grace" (ch. 13). In fact, the council's sixth canon explicitly condemns those who say "that it is not in human power to make our ways evil, but that God produces the evil works just as [God] produces the good ones, not only by allowing them but properly and directly, so that Judas' betrayal is no less God's work than Paul's vocation."

Summary

Christians as well as the adherents of the other religions share a common structure of human existence that is Christocentric, and they inhabit a Christocentric universe. Furthermore, they are all endowed with a divine gift that modifies them from within and that also impacts on their concrete social and religious institutions. This gift—the supernatural existential—is God's offer of grace, flowing from his universal salvific will. It orients the adherents of the world religions, antecedent to their free decision, to the Absolute, the Transcendent, to the God of Abraham, Isaac, Jacob, to the Father of Jesus. This gift is the offer of salvation, that is, union with God in this world and everlastingly with him in the world to come.

Notes

1. The treatment of human existence is based on Richard McBrien, *Catholicism: Completely Revised and Updated* (San Francisco: HarperCollins, 1994), 157–99.

2. Saint Irenaeus of Lyons, *Against the Heresies,* trans. Dominic J. Unger (New York/Mahwah, NJ: Paulist Press), vol. I, bk. I, ch. 10, I.

3. Martin Luther, *Lectures on Romans,* Library of Christian Classics, vol. 15, trans. Wilhelm Pauck (London: S.C.M. Press, 1961).

4. Martin Luther, "Lectures on Psalms: On Psalm 51.I," trans. Jaroslav Pelikan, *Luther's Works,* vol. 12 (St. Louis: Concordia Publishing House, 1955).

5. See his commentary on the First Commandment in *The Large Catechism of Martin Luther,* trans. Robert H. Fisher (Philadelphia: Fortress Press, 1959), 9–15.

6. References to the works of Calvin are taken from McBrien, *Catholicism,* 305.

7. Council of Trent, *Decree on Justification* [DS], 1525.

Chapter Eleven

TRUE RELIGION

In our historical and phenomenological study and in our theological investigation up to this point we have found:

- That the Sacred, the Transcendent, appears to be present and active in the founders, the adherents, and the concrete structures of the world religions during the relatively short period of the Axial Age
- That the essence of the common human existence of those who practice the world religions is Christocentric, just as the world they inhabit is Christocentric
- That the natural desire for God and the supernatural existential are present and operative in their depths as well as in the concrete forms of their religious institutions; that they are embraced by God's universal salvific will

In light of these findings, it is reasonable to make the following judgment motivated by faith: God was in reality operative in the founders, early adherents, and institutions of the world religions and continues to be effective in them. Therefore, like Christianity, the other world religions are true religions: that is, God's truth and grace are operative in them; they are authentic means of striving for self-transcendence and gaining access to salvation. This appeared to be the case in our historical and phenomenological reflection, but there we bracketed whether or not it was grounded in truth. Here we no longer bracket the issue of truth; rather, we conclude, as a result of our reflection on the sources of faith, that what appeared to be true is so in reality.

We will elaborate on the truth of the non-Christian world religions, but since this matter is at the heart of the current controversy in

Catholic circles about religious pluralism, we first place our thinking in historical perspective. We take a look backward now at different kinds of Catholic thinking that have been used through the ages to try to appraise the meaning and value of the other religions. A short review of the history of Catholic attitudes toward the non-Christian religions will enable us better to understand the positive appraisal we have made of the truth and value of the other religions and how that appraisal is in accord with the modern official teaching of the church.[1]

A Historical Review of Catholic Thought

In regard to other religions, the writers of the New Testament and the communities for whom they wrote were concerned mostly with their relationship with Judaism. In the second century, however, the communities of Jesus' followers moved deeper both physically and culturally into the Greco-Roman world, and there, in that gentile environment, Christians were a minority, a frequently endangered minority. Consequently they were obliged to explain to themselves and their neighbors how they as disciples of Jesus related to their broader culture with its diversity of religions and philosophies.

During the first three centuries CE, the early Christian theologians, the great church fathers, tried to make sense of the broader "pagan" cultures by means of a central theme taken from the New Testament, namely, the Word of God. They coined a new expression, the *logos spermatikos*; literally *logos* means "word," and *spermatikos* means "seedlike." While Christians all experienced that the Word of God was "made flesh" in Jesus of Nazareth, the fathers claimed that to those in the Greco-Roman world before and after Jesus, the same Word of God was scattered like seed. The Word was concentrated in Jesus, but it was strewn to the winds of history. All humankind partakes of the universally sown Word. A great father of the church, Justin Martyr, wrote that anyone who hears God's call in this Seed-Word and tries to live according to its lead is really already a Christian, even if he or she never heard of Jesus. And Tertullian declared that because of God's universal presence and call, the spirit of each man and woman is "naturally Christian." There was then a strong affirmation of God's loving, saving presence beyond the church. However, all the early Christian writers did insist that the Seed-Word in other cultures and religions needs to be made clear and fulfilled in the fully embodied Word in Jesus.

But soon a drastic change occurred: historical developments brought about a shift from a stress on God's universal love and presence to an emphasis on the specific importance of the church. After Emperor Constantine, and under Emperor Theodosius (379–395), the frequently persecuted minority community of Christians suddenly became the official state religion. The high priest, the bishop of Rome, became the *Pontifex Maximus* who wielded both spiritual and political power. The church's welfare was now joined to that of the state. This meant that the enemies of the state, who were non-Romans and non-Christians, became the church's enemies. Consequently, there was a change in attitude toward those "outside" the church.

This change was greatly influenced by Augustine of Hippo. He realized and insisted in his preaching and writing that persons are saved only by grace. Without grace in this life and the next, humankind is lost. In Augustine's perception, the "barbarian" tribes, who were threatening the Roman Empire and the church, represented examples of lost humanity. He progressively came to the conviction that necessary saving grace is found *not* outside the church but only *within* it. He developed his teaching of "double predestination," according to which God from all eternity predestines some to salvation within the church, and the rest—"the damned masses"—to perdition. This meant that those in the "heathen" religions and all Jews and all heretics and schematics who die outside the church would go into the everlasting fire prepared for Satan and his angels.

This negative position taken in regard to those outside the church lasted until around the sixteenth century. During this long period, this famous dictum, first declared by theologians like Origen (d. 254) and especially Cyprian (d. 258), was in force: "Outside the church, there is no salvation." At first it was directed to persons already in the church as a warning that if they had any thought of leaving, it was at their eternal risk. But after the fifth century, and through the Middle Ages, this proclamation was directed at non-Christians to communicate to them that those who are not in the church are out of a heavenly destiny.

The condemnatory "Outside the church, there is no salvation" was proclaimed through the centuries, not only from the pulpits or in lecture halls, but also in the solemn and official declarations of the popes and councils of bishops. To this dictum the Fourth Lateran Council

(1215) added an adverbial phrase, so that it read "outside the church, no salvation at all *(omnino)*." In his bull, *Unam Sanctam* (1302), Pope Boniface VIII clarified further that to belong to the one church and enjoy salvation one had to accept papal authority. Then the Council of Florence (1442) repeated the condemnation and added, "No persons, whatever almsgiving they have practiced, even if they have shed blood for Christ, can be saved, unless they have remained in the bosom and unity of the Catholic Church."

These uncompromising views, it should be noted, were historically and psychologically conditioned. Historically, Christians thought that the gospel had been preached to all the ends of the Earth. Psychologically, they could not conceive that in hearing it, anyone could not be convinced of its overwhelming truth and beauty; to refuse the truth of the church would come only from ill and sinful intentions. But after Columbus discovered the new world, the masses of new peoples in the Americas shook the foundations of those conditioned convictions. These peoples and tribes had never heard of the good news of Jesus. And when they did hear the gospel and experienced the impact of the colonizing Christians, they preferred their own traditional religious views and practices. So it was that the Council of Trent (1545–1563), with the help of theologians like Robert Bellarmine and Francisco Suarez, arrived at a formula, "baptism of desire," according to which pagans who could not be baptized with water could be baptized "through desire." This meant that on the condition of following their conscience and living morally, they were implicitly manifesting a desire to enter the church and could thus be prepared for a heavenly reward.

While this was a new attitude for the time, it was also a return to the view of the "seeds of the Word" sown through history. It meant a shift from "Outside the church, there is no salvation" to "Without the church, no salvation." By following God's voice in their conscience, men and women outside the church were somehow also inside or related to the church. This positive view of persons of other religions was repeated and developed by popes from the seventeenth century right up to the middle of the twentieth century. And especially during the first half of the twentieth century, theologians formulated concepts by which they could include within the church any devoted "pagan" outside the church. Buddhists or Hindus or Muslims who lived according to their conscience and had a love for their neighbors belonged to the "soul" of the church, or, they were "attached," "linked," "related to" the church; or they were "imperfect," "tendential," "potential" members of the church.

These were genuine efforts to affirm God's universal love, while at the same time maintaining the necessary role of the church. However, all these efforts made from the sixteenth to the twentieth century never included a more positive attitude toward the religions of those outside the church. Throughout all this time, theologians and church leaders and presumably ordinary Catholics did not dare to imagine that God could make use of other religions to offer grace, revelation, and salvation. The church fathers, too, while recognizing that the "Seed-Word" was sown through history, never said that the religions could be suitable ground for this Word. If the Word or Spirit of God was growing and affecting peoples' lives outside the boundaries of the church, it was happening to individuals by means of some kind of personal or mystical experience. Since there was only one authentic Savior, there could only be one true religion. God could make use only of Christianity. This was presumed until the 1960s. And then Pope John XXIII convened the council that stands as a milestone in the history of what the church has expressed in regards to other religions and its relation to them.

Second Vatican Council

The Second Vatican Council (1962–1965) set out on the path toward a new Christian theology of religions. Never before had any church in its official documents spoken so extensively and positively about the other religions; never before had Christians been called upon to take these religions seriously and dialogue with them. In comparison with the "Outside the church, there is no salvation" view that held sway from the fifth to the sixteenth century, Vatican II is a true milestone.

Where previous official statements of the Catholic Church were tentative about the possibility of salvation in Christ by the grace of the Holy Spirit for those outside the Christian community, Vatican II is clear and unambiguous. For example, the *Dogmatic Constitution on the Church, Lumen Gentium* [LG], states:

> Those also can attain to salvation who through no fault of their own do not know the Gospel of Christ or His Church,

yet sincerely seek God and moved by graced strive by their deeds to do His will as it is known to them through the dictates of conscience. Nor does Divine Providence deny the helps necessary for salvation to those who, without blame on their part, have not yet arrived at an explicit knowledge of God and with His grace strive to live a good life. (16)

What the council states about religious people outside the church is based on the council's reendorsement of what had been taught since the Council of Trent: that God's love and saving presence cannot be confined within the boundaries of the church. For the first time in the history of the church, the council's *Declaration on Religions* sets forth descriptions of how each of the major historical religions seeks to respond to "those profound mysteries of the human condition." It explicitly recognizes and praises the "profound religious sense" that enlivens all these traditions. It affirms that their teachings and practices represent what is "true and holy" and "reflect a ray of that Truth which enlightens all men." And the declaration then gives an exhortation to all Catholics that they had never before received from their pastors: "that through dialogue and collaboration with the followers of other religions, carried out with prudence and love and in witness to the Christian faith and life, they recognize, preserve and promote the good things, spiritual and moral, as well a the social-cultural values found among these men" (*Nostra Aetate* [NA] 2).

In the *Decree on the Church's Missionary Activity* (*Ad Gentes* [AG]), other positive and new things are said about other religions. It uses a phrase directly taken from Karl Rahner's 1962 essay,[2] when it recognizes in the religions "elements of truth and grace" (*AG* 9). It also applies the expression of the church fathers by affirming that in the other religions one can detect "seeds of the Word," the same Word embodied in Jesus (*AG* 11, 15). These seeds of the Word promote the growth of authentic "seeds of contemplation" (*AG* 18), a "sort of secret presence of God" (*AG* 9). In the religions, in fact, there are "precious things, both religious and human" (*Pastoral Constitution on the Church in the Modern Word, Gaudium et Spes* [GS] 92). How different these statements are from those of Pope Boniface VIII or the Council of Florence.

The Council and Karl Rahner

What Vatican II has to say about the other religions resonates with and seems to be influenced by the view of German theologian Karl Rahner. Let us look at what he has to say. During the second half of the twentieth century, in the writings of Karl Rahner, the Catholic theological community took a radical turn in its way of understanding and relating to persons of other faiths. Rahner, a Jesuit, is arguably the most famous and influential Catholic theologian of the twentieth century. He became convinced that God's world was much more extensive than the Christian world. In much of his writings he aimed at enlarging the scope of the Christian vision so that it could detect the active presence of God deep within every human being and throughout the expanse of history. Around the beginning of the 1960s he turned his attention to the non-Christian religions and saw in them what few Christians had ever seen. In a lecture first given in 1961, and later published in an article, he was the first to explore the path toward a new and revolutionary Christian theology of religions.[3]

In Rahner's view, the other religious paths themselves are recognized as mediations or ways of Christ's salvation; God's grace is active in the other religions. The reason he gave for such a view was a key ingredient of Catholic experience and theology. Catholic theological thinking has always taken seriously the claim made by contemporary anthropologists and psychologists, namely, that human persons are embodied and social beings. Everything humans know and believe and commit themselves to comes to them, not through some kind of spiritual injection, but through their bodies and through other people. This is true also for religious human beings. It has to be the way God deals with men and women...through their bodies and other people. Rahner concluded, therefore, that God's presence has to take some kind of physical, bodily form.[4]

Among the many bodies that God's presence can assume in human history, it can be expected, Rahner claims, that one of the foremost and most effective will be the religions of the world. It is surely in the religions that humans engage in the search for profound meaning. If it is believed that God acts throughout human history, and that his action must take physical, material form, then the religions of the world are the first areas that should be investigated for clues of the divine Spirit and truth. Catholics traditionally and characteristically insist on the necessity of the church precisely because they believe that God meets them in physical, social forms they call "sacraments." The church itself is held to be the "primary sacrament." So, then, a general truth for Catholics is, Rahner asserts, a general truth for others. Like Christians, Buddhists and Hindus need sacraments in the sense of embodiments of God's grace, and they find them especially in their religions. The other religions, therefore, can be "ways of salvation." People are being drawn by God to himself in and through the beliefs and practices of Hinduism, Buddhism, Islam, and the indigenous religions. The non-Christian religions can be "a positive means of gaining the right relationship to God and thus for the attaining of salvation, a means which is therefore positively included in God's plan of salvation."[5] Not *despite* their religions, but *because* of their religions. And when his tightly developed theological argument is closely followed, Rahner really was establishing not just the *possibility* but the *probability* that God is speaking in languages other than "Christian."

Quite clearly, what Vatican II has to say about other religions resonates with Rahner's new theology of religions. But one of the exceptions in this regard concerns a key ingredient of Rahner's new vision of the religions. The council did *not* follow Rahner in expressly concluding that the other religions may be viewed as possible or probable "ways of salvation" instruments by which God draws people to himself. In this much-cited selection from *Lumen Gentium,* the focus is on those who "strive to lead an upright life," not on those, for example, who are Hindus or Muslims. But what about the beliefs and religious practices of those outside the Christian community? Are the "individual persons of good will" saved *by* the instrumentality of their religious observances or *despite* them? Does the saving grace that is "active invisibly" in the hearts of individuals ever become visible and concrete in the religious practices and traditions of these individuals?

While the council fathers are generally clear about the possibility of salvation for those outside the Christian community, they maintain an intentional ambiguity about the *way* in which such people are saved. For example, in the *Declaration on the Relation of the Church to Non-Christian Religions* (*Nostra Aetate* 2), it is simply stated that the Catholic Church "rejects nothing of those things which are true and holy" in other religious traditions, but no more. In the *Decree on the Church's Missionary Activity*

(*Ad Gentes* 11), the council fathers teach that Christians must "lay bare the seeds of the Word which lie hidden among their fellows [of other religious traditions]." Are Buddhists saved by Christ in a way that is unconnected to their practice of the Dharma? Does the Holy Spirit sanctify the life of a Jain apart from the Jain's practice of *ahimsa*? There are passages in the council documents consistent with the view that God's truth and grace are not confined to Christianity but are ubiquitous.[6] These statements do move in a direction toward a view proposed by Karl Rahner.

But James Fredericks advises that such statements in the council texts "should not be over interpreted. They move in a Rahnerian direction to the extent that they recognize grace to be operative and efficacious in the lives of people who are not Christians. They do not go as far as Rahner would in recognizing the other religious paths themselves as mediations of Christ's salvation."[7] Commenting on the council's restraint in regards to the question of how non-Christians are saved, Karl Rahner argued that this is an essential problem left open by the council for theologians. "The essential problem for the theologian has been left open [by Vatican II]….The theological quality of non-Christian religions remains undefined."[8]

The bishops, in other words, did not affirm nor deny that the religions may be actual instruments by which the Spirit flows into the lives of peoples outside the church. Why this cautious position taken by the bishops? Paul Knitter suggests:

> Perhaps the reason they didn't decide this question is that they deliberately chose not to. Vatican II, from the very start, was defined by Pope John XXIII as a pastoral, not a doctrinal, council. That means it wanted to speak to the people, not to the theologians. Regarding the other religions, its intentions were "to foster between them and Christianity new attitudes of mutual understanding esteem dialogue, and cooperation."[9] Trying to pass judgment on controversial theological issues could well get in the way of this personal agenda.[10]

But there is another point that the council did not hesitate to clarify, and in so doing it echoed another of Rahner's ingredients in his theology of religions. In the words of the *Dogmatic Constitution on the Church*

(Lumen Gentium): "Whatever good or truth is found amongst them is looked upon by the Church as preparation for the Gospel" (16). In order to be faithful to its own identity and experience, Vatican II emphasizes the uniqueness of what God has done in Jesus and continues to do in the church. Since it is only Jesus "in whom people find the fullness of religious life and in whom God has reconciled all things to Himself (2 Corinthians. 5:18–19)" (*NA* 2), the other religions achieve their fullness exclusively in Christ. And for Catholics, this means the church. The church, then, is necessary for the fullness of salvation: for "it is only through Christ's Catholic Church, which is the all-embracing means of salvation, that they can benefit fully from the means of salvation" (*LG* 14; *Decree on Ecumenism* [*Unitas Redintergratio, UR*] 3).

While Vatican II is clearly a milestone in Christian attitudes toward the other religions, it is a faithful milestone: "While it certainly pointed in directions never before explored by Christians, it also wanted to make sure that those directions did not lead away from the heart of the Gospel and the special place of Jesus Christ in expressing God's love for all."[11]

After Vatican II, Catholic laity, theologians, and pastors continued to explore and develop the new vision in regards to the other religions. And the church's Magisterium did not hesitate to oversee and evaluate this development.

Dominus Iesus

In light of the tendencies within the council documents themselves, we now look into *Dominus Iesus (DI)* and its use of the council texts in developing an appraisal of the truth of the non-Christian religions.[12] In treating of the matter, one of the issues addressed in the declaration concerns the distinction between faith and belief. In number 7, a clear distinction is made between what it calls "belief," as found in the other religions, and "theological faith," as found in Christianity. A warning is given that this distinction must be firmly held.

Theological faith is the appropriate response to God's revelation and is the consequence of grace. Citing the *Catechism of the Catholic Church,* numbers 144, 150, 153, the declaration explains that theological faith is

[T]he obedience of faith that implies acceptance of the truth of Christ's revelation, guaranteed by God, who is the Truth itself. "Faith is first of all a personal adherence of man to God. At the same time, and inseparably, it is a *free assent to the word of truth that God has revealed.*" Faith, therefore, as a *"gift of God"* and as *"a supernatural virtue infused by him,"* involves a dual adherence: to God who reveals and to the truth which he reveals, out of the trust which one has in him who speaks. (*DI* 7)

In its full theological sense faith is "…the acceptance in grace of revealed truth, which 'makes it possible to penetrate the mystery in a way that allows us to understand it coherently'" (*Fides et Ratio* 13) (*DI* 7).

Belief, as found in the other religions, is not a free assent to the whole truth God has revealed. It is rather "that sum of experience and thought that constitutes the human treasury of wisdom and religious aspiration, which man in his search for truth has conceived and acted upon in his relationship to God and the Absolute" (*DI* 7). The declaration seems to be quite aware of the implications this distinction brings to the appraisal of the truth and salvific value of the other religious paths. Number 7 closes by remarking that contemporary theologians sometimes confuse theological faith with belief as found in other religions and do not realize that the other religions can only provide "religious experience still in search of the absolute truth and still lacking assent to God who reveals himself." This seems to have a resonance with the traditional Scholastic distinction between the natural knowledge of God as found in the other religions and the supernatural faith enjoyed by Christians.

Fredericks notes that number 8 of *Dominus Iesus* ends by citing Pope John Paul II in a way that does not seem wholly compatible with the strict distinction asserted between faith and belief. Quoting the pope's *Redemptoris Missio* [*RM*], number 55, *Dominus Iesus* acknowledges that God "does not fail to make himself present in many ways, not only to individuals, but also to entire peoples through their spiritual riches, of which their religions are the main and essential expression…." From this, the declaration concludes that "the sacred books of other religions, which in actual fact direct and nourish the existence of their followers, receive from the mystery of Christ the elements of goodness and grace which they contain." Noting an incompatibility, Fredericks inquires:

> If the grace contained in the Sutras and in the Upanishads, the Qur'an, and the Dao-de-jing is from Christ and not merely the product of human wisdom untouched by grace, how then can Christians maintain a stark, un-nuanced distinction between "theological faith," on the one hand, and "belief" in the other religions which is merely "that sum of experience and thought that constitutes the human treasury of wisdom and religious aspiration?"[13]

And then in reference to *Ad Gentes* 7, where it is made clear that God can lead non-Christians to "that faith without which it is impossible to please him," Fredericks concludes, "In fine, the sharp distinction between theological faith and mere religious belief, which Dominus Iesus claims to be 'firmly held,' remains problematic when interpreted against the complexities of the documents of Vatican II."[14] This, too, is the view of Cardinal Dulles, who also refers to *Ad Gentes* 7 as an indication that the declaration's distinction between theological faith and belief in the other religions is not in keeping with the council.[15] This same distinction receives a critical appraisal from Richard McBrien,[16] Francis X. Clooney,[17] and Philip Kennedy.[18] It would seem, then, that the problematic issue of religious belief and theological faith requires, and will receive, further scrutiny by the church and its theologians.

Dominus Iesus does make an accurate assessment of Vatican II's teaching regarding the salvation of other religious believers. In number 20 the declaration affirms the certainty that other religious believers *can* be saved by the grace of Christ. Then in the following number it goes on to remark that Vatican II limited itself to the statement that God bestows this grace "in ways known to himself" (*AG* 7). *Dominus Iesus* specifies that the saving grace of Christ received by the other religious believers comes to them through the instrumentality of the church.

> The Church is the "universal sacrament of salvation," (*LG* 48) since, united always in a mysterious way to the Savior Jesus Christ, her head, and subordinated to him, she has, in God's plan, an indispensable relationship with the salvation

of every human being. For those who are not formally and visibly members of the church, "salvation in Christ is accessible by virtue of a grace which, while having a mysterious relationship with the church, does not make them formally part of the church but enlightens them in a way which is accommodated to their spiritual and material situation. This grace comes from Christ; it is the result of his sacrifice and is communicated by the Holy Spirit" (*RM* 10); it has a relationship with the church, which "according to the plan of the Father, has her origin in the mission of the Son and the Holy Spirit" (*AG* 2). (*DI* 20)

The writers of the declaration propose, finally, that the theological status of the other religious paths—their value as mediations of salvation—remains an open question for the church's theologians whose "work is to be encouraged, since it is certainly useful for understanding better God's salvific plan and the ways in which it is accomplished" (21). Pope John Paul II himself made a significant contribution to this question, a contribution that goes beyond and develops the teaching of Vatican II.

The Magisterial Teaching of John Paul II

A strong and persistent call for greater openness to other religions came from Pope John Paul II. That he went beyond the approach of Pope Paul VI is evident in what he had to say and what he did. He consistently reached out to adherents of the other religions, from his bringing together of different religions in Assisi to pray for peace in 1986 to the trip he made, when ailing and weak, to Israel and Palestine to promote greater interaction between Muslims and Jews and to petition for forgiveness for Catholic sins of the past.

It seems that the foremost source of the Pope's concern for interreligious dialogue was his theology of the Holy Spirit. For John Paul, the fundamental reason why there are such spiritual treasures in the religions of the world, why beneath the surface of their vast differences there is an undercurrent of unity, why dialogue among these religious families is so necessary and so promising is the reality of the one Spirit alive and active, before Christ and after him, within the religious searching and findings of humankind. This Spirit, the pope reminds his fellow Christians, is full of surprises, for s/he "blows where [s/he] will" (John 3:8) (*Redemptoris Hominis* 11). There are many religions, but there is one Spirit seeking to bear fruit in them all.[19]

John Paul's concern for this subject can be seen in his first encyclical letter, *Redemptoris Hominis* (1979). After that, his interest developed and led him toward a greater esteem of non-Christian believers as religious persons, and subsequently, a greater appreciation of the other religions themselves. In the encyclical, the pope perceives in the beliefs of those who follow other religious paths an "effect of the Spirit of truth operating outside the visible confines of the Mystical Body" (8). Then in an encyclical letter on the Holy Spirit, *Dominum et Vivificantem* (1986), John Paul II, quoting *Gaudium et Spes* 22, teaches that Christians "ought to believe that the Holy Spirit offers to every man the possibility of being associated, in a way known only to God, with the Paschal Mystery" (53).

John Paul II further developed his teaching about other religious traditions in light of the work of the Holy Spirit in 1990 with the promulgation of *Redemptoris Missio,* the encyclical letter *On the Permanent Validity of the Church's Missionary Mandate.* In number 28 he states, "The Spirit…is at the very source of the human person's existential and religious questioning which is occasioned not only by contingent situations but by the very structure of his being." The pope did not restrict the activity of the Spirit to the purely interior, private realm of the individual. "The Spirit's presence and activity affect not only individuals but also society and history, peoples, cultures and religions." In the same number 28 he summarized the essential elements of his understanding: the Spirit is universally present and active in the hearts of every person; to every person the Spirit offers the possibility of sharing in the Paschal Mystery; the Spirit is the source of every human being's religious quest, which arises from the structure of his being; the activity of the Spirit affects not only individuals but also religious institutions. In the next section the pope reflected on the implication of these truths for Christians. Because the Spirit "blows where he wills" (John 3:8), we must "broaden our vision in order to ponder his activity in every time and place" (28).

The pope, then, did not limit the grace-giving activity of Christ to the exclusively private and interior realm of the individual but acknowledged that Christ's truth and saving grace are received by non-Christians by means of their religious traditions. Thus John Paul began the process of dislodging the theological jam caused by the controversy about whether Vatican II did or did not view the other religions as genuine conduits of grace. But it should be emphasized that nowhere in the development of his theology of the Holy Spirit does the pope propose that other religious paths are in their own right *means* of salvation. Nor did he state that the church can ever be entirely distinguished from Christ and the Spirit. Rather the pope spoke of "participated forms of mediation," that is, the participation of the other religions in the saving mystery of Christ that is fully present in the church. The phrase, "participated forms of mediation," should be seen in light of Vatican II's *Lumen Gentium:* "The unique mediation of the Redeemer does not exclude, but rather gives rise to a manifold cooperation which is but a sharing in this one source" (62). This text does not speak of the other religions per se, but rather of elements in the spiritual and material situation of other religious believers. The pope used the concept of "participated forms of mediation" in *Redemptoris Missio* to assert the centrality of Christ in the salvation of all: "Although participated forms of mediation of different kinds and degrees are not excluded, they acquire meaning and value *only* from Christ's own mediation, and they cannot be understood as parallel or complementary to his" (5). While the pope taught that the Spirit is at work outside of Christianity in the other religious paths, he persistently related the operation of the Spirit outside of Christianity to the Christ event, that which the church alone bears full and explicit witness. The pope's implication, then, is that in regard to their truth-value, religions are not equal.

John Paul II's theology of the Holy Spirit surely has importance for Catholic thought about the theological status of the non-Christian religions. But *Dominus Jesus* surprisingly has little to say about it. And while John Paul may have very well agreed with the declaration's specification of his thought, it leaves, as Fredericks accurately notes, a distorted impression of the pope's views of the presence and efficacy of the Holy Sprit in the religious lives of those who follow other religious paths. A more prominent and positive reflection of the pontiff's pneumatological approach to the question of religious diversity is given in other forms of official church teaching, that is, in the 1991 *Dialogue and Proclamation* (*DP*) issued jointly by the Commission on Interreligious Dialogue and the Congregation for the Evangelization of Peoples, as well as in the 1997 statement of the International Theological Commission.

Other Forms of Official Church Teaching

Even if for some it is not so "evident" that John Paul affirmed other religious traditions as instruments of divine saving grace, in *Dialogue and Proclamation* spokespersons for the Catholic Church removed the ambiguity. They talked about other religions as never before. They explicitly recognized "the active presence of God through His Word" and "the universal presence of the Spirit" not only in persons outside the church but also in their religions. Consequently, it is "in the sincere practice of what is good in their own religious traditions…that the members of other religions correspond positively to God's invitation and receive salvation" (*DP* 29). Even more unambiguously, *Dialogue and Proclamation* states that the religions of the world play "a providential role in the divine economy of salvation" (17). "'Correspond positively…divine economy…'—this is theological language for indicating that in and through other religions, people truly are able to find and connect with God."[20]

Making such forward steps even more assuredly, the official and prestigious Vatican International Commission issued a statement in 1997 entitled "Christianity and the World Religions." John Paul's teachings are summarized numbers 81 and 83 of this document, and then in number 84 the following conclusion is reached:

> Given this explicit recognition of the presence of the Spirit of Christ in the religions, one cannot exclude the possibility that they exercise as such a certain salvific function, that is, despite their ambiguity, they help men achieve their ultimate end. In the religions is explicitly thematized the relationship of man with the Absolute, his transcendental dimension. It would be difficult to think that what the Holy Spirit works in the hearts

271

of men taken as individuals would have salvific value and not think that what the Holy Spirit works in the religions and cultures would not have such value. The recent Magisterium does not seem to authorize such a drastic distinction.[21]

What the recent Magisterium does not appear to support is the radical distinction between *nature* and *grace*, the natural and the supernatural orders, or more to the point, between the beliefs of Hindus, Buddhists, Jews, Muslims and the faith of Christians. This distinction is at the heart of the controversy over *Dominus Iesus*.

Summary

The church teaches that the other religions can be bearers not just of "truth and goodness" but also of the saving presence of the Spirit. According to the official teaching of the church, God's truth and the saving grace of Christ are received by non-Christians by means of their religious institutions, not in their own right, but as "participated forms of mediation" in the saving mystery of Christ, which is fully present in the church. Any further specification of the status of the non-Christian religions remains an open question for the church's theologians, whose "work is to be encouraged, since it is certainly useful for understanding better God's salvific plan and the ways in which it is accomplished" (*DI* 21).

In light of both the Magisterium considered previously and the historical, phenomenological, and theological study presented in part I of this book, we go on now to elaborate on our appraisal of the truth of the non-Christian world religions.

The Truth of the Non-Christian World Religions

To the adherents of the non-Christian traditions, by means of their own religious practices and in view of their salvation, the one true God, in and through Jesus Christ and the Holy Spirit, communicates himself and his truth. Elements of God's revelation are truly expressed in the other religions; they contain many authentic values; they contain elements of the supreme truth and seeds of God's word. By means of the same practices and institutions, God offers to the adherents of the non-Christian religions the grace freely to accept his revelation in faith and to respond to it in religious activity.

In other words, through the instrumentality of their own religious paths, non-Christians are enabled by God freely to accept or activate his offer of grace—the supernatural existential—and thus to be saved. Their religious traditions are authentic means of salvation because God has included them in the plan of salvation he works out in history, the plan that reaches its climax in the saving life, death, and resurrection of Jesus. They are by the will of God connected to that plan. Apart from it they would not be means of salvation. They are also mysteriously related to the church of Jesus.

Christ at Work in the Non-Christian Religions

It is not enough to recognize the possibility of God's salvific power in and through Christ reaching personally and in a hidden way to non-Christian individuals who, through the sincerity of their religious life, open themselves to him whom they do not know. It must be acknowledged that the other religions have salvific power as objective institutions and historical practices and phenomena. Nor is it enough to recognize that they have played a role, intended by God's providence, in preparing humankind for the gospel. They have had salvific value in the past and, even today, centuries after the Christian economy of salvation has been established, they still have salvific value for millions of their adherents.

The concrete religions bear in themselves supernatural, gracious moments, and by practicing them persons attain to God's grace. This is not to say that non-Christians are not saved by Christ; rather it means that Christ's power is hidden at work in the world religions: non-Christians are saved by Christ in the religions they profess. While it is true that there exists no salvation without Christ, salvation without the gospel is a reality, because for adherents of the other religions who have not personally encountered the gospel message these religions are the channel of Christ's salvific power.[22]

Revelation and Faith

Although truth is to be found not only in Christianity but in the other religions as well, there are distinctions to be made from the point of view of revelation and faith.[23] In the non-Christian traditions, revelation is to be understood in a qualified and analogous sense. For there the self-revelation of God is not experienced in explicit Christian categories, that is, in Christ and his Spirit. Rather it is experienced in the specific categories proper to the other religions. In other words, God's salvific power in and through Christ reaches personally and in a hidden way to non-Christian individuals. But this analogous revelation is authentic revelation. This is so because God's self-offer in Christ—the supernatural existential—alters every person's consciousness, so God truly reveals himself to everyone. In the graced consciousness of the adherents of those religions outside the Judeo-Christian tradition, God's self-offer is marginally, preconceptually, connaturally, and unthematically known as the graced lens through which everything else is known. This is implicit and transcendental but real knowledge of God's self-offer, his self-disclosure.

The faith that is the foundation of the other religions is to be understood in light of God's self-offer. Since the implicit but real knowledge of God's self-offer or disclosure in Christ is embodied in every person's consciousnesses, it enables every person to respond freely to it in an authentic supernatural faith, without which salvation is impossible. This may be called an *implicit* faith as distinguished from the baptized Christian's *explicit* faith in Jesus Christ. It is not a free assent to the whole truth God has revealed; and it does not give access to a coherent comprehension of the mystery of God. But this qualified and analogous faith—this belief—is, nevertheless, a grace of God by which those who profess it are saved. It is a precious gift that enables the recipients to nourish their spirit within them, to reach for enlightenment, release, and salvation. Since revelation is universal, genuine faith is a possibility in the non-Christian religions and indeed universally. A purely natural person to whom God has not revealed himself is nonexistent.

And since the social and historical dimensions are integral to all human persons, God's self-communication and self-revelation penetrate not only the hidden depths of every person's being and consciousness, they also incarnate and interpret themselves—with varying degrees of success—in diverse societies throughout history. The non-Christian religions are the more or less successful historical, social incarnations and interpretations of God's self-communication and revelation. Nevertheless, the one history of the one human race is directed by Christ's Spirit to reach its full incarnation and revelation in the person of Jesus Christ and his church.

It should be emphasized that the act of faith itself, which is always and everywhere possible, has a Christocentric character. No time or place existed in which Jesus Christ was not present and operative in non-Christian believers and their religions. Saving revelation and faith found in non-Christian religions cannot be separated from the person of the Lord Jesus Christ. Only the Spirit of Jesus makes faith possible. Since the Spirit is given "in view of Christ's merits," a real intrinsic connection exits between the person of Jesus Christ and the grace of the Spirit present always and everywhere. From the initial creation of the world, the Spirit of Jesus has been the inner dynamism of a revelation and salvation always mediated historically and socially. The history of revelation and salvation is one, and it is always directed by the Spirit to the climax in the crucified and risen Christ.

The church teaches explicitly that God calls all to salvation and that a person is saved through faith. For authentic faith to exist, even a qualified faith, authentic revelation must exist, at least an implicit revelation. Therefore, both revelation and faith can be found in people outside the Judeo-Christian tradition. There must be saving faith that is not explicitly centered on Christ. Thus non-Christian salvation in faith, hope, and love exists. And if a non-Christian attains salvation, then non-Christian religions must play a positive role in its attainment. The social-historical nature of the human person demands that even the most interior decisions be somehow mediated by the concreteness of one's social and historical life—in this case a person's non-Christian religion. Accordingly, God calls people to faith and salvation through communities, institutions, and agencies other than the church.

What Caused the Axial Period?

We return here to questions that arose as a result of our historical and phenomenological study. How is it that during the millennium before Jesus Christ separate regions of the world brought forth creations upon which the entire history of the human spirit has rested ever since? How is it that during the Axial Period human beings, for the first time in history, began to strive for self-transcendence and salvation? Is it a coincidence? Or do we interpret the events of the Axial Age as evidence of some underlying intentional, spiritual force, of some plan of divine providence?

The Christian tradition gives evidence that makes it reasonable to judge in faith that the extraordinary events of the Axial Period were *not* a coincidence. Nor can they be sufficiently accounted for by the historical, social, and political developments that impacted on the Axial sages and their followers. These influences surely played a role in bringing about the great world religions and other creative works of the Axial Age. But according to traditional Christian faith, the transcendent truth, beauty, and goodness embodied, in varying degrees, in those religions cannot be the result solely of human ingenuity and inventiveness. Ultimately they are the products of humankind's response of graced faith in divine revelation. The theological reflection presented in this book—a reflection grounded in scripture, tradition, Magisterium, and the history and phenomenology of religions—has endeavored to demonstrate the following claim: there is sufficient evidence to support the belief that the post-Axial religions were the result of Jesus' operating in a hidden and mysterious manner in human history, respecting the freedom and responsibility of men and women, effectively making self-transcendence and salvation possible to men and women of goodwill in and through the objective institutions and practices of the world religions. There are grounds to believe that in the post-Axial religions, Jesus was enabling and continues to enable the adherents of those spiritual traditions, on the one hand, to recognize and deal with the moral weakness and failure of humankind, the insecurity and liability-to-suffering of all life; on the other hand, to experience loving union with God in an existence that is radically different and of a limitlessly better quality. There is every good reason to believe that the events of the Axial Period were not a coincidence, but, rather, the results of God's offering to human creatures, by mediation of the world religions, the possibility of gradually undergoing a personal transformation from self-centeredness to Sacred-centeredness.

Notes

1. The historical review of Catholic thought is based on Paul F. Knitter, *Introducing Theologies of Religions* (Maryknoll, NY: Orbis, 2002), 63–78.

2. Karl Rahner, "Christianity and the Non-Christian Religions," *Theological Investigations* V, trans. Karl-H. Kruger (Baltimore: Helicon Press and London: Darton, Longman and Todd, 1966), 115–34.

3. Published later as Karl Rahner, "Christianity and the Non-Christian Religions," in *Theological Investigations* (Baltimore: Helicon Press, 1966), 63–78.

4. The discussion in the following paragraphs is from Karl Rahner, *Foundations of Christian Faith* (New York: Crossroad, 1978), 178–203, 318.

5. Rahner, "Christianity and the Non-Christian Religions," 125.

6. For example, *Gaudium et Spes* 22; *Ad Gentes* 3.

7. James Fredericks, "The Catholic Church and the Other Religious Paths: Rejecting Nothing That Is True and Holy," *Theological Studies* 64 (2003), 231.

8. Karl Rahner, "On the Importance of the Non-Christian Religions for Salvation," in *Theological Investigations*, vol. 18 (London: Darton, Longman, & Todd, 1984), 29.

9. Jacques Dupuis, *Toward a Christian Theology of Religious Pluralism* (Maryknoll, NY: Orbis, 1997), 158; see also 169–70.

10. Knitter, *Theologies of Religions*, 77–78.

11. Ibid., 78.

12. See *Origins* 30:14 (September 12, 2000), 220–22.

13. James Fredericks, "Catholic Church and Other Religious Paths," 232. Gerald O'Collins notes this same incompatibility. He points out that the declaration rejects any religious "pluralism" that goes beyond recognizing the fact of different religions to endorse a "pluralism in principle" (4). Nevertheless, the same declaration acknowledges that God's Spirit touches "not only individuals" but also "cultures and religions" (12). O'Collins states, "Granted that God never acts merely 'in fact' but always 'in and on principle,' such statements about the Spirit's activity in various religions and all that that comes from God to the religions imply some kind of religious 'pluralism' which exists in principle. After rejecting one meaning of 'pluralism in principle' (that which argues for separate and equal paths of salvation) the declaration appears to finish up endorsing another meaning of pluralism in principle, that which maintains that God's saving initiatives can be seen not only in Christianity but also in the religions of the world." Gerald O'Collins, "Watch Your Language" [review of *The Meeting of Religions and the Trinity* by Gavin D'Costa], *Tablet* (November 4, 2000), 1490.

14. Fredericks, "Catholic Church and Other Religious Paths," 233.

15. Avery Dulles, "*Dominus Iesus*: A Catholic Response," *Pro Ecclesia* 10 (Winter 2001), 5.

16. McBrien identifies the declaration's refusal to acknowledge the existence of true theological faith (as opposed to "belief") in other religions as "perhaps the most serious problem with *Dominus Iesus*'s approach to other religions...." He states, "If one truly believes in God, who is the one and only object of faith, it is because that person has somehow received the gift of faith from God, even if it should have no explicit reference to Jesus Christ." "*Dominus Iesus:* An Ecclesiological Critique," *Bulletin/Centro Pro Unione* 59 (Spring 2001), 22.

17. Clooney points out that the "faith-belief" distinction does not seem to do justice to the declaration's richer affirmation that faith is a *dual* adherence, "to God who reveals *and* to the truth which he reveals." He states that "given the declaration's explanation of faith as a 'personal adherence of man to God' too, the denial of 'faith' to the people of other religious traditions must be interpreted as also indicating that in other religious traditions there can be no relationship with God of the sorts that amounts as personal adherence, which is also faith." This would be contrary, Clooney proposes, to what the declaration asserts that God "does not fail to make himself present in many ways, not only to individuals, but also to entire peoples through their spiritual riches." If God is present to people in their own religions, Clooney continues, "God surely is present in such a way that those people can respond to God and to adhere to God even before assenting fully to revelation as understood in the teachings of the Roman Catholic Church." However, if God does not fail in the divine intention to communicate with all human beings, and if knowing God invites humans to adhere to God, "then it does not seem entirely reprehensible to say that the devout Muslim or Hindu who adheres to God does in some way have not only 'a life of belief' but also 'a life of faith' as defined in the declaration." "Implications for the Practice of Inter-Religious Learning," *Sic et Non: Encountering Dominus Iesus,* Stephen J. Pope and Charles Hefling, eds. (Maryknoll, NY: Orbis, 2002), 158–59.

18. Kennedy suggests that the declaration's distinction between theological faith and belief seems to slight some world religions. Since Judaism, Christianity, and Islam are all Abrahmaic religions by definition, Christians as well as Jews and Muslims believe in the God of Abraham, Isaac, and Jacob. "Therefore, the faith of Jews and Muslims is properly theological faith because it is given to God. While Christians espouse a Trinitarian understanding of God, wherein the Second Person is the incarnation of a passionate Logos unto death, their God nevertheless remains the God of Abraham." Cited in Martin E. Marty, "Rome and Relativism," *Commonweal* 125:18 (September 20, 2000).

19. Knitter, *Theologies of Religions,* 81.

20. Ibid., 82.

21. International Theological Commission, "Christianity and the World Religions," *Origins* (August 14, 1997), 84. In number 87 of this document the following elaboration is added: "The affirmation of the possibility of the existence of salvific elements in the religions does not imply in itself a judgment about the presence of these elements in each one of the specific religions. On the other hand, the love of God and of one's neighbor, made possible in the final analysis by Jesus the sole mediator, is the only way to reach God himself. The religions can be carriers of saving truth only insofar as they raise men to true love. If it is true that this can be found in those who do not practice any religion, it nonetheless seems that true love for God must lead to adoration and religious practice in union with other men."

22. Jacques Dupuis, a Belgian Jesuit who has spent most of his long life in India and who is one of the most cited and respected contemporary Catholic theologians exploring the world of other religions, has made a significant contribution to the theological reflection on God's saving action outside of the confines of the church. His thinking is compatible with the church's teaching and merits serious attention from those concerned with the ongoing project of developing a theological appraisal of religious pluralism. Gerald O'Collins, with good reason and insight, argues, "What Dupuis has written about the universal mission of the divine Spirit fills out nicely...what John Paul II has taught about the Spirit operating beyond the visible Church and enriching the world cultures and religions." Gerald O'Collins, "Jacques Dupuis's Contributions to Interreligious Dialogue," *Theological Studies* 64 (2003), 395. In regards to God's salvific activity outside of the church, Dupuis has several qualifications.

First, he relates the ways of salvation provided by the other religions to the entire Christ event, the incarnation, life, death, resurrection, present activity, and future coming of Christ. Second, he asserts that what the Spirit is about and discloses in other religions may be truly different from, but never contradictory to, what one finds in God's revelation in Jesus. The implication is that God has more to disclose to humankind than what God has communicated in Jesus: "More divine truth and grace are found operative in the entire history of God's dealing with humankind than are available simply in the Christian tradition." Christians "do not possess a monopoly on truth." Dupuis, *Christian Theology of Religious Pluralism*, 388; 382. Dupuis's views will be seen in fuller light further on when we focus on his understanding of Jesus Christ as "the fullness of God's revelation." (Because the quotations in the following paragraph are taken mostly from *Toward a Christian Theology of Religious Pluralism*, page numbers only are given in parentheses.)

Third, Dupuis maintains that the salvific action mediated by means of the other religions happens as intended by God and as part of the single divine plan of salvation for the whole world. The Father is the efficient cause of humankind's salvation. The other religions, then, have a "lasting role and specific meaning in the overall mystery of the divine-human relationship" (211). God, then, does not intend all people to find their fulfillment in the Christian Church. Religious plurality is not just a "matter of fact" but a "matter of principle." "Plurality needs to be taken seriously and to be welcomed....Its place in God's plan of salvation for humankind must be stressed" (201). Fourth, Dupuis highlights the final causality in the divine plan for salvation. According to that plan, all things and all religions converge toward the final kingdom of God and the risen and glorious Son of God: "An eschatological 'reheading'...in Christ of the religious traditions of the world will take place at the eschaton, and it will respect and preserve the irreducible character which God's self-manifestation through his Word and his Spirit has impressed upon each tradition" (389).

Finally, Dupuis acknowledges that the fullness of the means of salvation is to be found only in the church. What then is the role of the church for the salvation of those who are not baptized and go to God after a life spent in practicing their religious faith? What is the "necessity" of the church for the salvation of all human beings? "This necessity does not...imply a universal mediation in the strict sense, applicable to every person who is saved in Jesus Christ. On the contrary, it leaves room for 'substitutive mediations'...among which will be found the religious traditions to which the 'others' belong....However, according to the recent Magisterium, the church remains the 'ordinary way' for people's salvation (*Evangeli Nuntiandi* 80) inasmuch as it possesses the 'ordinary means' of salvation (ibid.) or the 'fullness of the means of salvation' (*Redemptoris Missio* 55), even though the members of the other religious traditions can be saved in Jesus Christ 'in a way known to God' (*Ad Gentes* 7; cf. *Gaudium et Spes* 22)....The 'universal instrumentality' of the church in the order of salvation mentioned in *Lumen Gentium* 9 and *Redemptoris Missio* 9 is understood, in the case of nonmembers, as expectation and hope, based on their orientation to it." Jacques Dupuis, *Christianity and the Religions: From Confrontation to Dialogue* (Maryknoll, NY: Orbis, 2002), 212.

23. An important source of my treatment here of revelation and faith is Harvey D. Egan, "A Rahnerian Response," *Sic et Non: Encountering Dominus Iesus*, Stephen J. Pope and Charles Hefling, eds. (Maryknoll, NY: Orbis, 2002).

Chapter Twelve

THE UNIQUENESS OF CHRISTIANITY

Christianity and the non-Christian world religions are similar in that they are all "true" religions. But among them, there are, of course, significant differences from the point of view of the experience and interpretation of the Sacred, creeds and dogmas, liturgical practices, theology and spirituality, and so on. Since God makes himself available to all human persons, why are there many religions rather than just one? Richard McBrien explains these differences:

> Just as God is in principle available to every person (Rahner's "supernatural existential") and to every people (since we are essentially social), so also religion, as the structured response to the experience of God, is available to every person and people. But since "no one has ever seen God" (John 1:18), we can never be absolutely certain that we have had an actual experience of God or that we have correctly perceived, interpreted, and expressed that experience. Furthermore, God can become available to us only on terms consistent with our bodily existence, i.e., sacramentally. Every experience of God or, from the other side, every self-disclosure of God, is inevitably conditioned by the situation of the person or community to which God has become available in a special way. Those communities are differentiated by time, place, culture, language, temperament, social and economic conditions, etc. Revelation, therefore, is always received according to the mode of the receiver, to cite a central Thomistic principle ("Duodenum recipitur in aliquo recipitur in eo secundum modum recipientis," *Summa*

Theologica, 1. q. 79, a. 6). Since religion is our structured response to the reception of God's revelation, our response will be shaped by that mode of reception. Indeed, the Son of God became incarnate in a particular time and place, in a particular culture and religious situation, in a particular man and a particular family, nation and ethnic community."[1]

While many differences exist among the religions, it is important for us in this study to focus on the basic difference between Christianity and the other religions. In what fundamental way is Christianity *unique*?

Central to the understanding of its uniqueness is Christianity's conviction that it alone is founded on Jesus Christ, who is believed to be the only and unparalleled redemptive mediator between God and humankind, the universal savior intended for all persons, as well as the perfection and fullness of God's revelation of truth. These beliefs are well grounded in the testimony of the scriptures and in the teaching of the church.

Scriptures and Teaching of the Church

In regard to Jesus Christ as God's revelation of truth, scripture asserts that in the mystery of the incarnate Son of God, who is "the way, the truth, and the life" (John 14:6), the full revelation of the divine truth is given: "No one has ever seen God. It is God the only Son, who is close to the Father's heart, who has made him known" (John 1:18); "For in him the whole fullness of deity dwells bodily" (Col 2:9). The Second Vatican Council teaches, "By this revelation, then, the deepest truth about God and the salvation of man shines out for our sake in Christ, who is both the mediator and the fullness of all revelation" (*Dei Verbum* [*DV*] 2). Furthermore,

> Jesus Christ, therefore, the Word made flesh, was sent "as a man to men." He "speaks the words of God" (John 3:34), and completes the work of salvation which his Father gave him to do (see John 5:36; 17:4). To see Jesus is to see his Father (John 14:9). For this reason Jesus perfected revelation by fulfilling it through his whole work of making himself

present and manifesting Himself: through His words and deeds, His signs and wonders, but especially through his death and glorious resurrection from the dead and final sending of the Spirit of truth. Moreover, He confirmed with divine testimony what revelation proclaimed, that God is with us to free us from the darkness of sin and death, and to raise us up to life eternal....The Christian dispensation, therefore, as the new and definitive covenant, will never pass away, and we now await no further new public revelation before the glorious manifestation of our Lord Jesus Christ (see 1 Timothy 6:14 and Titus 2:13). (*DV* 4)

Pope John Paul II taught that Jesus contains the fullness of what God wants to make known to humanity.

In Christ and through Christ God has revealed himself fully to mankind and has definitively drawn close to it; at the same time, in Christ and through Christ man has acquired full awareness of his dignity, of the heights to which he is raised, of the surpassing worth of his own humanity, and of the meaning of his existence." (*Redemptoris Hominis* [*RH*] 11)... God's revelation becomes definitive and complete through his only-begotten Son....In this definitive Word of his revelation, God has made himself known in the fullest possible way. He has revealed to mankind *who he is*." (*Redemptoris Missio* [*RH*] 5).

In regard to Jesus being the sole redemptive mediator of human-kind, scripture asserts with clarity, "And we have seen and do testify that the Father has sent his Son as the Savior of the world" (1 John 4:14); "Here is the Lamb of God who takes away the sin of the world" (John 1:29b). In his speech before the Sanhedrin, Peter proclaims, "There is salvation in no one else, for there is no other name under heaven given among mortals by which we must be saved" (Acts 4:12). And Saint Peter claims that Jesus Christ "is Lord of all," "judge of the living and the dead," and therefore "whoever believes in him receives forgiveness of sins through his name" (Acts 10:36, 42, 43). In addressing himself to the community of Corinth, Paul writes, "Indeed, even though there may be so-called gods in heaven or on earth—as in fact there are many gods and many lords—yet for us there is one God, the Father, from whom there are all things and for whom we exist, and one Lord, Jesus Christ, through whom are all things and through whom we exist" (1 Cor 8:5–6). Moreover, John states, "For God so loved the world that he gave his only Son, so that everyone who believes in him may not perish but may have eternal life. Indeed, God did not send his Son into the world to condemn the world, but in order that the world might be saved through him" (John 3:16–17). According to the New Testament, the universal salvific will of God is closely connected to the sole mediation of Christ: "[God] desires everyone to be saved and to come to the knowledge of the truth. For there is one God; there is also one mediator between God and humankind, Christ Jesus, himself human, who gave himself as a ransom for all" (1 Tim 2:4-6). And about Jesus as redemptive mediator the Second Vatican Council teaches:

> The Church believes that Christ, who died and was raised up for all, (2) can through His Spirit offer man the light and the strength to measure up to his supreme destiny, Nor has any other name under the heaven been given to man by which it is fitting for him to be saved (3). She likewise holds that in her benign Lord and Master can be found the key, the focal point and the goal of man, as well as of all human history. (*Gaudium et Spes* [GS] 10)

Pope John Paul taught that if God's saving love fills the universe, its pipeline is Jesus—only Jesus. "Christ is the one savior of all, the only one able to reveal God and lead to God….Salvation can come only from Jesus Christ" (*RM* 5). Consequently, Jesus is both "history's center and goal" (*RM* 6; *Dialogue and Proclamation* [DP] 22, 28) and he who "reconciles" or repairs the "rupture in the relationship between Creator and creation…after original sin."[2]

The scriptures and the teaching of the church, then, give testimony that Jesus is the summit and fullness of God's revelation and the universal savior intended for all humankind. This means that in principle a person's knowledge of God in Christ is completely adequate. Nothing is to be discovered about God (about God's mercy, love, fidelity, justice) that had not already been disclosed through Christ. The Christ-event is the definitive and normative self-communication of God by which all other communications are to be measured and tested. In the Christ-event is found the sole and unparalled redemptive mediation between humankind and God.

Only Jesus Christ is the absolute savior, the fullness of God's revelation and salvation. Only Jesus of Nazareth is the one mediator between God and humankind—the one ultimately sought by that "seeking Christology" written into every person's being and consciousness by the grace of God's Christocentric self-communication. Christianity, established on the reality of Jesus Christ, is therefore unique among the religions of the world. The preeminence of Christianity resides not in Christians themselves but in Jesus' person, his message, and his saving life, death, and resurrection. An authentic pluralism is compelled to acknowledge the uniqueness of God's revealing and saving activity in Jesus Christ.

Dominus Iesus

These traditional truths, so important to the recognition of the unique character of Christianity, have been challenged by some theologians in the contemporary debate about religious pluralism. *Dominus Iesus* took a critical stance to their claim that these truths have been superseded.

It appears that the declaration had in mind the "pluralistic" theology of religions, often associated with John Hick's philosophy of religion.[3] Hick's type of theological thinking is based on the hypothesis that "the great world traditions constitute different conceptions and perceptions of, and responses to, the Real from within the different cultural ways of being human."[4] Religious terms for ultimate reality, like *Brahman, Sunyata* and the *Dao, Yahweh, Allah, Shiva,* and *Kali* are different ways human beings have of naming and connecting with what Hick calls the "Real." As a consequence, *all* religions must be seen as partial and incomplete interpretations of a transcendent Reality that fully surpasses humankind's ability to name. No religion may legitimately claim to have the definite and entire revelation of God and therefore affirm superiority to any other religion as a path to salvation. Regarding this relativistic thinking about religious diversity and its implication for Christianity's evangelizing efforts, *Dominus Iesus* states that "the Church's constant missionary proclamation is endangered today by relativistic theories which seek to justify religious pluralism, not only de facto but also de jure (or 'in principle')" (4).

The pluralistic theology of religions has implications also for traditional Christology. These have been articulated, for example, in the recent work of Roger Haight.[5] To the question, "Is Christianity really a religion destined for all people?" Haight's response tends toward the side of pluralism. He proposes that

> Christians must believe that Jesus is a normative revelation from God, but they may also hold that God is normatively disclosed in other religious traditions as well. Jesus may mediate salvation for Christians, but he is not salvific for people who follow other religious paths. Consequently, Jesus of Nazareth is not a universal savior, the unique and unparalleled redemptive event intended for all. Other mediations of salvation proper to the other religious traditions exist and are not to be subsumed within the mediation Christians affirm. Many distinct and independent paths lead to a sole common salvation in God. Jesus, therefore, is not necessarily the only mediation of the divine empowered by the Spirit.[6]

Dominus Iesus takes a critical stance against contemporary theological thinking that claims Jesus of Nazareth "reveals the divine not in an exclusive way, but in a way complementary with other revelatory and salvific figures" (9). This position is rejected for being in profound conflict with the Christian faith: "There are also those who propose the hypothesis of an economy of the Holy Spirit with a more universal breadth than that of the Incarnate Word, crucified and risen. This position also is contrary to the Catholic faith, which, on the contrary, considers the salvific incarnation of the word as a trinitarian event" (12). In support of this view the declaration cites *Gaudium et Spes* 22: "The Holy Spirit offers to all the possibility of being made partners, in a way known to God, in the paschal mystery." *Dominus Iesus* also cites *Redemptoris Missio* where the pope notes that the Spirit, who is at work universally for the salvation of all human beings, "is the same Spirit who was at work in the incarnation and in the life, death, and resurrection of Jesus and who is at work in the church. He is therefore not an alternative to Christ nor does he fill a sort of void which is sometimes suggested as existing between Christ and the Logos" (29). It is necessary above all, the declaration states, to insist on the definitive and complete character of the revelation of Jesus Christ.

> In fact it must be *firmly believed* that, in the mystery of Jesus Christ, the incarnate Son of God, who is "the way, the truth and the life" (John 14:6), the full revelation of the divine truth is given: "No one knows the Son except the Father, and no one knows the Father except the Son and anyone to whom the Son wishes to reveal him" (Matthew 11:27); "No one has ever seen God; the only Son, who is in the bosom of the Father has revealed him" (John 1:18); "For in Christ the whole fullness of divinity dwells in bodily form" (Colossians 2:9–10). (*DI* 5)

Conclusion: Christianity as Normative

Since Christianity, and only Christianity, is the response to faith in Jesus—who is the only mediator of salvation between God and humankind as well as the summit and fullness of God's revealed truth[7]—it is the normatively true religion.[8] The non-Christian religions, then, are relatively true and lesser and extraordinary means of salvation. While the other religions do not have the fullness of truth—ambiguities and errors are found within them—they nevertheless are true and valid insofar as they implicitly share and practice the truth and values of Christianity.

It should be noted here that in *Dominus Iesus* 22 the following qualification is included: "If it is true that the followers of other religions can receive divine grace, it is also certain that *objectively speaking* they are in a gravely deficient situation in comparison with those who, in the Church, have the fullness of the means of salvation." However, citing *Lumen Gentium* 14, the declaration goes on to caution that "'all the children of the Church should nevertheless remember that their exalted condition results, not from their own merits, but from the grace of Christ. If they fail to respond in thought, word and deed to that grace, not only shall they not be saved, but they shall be more severely judged.'"

Convinced of the unique and normative status of Christianity, the declaration speaks in number 22 of the church's duty to bring the Christian gospel to the world. She is "duty bound to proclaim without fail Christ, who is the way, the truth and the life (John 14:6). In him, in whom God reconciled things to himself (2 Corinthians 5:18–19), men find the fullness of their religious life" (*Nostrae Aetate* 2). And in number 5 the declaration states that

> the encyclical *Redemptoris Missio* calls the Church once again to the task of announcing the Gospel as the fullness of truth: "In this definitive Word of his revelation, God has made himself known in the fullest possible way. He has revealed to mankind who he is. This definitive self-revelation of God is the fundamental reason why the church is missionary by her very nature. She cannot do other than proclaim the Gospel, that is, the fullness of the truth which God has enabled us to know about himself." (*RM* 5).

The Teaching of Pope Benedict XVI on Theology of Religions

Benedict XVI's career began in 1959 with his position as professor of systematic theology.[9] His life as teacher and scholar was strongly influenced by his experiences as consultant in Vatican II (1960–64); there he witnessed many developments inside the council, enabling him to help formulate certain texts and, later on, to comment on them with authority. Regarding his teaching on the non-Christian religions, we call attention, first, as an introduction, to a sermon Professor Ratzinger preached in 1964. It was entitled," Are Non-Christians Saved?" In light of the controversy that arose as a consequence of his later teaching on the subject as pope, it seems appropriate to make reference to this sermon.

"Are Non-Christians Saved?"

Everything we believe about God, and everything we know about man, prevents us from accepting that beyond the limits of the Church there is no more salvation, that up to the time of Christ all men were subject to the fate of eternal damnation. We are no longer ready and able to think that our neighbor, who is a decent and respectable man and in many ways better than we are, should be eternally damned simply because he is not a Catholic. We are no longer ready, no longer willing, to think that eternal corruption should be inflicted on people in Asia, in Africa, or wherever it may be, merely on account of their not having "Catholic" marked in their passport.

Actually, a great deal of thought had been devoted in theology, both before and after Ignatius, to the question of how people, without even knowing it, in some way belonged to the Church and to Christ and could thus be saved nevertheless. And still today, a great deal of perspicacity is used in such reflection.

Yet if we are honest, we will have to admit that this is not our problem at all. The question we have to face is not that of whether other people can be saved and how. We are convinced that God is able to do this with or without our theories, with or without our perspicacity, and that we do not need to help him do it with our cogitations. The question that really troubles us is not in the least concerned with whether and how God manages to save *others.*

The question that torments us is, rather, why it is still actually necessary for us to carry out the whole ministry of the Christian faith—why, if there are so many other ways to heaven and to salvation, should it still be demanded of us that we bear, day by day, the whole burden of ecclestical dogma and ecclesiastical ethics?...[10]

This sermon given during the time of Vatican II is a foreshadowing of Professor Ratzinger's later teaching on the theology of religions.

Cardinal Ratzinger and Dominus Iesus

Ratzinger's tenure as professor of theology ended in 1977 with his appointment as archbishop of Munich and Freising. In 1981, Pope John Paul II called him to Rome to assume the post of cardinal prefect of the Congregation of the Doctrine of the Faith. He occupied this post until he was elected pope in 2005.

The decade from 1992 to 2002 was one in which the Congregation for the Doctrine of the Faith, and therefore also its cardinal prefect, gave much attention to the theology of religions. There were several theologians who set forth unorthodox answers to the questions of religious diversity, and correcting them played the same role in the efforts of the congregation in these years as correcting the publications of some liberation theologians had during the preceding two decades.

And then, on August 6, 2000, the declaration *Dominus Iesus*, elaborated under the supervision of Joseph Cardinal Ratzinger, was published with the ratification of Pope John Paul II. There is hardly any doubt that Ratzinger had more a part in its composition than anyone else, and that its integral content represents his own theological thought. As we have seen, the document's main concern was precisely to combat inappropriately pluralistic theologies with a strong statement of the following basic claims of christological and ecclesiological orthodoxy: the unique and total salvific significance of the life, passion, death, and resurrection of Jesus; the close unity of the redeeming work of the incarnate Logos with that of the Holy Spirit; the profound intimacy between the church of Christ and the visible and hierarchically structured Catholic Church in full communion with the bishop of Rome; and the necessity of preserving the church's evangelical mission to bring the gospel to all and its imperative to engage in serious dialogue with other religions.

Cardinal Ratzinger's firm and explicit personal affirmation of *Dominus Iesus* should be noted. On September 14, 2000, he sent a letter, signed by himself, to the presidents of Bishops' Conferences explaining the purpose and authority of the declaration. He states that the declaration

> presents the principle truths of the Catholic faith in these areas; such truths require, therefore, irrevocable assent by the Catholic faithful; the text also...points out important questions that remain open to theological investigation and debate. Since it is a document of the Congregation for the Doctrine of Faith, the declaration has a universal theological nature.

Ratzinger goes on to indicate that he

is confident that the conference itself, as well as individual bishops, will do everything possible to insure its distribution and favorable reception....Particularly in the areas of ecumenical and interreligious dialogue and in Catholic universities and faculties of theology, it is essential that the doctrinal contents of this declaration become a point of reference as well as a solid and indispensable foundation for pastoral and missionary work which is convincing, effective and consistent with Catholic teaching.[11]

The thinking of Joseph Ratzinger on theology of religious pluralism is surely found expressed in *Dominus Iesus*. Further insights into his views on this subject can be found in one of his books, *Truth and Tolerance*, which was published in 2003.

Cardinal Ratzinger's Writings as a Theologian

During his career as prefect of the Congregation of the Doctrine of the Faith, Cardinal Ratzinger continued his theological writing. And when he reached the age of seventy-five, he evidently was ready to sum up his life's scholarly work. As he began to edit his writings, he made no major changes in his original texts. A text he edited and published shortly before his elevation to the papacy is of particular significance for us: *Truth and Tolerance: Christian Belief and World Religions.*[12]

This text is a collection of thirteen of his previously published essays on the various questions concerning the theology of religions. Some of these questions are, May a non-Christian religion be a real means of salvation for its adherents? May eternal salvation be separated from the life, death, and resurrection of Jesus? What may be said in regard to a devout non-Christian's relation to God? How can the Catholics Church's demand for the evangelization of non-Christians be reconciled with its requirement for serious dialogue with those who practice the other religions? What is the meaning of interreligious prayer? The essays of *Truth and Tolerance*, mostly from the 1990s, with his more recent comments and elaborations added, are learned restatements of basic Catholic orthodoxy on these questions raised by religious diversity.

As Cardinal Ratzinger himself indicates in *Truth and Tolerance,* when *Dominus Iesus* was published in 2000, there came "a cry of outrage from modern society, but also from great non-Christian cultures such as that of India; this was said to be a document of intolerance and of a religious arrogance that should have no more place in the world of today."[13] There was also (and this is not spoken of in the book) criticism of *Dominus Iesus* from prominent members from within the hierarchy. At least two cardinals, Edward Cassidy, then president of the Pontifical Council for Promoting Christian Unity, and Walter Kasper, the current president, publicly distanced themselves from the declaration.

In light of this context of tense conflict, the collection of Ratzinger's essays, which was published in German and Italian in 2003 and in English in 2004, is important. It holds firmly to the line of the fundamental claims of christological and ecclesiological orthodoxy expressed in *Dominus Iesus.* Consequently, it is a precise indication of what the former theologian and Vatican administrator who is now the pope thinks about the theology of religions, and it makes clear what is at issue between the pope and the critics of *Dominus Iesus. Truth and Tolerance* also expresses elements of Ratzinger's thought not directly related to the purpose of *Dominus Iesus.* Some of these elements we consider next.

Ratzinger and Rahner

For the lead essay of the collection, Ratzinger placed a piece he had written nearly forty years previously for the *Festschrift* dedicated to Karl Rahner on the occasion of his sixtieth birthday: "The Unity and Diversity of Religions: The Place of Christianity in the History of Religions." This time Ratzinger added some "preliminary remarks" that set forth his criticisms of Rahner, which he had intentionally omitted in the Festschrift as a mark of respect for his countryman. These criticisms refer to Rahner's famous lecture of 1961 on "Christianity and the Non-Christian Religions." Ratzinger speaks of two points in Rahner's approach with which he did not agree: first, Rahner's restricting his interest in the non-Christian religions to the salvation of the individual person, without much concern for the significance that other religions have in themselves; second, all religions, consequently, were equally summed up by Rahner in the single abstract concept of "religion." In fact, for the solution offered by Karl Rahner, the history of religions, as well as any concrete religion, becomes irrelevant. Ratzinger acknowledges that in light of the enormous amount of research being done in the field of the history of religions, a single theologian is unable to master all religions in detail. In his book, however, Ratzinger does reflect on the significance the other religions have in themselves. His reflection includes efforts to discover "whether there was any kind of continuous historical development here and whether any basic types of religion could (be) recognized, which we could then more easily evaluate" (18). He also reflects on the unique character of Christianity, "to show more clearly the place of Christianity in the history of religions" (16).

Two Types of Religions

One of the basic points argued by Ratzinger in his book, *Truth and Tolerance*, is that an impartial exploration of the world's religions discloses a fundamental difference between two types of religions: those that offer a "mysticism of identity" (33–34) and those that advocate a "personal understanding of God." In his review of the cardinal's book, Paul Griffiths, Schmitt Professor of Catholic Studies at the University of Illinois at Chicago, proposes that "Ratzinger tends too easily to identify religions of the former type [those that offer a 'mysticism of identity'] with those of Asia, especially Hinduism. This is dubious, descriptively and historically: Many Hindus have had what Ratzinger means by a personal understanding of God, and at least some Christians, Jews, and Muslims have lacked it." But Griffiths adds that the distinction is, nevertheless, "a powerful one and serves well Ratzinger's purpose of emphasizing difference and underscoring distinction: All religions do not commend the same goal or offer the same understanding of God and the human; and it is among the tendencies of those who advocate religious pluralism to obscure this."[14]

Uniqueness of Christianity

Ratzinger explains the uniqueness of Christianity in a precise and traditional way. Christianity's distinctiveness does not enter history like a bolt from the heavens. Nor does it simply abolish or lay waste the world's religions and cultures. Rather, as the principle and fullest presence in the world of the institutional form of the Christ's body, the church provides those who do not yet know her with the enticement of a fuller and richer understanding of what they already know, both religiously and culturally. The possibility of conversion offered by Christianity is, consequently, an offer that carries with it a culturally and religiously unique fulfillment of cultures as they existed before conversion. The church is called, therefore, to address Buddhists, Marxists, secular hedonists, and neo-Stoics in the same voice and with the same two attitudes: as a humble yet confident presenter of an outstanding gift, and at the same time, as an eager and sincere listener. These attitudes are those of proclamation and dialogue; they are inextricably linked in Ratzinger's thought, as they are also in the documents of Vatican II. Ratzinger notes that the only two partial exceptions are conversations with those to whom the church is already closely related—that is to say, the Jewish people and the Muslims. But he says little about the Jews or the Muslims in these essays.

Religious Truth

In the second half of *Truth and Tolerance*, Ratzinger turns to the question of religious truth. If God is triune, if Jesus of Nazareth was the second person of the Holy Trinity, and if the Catholic Church is the institution in which Christ's church subsists—if all these traditional beliefs are true, then the positions rejected in *Dominus Iesus* must be false. But he also concerns himself with the larger philosophical difficulties in regard to skepticism and relativism. At some length he speaks of the connections of relativism with the rejection of the very idea of truth as correspondence of the knowing intellect to its known objects, and he explores the connection of skepticism with the idea that it is impossible to know which religion is true even if one were true. One way he does this is by reflecting on Christianity's rivals in the Roman world of late antiquity. But Ratzinger does not think that people today can simply adopt, for example, Saint Augustine's response to the neo-Platonists. He recognizes that for modern persons, as for their fourth- and fifth-century forbearers, arguments to support the Christian affirmation of the basic comprehensibility and rationality of the world will no longer be convincing to the cultured despisers of Christianity. While this position is correct, it is to be held together, Paul

Griffiths suggests, with Ratzinger's equally strong affirmation of Christianity's truth. The world is comprehensible by human rationality because of the nature of its creator and redeemer. "Faced with the Christian claim—with good arguments in support of it, for that matter—many will deny it. This interesting fact holds the key to at least some elements of the complex of questions raised by religious diversity."[15]

Buddhism and Hinduism

In the view of Paul Griffiths, many of Ratzinger's statements about Buddhism and Hinduism in *Truth and Tolerance* are characterized by a superficiality and generality he would himself criticize in comparable remarks about Christianity. But he adds, "These are matters that do not affect the merits of the work as a whole, which are great. *Truth and Tolerance* provides transparently lucid guidelines for the recognition of when orthodoxy has been abandoned. It rightly identifies the main intellectual and social pressures issuing in such abandonment."[16]

Summary

In his writings as theologian and his work as prefect of the Congregation of the Doctrine of the Faith, Joseph Ratzinger held to traditional christological and ecclesiological truths in his reflection on the theology of religions.

Papal Teaching of Benedict XVI

There have been many occasions that seem to prove that, as the Supreme Pontiff, Benedict XVI is highly motivated to foster and develop what was initiated by his predecessors, especially John Paul II. In John Paul's time, there were many symbolic acts of respect: visits of synagogues and mosques, the prayer in Assisi, the Wailing Wall in Jerusalem, and in Yad Vashem. What John Paul II began, Benedict continued: he visited the synagogue in Cologne; he visited Auschwitz, where suddenly a rainbow appeared; he prayed in the Blue Masque in Istanbul facing Mecca. At the same time, however, we witness disturbing conse-quences of his lecture at Regensburg.

On September 12, 2006, Benedict XVI delivered an academic lec-ture in Regensburg, Germany, that argued for both the reasonableness of faith and that faith separated from reason can result in behaviors con-trary to God's will. In this context, the pope quoted the opinion of a fourteenth-century Byzantine emperor, Manuel II Paleologus, that "not acting reasonably is contrary to God's nature." The emperor had illus-trated his assertion about unreasonable religious behavior by discussing the use of violence to coerce conversion, attributing such practices in polemical terms to Islam, and this language was quoted by the pope: "Show me just what Mohammed brought that was new, and there you will find things only evil and inhuman, such as his command to spread by the sword the faith he preached."[17]

The lecture sparked protests in many Islamic countries. Apparently the protestors had concluded or were advised that Benedict himself believed Islam to be, in the quoted words from the fourteenth century, "only evil and inhuman." Because the lecture did not include any examples of unreasonable Christian practices or repeat formal Catholic teaching from the Second Vatican Council that the church regards Muslims with esteem, the probability of unintended negative interpretations of the lecture was increased.

On September 16, 2006, the Vatican secretary of state, Cardinal Tarcisio Bertone, issued a statement about criticism in the Muslim world over Pope Benedict XVI's remarks about Islam and violence.

> As for the opinion of the Byzantine emperor Manuel II Paleologus…the Holy Father did not mean, nor does he mean, to make that opinion his own in any way. He simply used it as a means to undertake—in an academic context, and as is evident from a complete and attentive reading of the text—certain reflection on the theme of the relationship between religion and violence in general, and to conclude with clear and radical rejection of the religious motivation for violence, from whatever side it may come.[18]

Bertone stated that the position of the pope concerning Islam is unequivocally that expressed by the councilor document *Nostra Aetate:*

The Church regards with esteem also the Muslims. They adore the one God, living and subsisting in Himself; merciful and all-powerful, the Creator of heaven and earth, who has spoken to men; they take pains to submit wholeheartedly to even His inscrutable decrees, just as Abraham, with whom the faith of Islam takes pleasure in linking itself, submitted to God. Though they do not acknowledge Jesus as God, they revere Him as a prophet. They also honor Mary, His virgin Mother; at times they even call on her with devotion. In addition, they await the Day of Judgment with God will render their deserts to all those who have been raised up from the dead. Finally, they value the moral life and worship god especially through prayer, almsgiving and fasting. (3)

The Holy Father sincerely regrets, Bertone insisted, that certain parts of his lecture could have sounded offensive to the sensitivities of the Muslim faithful and were interpreted in a way that does not at all correspond to his intentions. On September 17, 2006, the pope stated, "At this time, I wish also to add that I am deeply sorry for the reactions in some countries to a few passages of my address at the University of Regensburg, which were considered offensive to the sensibilities of Muslims. These in fact were a quotation from a medieval text, which do not in any way express my own person thought." In a general audience on September 20, 2006, the pope stated:

In no way did I wish to make my own the words of the medieval emperor. I wished to explain that not religion and violence, but religion and reason, go together. I hope that my profound respect for world religions and for Muslims, who "worship the one God" and with whom we "promote peace, liberty, social justice and moral values for the benefit of all humanity" (*Nostra Aetate*, no. 23) is clear. Let us continue the dialogue both between religions and between modern reason and the Christian faith![19]

Notes

1. Richard McBrien, *Catholicism: Completely Revised and Updated* (San Francisco: HarperCollins, 1994), 380.

2. From the pope's November 1999 apostolic exhortation *Ecclesia in Asia* 11.

3. A comprehensive statement of Hick's pluralist approach is his book, *An Interpretation of Religion: The Challenge of Other Religions* (Oxford: Blackwell, 1989).

4. Ibid., 376.

5. Roger Haight, *Jesus: Symbol of God* (Maryknoll, NY: Orbis, 1999).

6. Philip Kennedy has also articulated implications of pluralistic theology for Christology. He holds that religious pluralism is an unavoidable fact of reality. Since God is illimitable, no historical reality can manifest the full richness of God. "Jesus Christ is not the complete revelation of God in history, but a partial manifestation of what God may be like. Since Jesus is not the unveiling of the fullness of God in the world, other religions may have their way about God's salvific nature. Even according to classical dogmatic theology, Jesus Christ is the enfleshment in history of the Second Person of the Trinity. The fullness of the Trinity is not incarnate in Jesus. Consequently, there is more to God, so to speak, than has been shown in Jesus Christ. God remains a Deus *absconditus*, a God who always escapes human attempts to picture God." Philip Kennedy, cited in Martin E. Marty, "Rome and Relativism," *Commonweal* 125:18 (2000). Gerald O'Collins has made a similar point about Christology. In one sense, surely, Jesus Christ embodies and communicates the fullness of revelation, but in another sense he does not. "The final vision of God is still to come. As St. John puts it, 'it does not yet appear what we shall be...when he appears, we shall be like him, for we shall see him as he is' (1 John 3:2). As we wait in hope for the complete and final revelation, we see and know 'dimly' and not yet fully. Looking forward to the fullness of God's saving self-manifestation. St. Paul writes: 'Now we see in a mirror dimly, but then face to face. Now I know in part: then I shall understand fully, even as I have been fully understood' (1 Corinthians.13:12)." Gerald O'Collins, "Watch Your Language" [review *The Meeting of Religions and the Trinity* by Gavin D'Costa], *Tablet* (November 4, 2000), 1490.

7. Jacques Dupuis has reflected with great insight and originality on Jesus Christ as the unique and only savior of humankind as well as the fullness of God's revelation. Since Dupuis's contributions will surely play an important role in the ongoing development of a theology of religions compatible with scripture, tradition, and Magisterium, as well as effective in promoting interreligious dialogue, it is included here.

Because Jesus' "personal identity" is that of the Word of God, Son of God, the second person of the Trinity, Dupuis states that "the Christian cannot stand without claiming for Jesus Christ a constitutive uniqueness." *Toward a Christian Theology of Religious Pluralism* (Maryknoll, NY: Orbis, 1997), 304. (Because the quotations in the next three paragraphs are taken mostly from this text, page numbers only are given in parentheses.)

This uniqueness of Jesus means that only he "opens access to God for all human beings" (387). It means, too, that in Jesus God has delivered the fullness of revelation: "It is the very person of Jesus Christ, his deeds and his words, his life, his death, and his resurrection—in a word, the total Jesus Christ-event itself—that constitutes the fullness of revelation. In him God has uttered to the world his decisive word" (248–49).

This fullness is not to be understood qualitatively, as though after Christ everything related to the divine mystery were already known and there was nothing further to learn. It is, rather, to be understood qualitatively, in the sense of being unsurpassed and unsurpassable in strength, concentration, and focus: "This plenitude...is not...one of extension and all-comprehension, but of intensity....It does not—cannot—exhaust the mystery of the Divine" (382). Our knowledge of God as revealed in Jesus is, then, not absolute: "It remains limited. On the one hand, Jesus' human consciousness, while it is that of the Son, is still a human consciousness and therefore a limited one. It could not have been otherwise. No human consciousness, even the human consciousness of the Son of God, can exhaust the Divine Mystery. On the other hand, it is precisely this human experience that Jesus had of being the Son, in relation to the Father, that enabled him to translate into human words the mystery of God that he revealed to us" (249). Consequently, the qualitative and limited fullness of God's revelation in Jesus "is no obstacle, even after the historical event, to a continuing divine self-revelation through the prophets and sages of other religious traditions, as for example, through the prophet Muhammad. That self-revelation has occurred, and continues to occur, in history. No revelation, however, either before or after Christ can either surpass or equal the one vouchsafed in Jesus Christ, the divine Son incarnate" (249–50). The revelation in Christ is central and normative for Christians.

While God's self-disclosure in Jesus has normative authority, it is nevertheless relational, in the sense that "the 'transhistorical' character of the risen humanity of Jesus Christ notwithstanding, the event [of God's becoming flesh] is limited by its insertion in history, without which its singular significance and density would vanish. It is, then, at once particular in time and universal in meaning and, as such, 'singularly universal,' yet related to all other divine manifestations to humankind in one history of salvation—that is, relational" (388). Therefore, while the fullness of what God wants to make known to humankind is focused in Jesus, to increase the depth of understanding, Christians have to relate what they have in Jesus to what the Spirit is disclosing in the other religions. The universal enlightenment of the Word of God and the disclosing of his Spirit "make it possible to discover, in other saving figures and traditions, truth and grace not brought out with the same vigor and clarity in God's revelation and manifestations in Jesus Christ. Truth and grace found elsewhere must not be reduced to 'seeds' or 'stepping stones' simply to be nurtured or used and then suppressed in Christian revelation. They represent additional and autonomous benefits" (388).

Dupuis clarifies the relationship between what God has to say through other religions and what God speaks in the Spirit. Since Christ, not the Spirit, is at the center of the way to God, whatever God discloses through other religions in the Spirit must be understood "in view of, and in relation to" what God has disclosed in Jesus Christ. It does not take the place of Christ (197).

"Complementarity" exists between the other religions and Christianity. Dupuis uses the term *complementarity* to indicate how some elements of the one Divine Mystery can be vividly expressed by the practices and sacred writings found beyond Christianity. Nonbiblical scriptures "may contain aspects of the Divine Mystery which the Bible, the New Testament included, do not highlight equally. To give some examples: in the Qur'an the sense of the divine majesty and transcendence, of adoration and of the human being's submission to the holiness of God's eternal decrees, and in the sacred books of Hinduism the sense of God's immanent presence in the world and in the recesses of the human heart." Jacques Dupuis, *Christianity and the Religions: From Confrontation to Dialogue* (Maryknoll, NY: Orbis, 2002), 135. While this complementarity may be considered reciprocal, it is not understood to mean "that anything is lacking with Christianity that it would have to receive from other religions, without which it would not enjoy the fullness of divine revelation, rather in the sense that God has provided gifts to human beings in the other religious traditions as well, which even though they find their fulfillment in the revelation of God in Jesus Christ, nonetheless represent authentic words of God, and additional autonomous gifts from God. Such divine gifts to human beings do not in any way impede the transcendence and unsurpassability of God's gift to humankind in Jesus Christ. The complementarity between the seeds of 'truth and grace' in the other religious traditions and the 'fullness' of the divine manifestation in Jesus Christ, attested by the Christian sacred scriptures, is thus to be understood as mutual 'asymmetrical' complementarity." Dupuis, *Christianity and the Religions,* 136.

8. Francis X. Clooney puts into context the traditional teaching that asserts Christianity as normatively true. "It is not a peculiarly Roman Catholic insight to hold that the content of faith is true or that truth about reality can be normatively apprehended. I have known many Hindus over the years who are quite willing to assert the truth of what they believe. In my years of study of Indian

Hindu theologies, too, I have encountered numerous claims by theologians as to the truth of a community's faith....When we claim that 'my faith is true, unique or even superior' we may be correct, but the claim itself is not unique or even particularly unusual. Catholics who make this claim are in important ways like Ramanuja and his community who make a comparable claim." "Implications for the Practice of Inter-Religious Learning," in *Sic et Non: Encountering Dominus Iesus*, Stephen J. Pope and Charles Hefling, eds. (Maryknoll, NY: Orbis, 2002), 160.

9. The sources for this section are the following:

Mathew Bunson, "Pope Benedict Speaks to Muslims," *Catholic Culture*, available at: http://www.catholicculture.org/library/view.cfm?recum=7536

Paul J. Griffiths, "Rehabilitating Truth" [review of *Truth and Tolerance: Christian Belief and World Religions* by Joseph Cardinal Ratzinger], First Things (May 2005), 49–51.

Michael Ireland, "Pope Benedict XVI Apologizes for Speech Offending Muslims," *StreamingFaith*, September 19, 2006, available at: http://www.stream ingfaith.com/community/news.aspx?NewsId=420&bhcp=1

"Pope Benedict and Islam," Boston College: Center for Christian-Jewish Relations, available at: http://www.bc.edu/research/cjl/eta-elements/texts/cjrelations/topics/Benedict_Islam.htm

Joseph Ratzinger, "Are Non-Christians Saved?" (1964), *Beliefnet*, available at: http://www.beliefnet.com/story/209/story_20936.html

Cardinal Joseph Ratzinger, "Letter of Cardinal Ratzinger regarding *Dominus Iesus*," Vatican, September 14, 2000, *Catholic Culture*, available at: http://www.catholicculture.org/library/view.cfm?recnum=31323

10. Ratzinger, "Are Non-Christians Saved?"

11. Ratzinger, "Letter of Cardinal Ratzinger regarding *Dominus Iesus*."

12. Joseph Cardinal Ratzinger, *Truth and Tolerance: Christian Belief and World Religions* (San Francisco: Ignatius Press, 2004).

13. Ibid., 9.

14. Griffiths, "Rehabilitating Truth," 51.

15. Ibid., 51.

16. Ibid.

17. Excerpts from the papal lecture, "Faith, Reason and the University: Memories and Reflections," September 12, 2006, Boston College: Center for Christian-Jewish Relations, available at: http://www.bc.edu/research/cjl/meta-elements/texts/cjrelations/topics/Benedict_Islam.htm

18. Ibid.

19. Ibid.

Chapter Thirteen

INTERRELIGIOUS DIALOGUE

In these modern times of religious pluralism, an important issue to be addressed by a theology of religions is interreligious dialogue. The leaders of the church have been telling their fellow members that the way Christians go about trying to be Christians includes a new item: dialogue with persons of other faiths. To be a Christian, it is necessary to seek conversations with people who are different. The Catholic Church, in order to be *catholic*, must be a dialogical church.

Vatican II, John Paul II, and the Vatican Congregations

In the documents of the Second Vatican Council, the Catholic Church teaches that Christians and all persons of goodwill are encouraged to dialogue with the non-Christian religions. In this dialogue, the question of truth is, of course, always pertinent (*Decree on the Church's Missionary Activity* 34; *Declaration on Christian Education* 11). But here the call to dialogue was an "exhortation"—something one might do after being observant of the essentials. Even before the council was concluded, Paul VI announced the formation of a "Secretariat for Non-Christians," now the Pontifical Council for Interreligious Dialogue. Much of Paul VI's teaching on dialogue is found in the encyclical *Ecclesiam Suam*, the "Magna Carta of dialogue."

John Paul II consistently asserted the importance of interreligious dialogue whenever he spoke of the other religious traditions. While the call to dialogue from Vatican II was an exhortation, in John Paul's *Redemptoris Missio (RM)* and in *Dialogue and Proclamation (DP)*, dialogue moved from the sidelines to the center. Catholics are now told that dialogue and proclamation are essential elements of promoting "the *mission* of the church." The word *mission* stands for the very purpose of the church, why the Christian religion exists, what it is obliged to do in the world. That mission is presented as two activities that are actually one: Christians are to make known the good news of God, and by doing so "transform humanity from within, making it new" (*DP* 8). So in order to carry out their mission and achieve their purpose, Christians are not only to proclaim, they must also dialogue. And this is something new.[1]

According to John Paul II and the Vatican congregations, *dialogue* means not just casual conversation, nor of sly means of conditioning the audience so as to convert them. Dialogue is "a methods and means of mutual knowledge and enrichment" (*RM* 55; *DP* 77). Since the pope stated "mutual enrichment," he meant both sides have something to learn and gain. In the dialogue, both sides must be prepared to be "questioned," "purified," thoroughly "challenged" (*DP* 32, 49; *RM* 56). Having been challenged and questioned, Christians who are engaged in dialogue with other believers are also to be ready to be changed and ready "to allow oneself to be transformed by the encounter" (*DP* 47). *Dialogue and Proclamation* goes even further: the change or transformation can really lead to conversion: "a deeper conversion of all toward God." And even more: "In the process of conversion, the decision may be made to leave one's previous spiritual or religious situation in order to direct oneself toward another" (*DP* 41). Apparently, this is not only about the possibility of a non-Christian becoming a disciple of Jesus. Dialogue according to the teaching of the church is dialogue in the fullest sense of the word.

The open dialogue to which Catholics are obliged has to accommodate the unique role of Jesus. That means that although the Vatican has strongly stated that both proclaiming and dialoguing are central elements in missionary ministry, in the end the proclaiming part holds a "permanent priority" over dialogue, because it constitutes "the missionary activity proper" (*RM* 44, 34). "Dialogue should be conducted and implemented with the conviction that the Church is the ordinary means of salvation and that she alone possesses the fullness of the means of salvation" (*RM* 55; also *DP* 19, 22, 58). Even though conversion can be a two-way street, John Paul II also made it clear that the conversion sought after by Christians is one that will lead to the formation of new Christian communities, and that means a conversion that results in baptism. This, according to John Paul, "is a central and determining goal of missionary activity" (*RM* 47–49).

Dominus Iesus

It must be noted that the promulgation of *Dominus Iesus* led immediately to problems with the Catholic Church's dialogue partners. As a consequence, Catholic bishops around the world felt obliged publicly to respond, reaffirming their commitment to dialogue with both Christians and other believers. These responses can be explained in part by the fact the *Dominus Iesus* says so little about dialogue, ecumenical or interreligious. It speaks of interreligious dialogue only in numbers 2 and 22.

The matter of most concern to the church's partners in dialogue is the claim in the declaration that interreligious dialogue is "part of the Church's evangelizing mission" (2, see also 22). Some Jews and Hindus, strongly opposed to Christian conversion, interpreted this linkage as a technique for gaining converts. *Dominus Iesus*, however, was not stating anything new in connecting interreligious dialogue with the church's evangelizing mission. An explicit foundation for this claim is found in other official documents.

Other Church Documents

While some of these documents renounce any intention to convert in the practice of interreligious dialogue, it must be acknowledged, as Fredericks notes, that ambivalence exists within official statements about how the church's mission to "convert all nations" is related to the need for interreligious dialogue. In his encyclical *Ecclesiam Suam*, Paul VI stated that although the purpose of interreligious dialogue was not the "immediate conversion of the interlocutor" (*Ecclesiam Suam* 79), the Christian in dialogue is still under the "apostolic mission" (80). And John Paul II, in an address in 1987 to the Secretariat for Non-Christians, remarked that interreligious dialogue and the proclamation of God's saving work are both elements of the church's one mission. Consequently, "Christ's followers must carry out his mandate to make disciples of all nations."[2] In the *Catechism of the Catholic Church*, it is stated that the missionary task of the church implies a "respectful dialogue" with followers of other religious paths in which Christians proclaim the gospel "in order to consolidate, complete and raise up the truth and the goodness that God has distributed among men and nations, and to purify them from error and evil...."[3] Fredericks suggests that statements like these "are neither comforting nor encouraging to the Church's dialogue partners. In spite of the Church's official statements renouncing dialogue as a covert technique of conversion, it is not surprising that other religious believers experience confusion and reticence."[4]

Clearly, interreligious dialogue should never be a covert attempt to convert the dialogue partner. Such attempts are not only dishonest but also not in keeping with the dignity of other religious believers called for by Christian faith. There is ample support for this view of dialogue in official church statements. In view for the need for honesty in dialogue, Paul VI taught that interreligious dialogue was not a "tactical snare."[5] In regard to the innate dignity of the dialogue partner, John Paul II stated that dialogue with other religious believers is essential for the church, because Christians "are called today more than ever to collaborate so that every person can reach his transcendent goal and realize his authentic growth and to help cultures to preserve their own religious and spiritual values in the presence of rapid social changes."[6] While interreligious dialogue finds it place within the large scope of church's evangelizing mission, it is indispensable that it be conducted openly and honesty, in such a manner as to preserve the dignity of it participants and to exclude any possibility of a "tactical snare."

Learning from Other Religions

It is also important that Christians recognize that while the church must not neglect its evangelizing mission in a world that needs to learn of the good news, there is much to learn from the non-Christian religious traditions. *Dominus Iesus* mentions that interreligious dialogue that "is part of the Church's evangelizing mission, requires an attitude of understanding and a relationship of mutual knowledge and reciprocal enrichment, in obedience to the truth and with respect for freedom" (2). Fredericks states that this reference to "reciprocal enrichment" is by far the most positive statement the declaration makes in regard to interreligious dialogue: "This statement is as close as *Dominus Iesus* comes to acknowledging that Catholics might have something to learn by entering into dialogue with those who follow other religious paths. Surprisingly few Vatican statements entertain the possibility that Catholics might benefit significantly from dialogue."[7] Yet there is solid basis, Fredericks adds, in official statements for the belief that interreligious dialogue can be enriching for Catholics. For example, in *Redemptor Hominis*, John Paul II noted that the church's "self awareness" (11) is formed by means of interreligious dialogue. In *Redemptor Missio*, interreligious dialogue is recognized as "a method and means of mutual knowledge and enrichment" (55). The same encyclical further notes that dialogue leads to "inner purification and conversion" (56). It should be noted that the conversion intended here by John Paul is conversion of Christians, not the conversion of the dialogue partner. Walter Kasper, formerly the cardinal prefect of the pontifical council responsible for dialogue with Jews, in a document interpreted widely as a response to *Dominus Iesus,* asserted that dialogue is not a "one-way street" but rather "an enrichment for us Christians" in which "we are not only givers, but also the learners and receivers."[8]

An important group of Catholic theologians insists that the other religions are to be perceived as having something to teach us, not only about themselves and their own "doctrines," but also about God, about human life, about Christ—that is, about *our* own doctrines. In this view, the other religions are not to be regarded, however benignly, as merely deficient expressions of Christianity or secondary instruments of salvation in Christ.[9] Francis X. Clooney urges the study of Jesus in light of the other religious traditions so that he may be seen newly radiant. "Learning from other religions…certainly does transform, enrich, and deepen our way of following Jesus. It drives out not only relativism and indifferentism but also arrogance and ignorance."[10] Other theologians who take this inclusivist approach include Karl Rahner, Hans Küng, Heinz Robert Schlette, Raimondo Pannikar, Gavin D'Costa, Joseph DiNoia, James Fredericks, Gerald O'Collins, and others represented, for example, in *Christian Uniqueness Reconsidered: The Myth of a Pluralistic Theology of Religions.*[11] Regarding interreligious dialogue, Richard McBrien concludes:

306

We are left, then, with fashioning an agenda for dialogue: to encourage other religions to bring out what is best and deepest in their own traditions and to encourage them along the course of self-criticism and renewal. But since dialogue is by definition a two-way process, the call to self-criticism and renewal applies equally to the Church. It should be led to appreciate anew its own traditions, to discover and learn from the traditions of the other religions, and "to do justice to the distinct claims advanced by the adherents of traditions with whom dialogue is envisaged" (J. A. DiNoia, *The Diversity of Religions: A Christian Perspective* [1992], p. 163)....
Christianity in dialogue with other religions will not shrink from emphasizing its own uniqueness, but dialogue will make it increasingly open to the religious richness and intrinsic salvific value of the other great traditions as well.[12]

Among the Catholic theologians who promote that much is to be learned from the study of the other religions, Gavin D'Costa and Jacques Dupuis have places of prominence.[13]

Gavin D'Costa

D'Costa suggests that a "turn to the Spirit" should provide the light in which to look at and dialogue with other religions. Christians, he reminds us, are not monotheists in exactly the same way Jews and Muslims are, for they believe in a God who is Trinitarian. In Christian experience, God relates to the world in ways that are truly different, and for these differing relationships different symbols have been used: Father (or Parent) expresses the Godhead as the creative source of all; the Word (or Son) indicates the divine as reaching outward to communicate the truth and saving power of God, particularly in Jesus of Nazareth, the incarnate Word and Son of God; the Spirit (the breath of God) carries on the message of Jesus and pervading all creation with the life-giving energy of God.

It is in the light of the Spirit that Christians should look upon and dialogue with the other religions. Viewing others from the perspective of the Spirit, Christians know, D'Costa declares, that the reality of God cannot be contained only in the activity of the Creator-Father or of the Word-Savior, but that the divine is also Spirit penetrating the other religions.[14] So their belief in the Holy Spirit leads Christians to hold the universality of God in all cultures and religions. And this means that they cannot know in advance what "fruits of the Holy Spirit" they will discover in the other religions; they cannot predetermine what that truth will be. Therefore, they will have to listen and to learn from them. Here D'Costa gives greater energy into the message we have seen from the Vatican: that the Christian Church must be a dialogical church.

> The church stands under the judgment of the Holy Spirit, and if the Holy Spirit is active in the world religions, then the world religions are vital to Christian faithfulness.... Without listening to the testimony [of the Spirit in other religions], Christians cease to be faithful to their own calling as Christians, in being inattentive to God.[15]

This need Christians have of the non-Christian religions is not simply so that they can be in awe at what the Spirit is doing in the other religions. D'Costa insists that the other religions are necessary for helping Christians to avoid bending religion into a tool used to take advantage of others.

In a Spirit-inspired approach to the other religions, Christians must be attentive about the way they use the word *fulfillment.* "Fulfillment, historically, does not work in only one direction."[16] For in the dialogue with other religions, the Christian "church is laying itself open to genuine change, challenge and questioning."[17] If theologians, then, are going to speak of "fulfillment," D'Costa would make it mutual fulfillment. Perhaps here he is not merely following the Vatican position, but stepping beyond it.

Since D'Costa urges a Trinitarian theology of religions, and since the Christian faith holds that the three persons are deeply interrelated, he tries to balance the universal outreach of the Spirit with the particular content of the Word of God in Jesus: "The riches of the mystery of God are disclosed by the Spirit and are measured and discerned by their conformity to and in their illumination of Christ....Jesus is the normative criterion of God, while not foreclosing the ongoing self-disclosure of God in history, through the Spirit."[18] This seems to imply that while the Spirit surely reaches beyond Jesus in extent, it cannot go beyond Jesus in content. "There is no independent revelation through the Paraclete [another name for the Spirit], but only an application of the revelation of Jesus."[19] Paul Knitter adds here with insight, "For some, there may be tension in what D'Costa is saying about how the universal activity of the Spirit is related to the particular Word of God in Jesus. Such tensions, D'Costa would say, are unavoidable for the Christian."[20]

Jacques Dupuis

In his research and in his experience of interreligious dialogue in India, Dupuis felt tensions in much of contemporary theology of religions. The problem for him comes from the fulfillment theory of most Christian approaches to the other religions—that is, from the position that views the other religions only as stepping stones or seeds or as preparation for Christianity. In Dupuis's view, this attitude has produced several undesirable outcomes. It is an obstacle to authentic dialogue because it does not allow for the level area that dialogue requires. Despite that adherents of the other religions are told that much truth, beauty, and goodness are embodied in the other religions, God and Christianity always win out. Also, the fulfillment theory places limits on what God may be accomplishing in other religions, for it permits only that kind of truth and goodness in them that can be fulfilled in the church. Finally, it results in making the church more important than God, more important than Jesus Christ and his vision of the kingdom of God. So in his magisterial and widely acclaimed book, *Toward a Christian Theology of Religious Pluralism,* Dupuis attempted to go beyond a fulfillment perspective to a theological position that he believed would allow for true dialogue by permitting God free rein.[21]

Dupuis's theology grounds the possibility for real complementarity between believers engaged in dialogue. "'Complementarity' is not understood here in the sense of the fulfillment theory, according to which Christian truth 'brings to completion'—in a one-sided process—the fragmentary truths it finds sown outside."[22] Dupuis wanted a theology that would truly make possible a "mutual complementarity," a "mutual enrichment and transformation"[23]—one in which the intended outcome is not for the adherent of the other religion to convert to the Christian's side, but rather, "more profound conversion of each to God."[24]

In harmony with Pope John Paul and with other theologians, Dupuis wanted to evolve a Spirit-based theology of religions: the Spirit is alive and active throughout history, especially in religious communities, before and after Christ. But Dupuis insists that what the Spirit is about in other religions may be truly different from, but never contradictory to, what is found in God's Word in Jesus Christ. God has more to say to humankind than what God said in Jesus. Dupuis's Spirit-based conclusions are grounded in traditional Trinitarian theology, where Christians declare that real distinctions exist between the three persons of the Trinity. This means that one person of the Holy Trinity cannot be reduced to or subordinated to another. If there is "real differentiation and plurality between the Word of God in Jesus and the Spirit of God in other religions,"[25] we can expect, insists Dupuis, that the religions are going to have "different" and "new" things to say to Christians...things that they have not yet heard.[26] Consequently, Christians do not "possess a monopoly of truth."[27]

Because of the abiding presence of the Spirit in the religions, Dupuis declared furthermore, Christians need to recognize that these other traditions have a "lasting role" and a "specific meaning" in what God intends to achieve with humanity.[28] In other words, God does not mean all people to find their fulfillment in the Christian Church. Religious pluralism reflects the way God wills them to be.[29] Christians then are to move beyond church-centeredness that so inflates the necessity of the Christian Church as to diminish the value of the other religions.

But Dupuis does admit that any Christian view of other religions must be Christ-centered. If God and the kingdom of God are at the center of Christian life, it is Jesus Christ who leads to that center.[30] He realizes that Christ-centeredness has resulted in the same kind of inflation of Christianity and deflation of others as has church-centeredness. He proposes what he believes to be a more dialogical understanding of Jesus Christ.

According to Dupuis, Christ has a "constitutive" uniqueness. This means that Jesus, and only Jesus, "opens access to God for all human beings."[31] This is so because while all of human persons are children of God, Jesus is the Son of God like no one else. His "personal identity" is that of the very Word of God, the Son of God, the second person of the Trinity.[32] Consequently, Christians must believe that in Jesus God has delivered the fullness of revelation.

Now to understand the essentials of Christian belief in a way that does not diminish other religions and permits for genuine dialogue with them, Dupuis makes some very fine distinctions. The "fullness" of God's truth in Jesus is "qualitative" not "quantitative": "This plenitude...is not...one of extension and all-comprehension, but of intensity....It does not—it cannot—exhaust the mystery of the Divine."[33] Knitter interprets this:

> Perhaps another way of putting what Dupuis is getting at is to understand the "fullness of truth" in Jesus not as giving us the whole picture (quantitative) but as so focusing the picture we have (qualitative) that we know what it is all about and can understand any further additions to it. It is the fullness of focus, of intensity, rather than one of detail and totality.[34]

Therefore, Dupuis clearly asserts that the fullness of God's truth in Jesus is "relational." The plenitude of what God intends to make known to humankind is focused in Jesus in such a way that to increase the depth of the picture Christians have to relate what they have in Jesus to what the Spirit is doing in the other religions. So Christians do not actually know the fullness of God's message in Christ unless they dialogue with others. With such a relational understanding of Christ's uniqueness, Dupuis holds that Christians can engage in authentic dialogue with others without diminishing or jeopardizing who Jesus is for them and for the world.

In regard to the relationship between what God communicates in Jesus and what God communicates in the Spirit, Dupuis specifies, "Christ, not the Spirit, is at the center as the way to God." What God has to say in the Spirit by means of other religions must be understood "in view of" Christ; it does not replace Christ.[35] So in interreligious dialogue, Christians may discover that other religions may have seen "certain dimensions of the Divine Mystery" more clearly than Christians have. They may see "at greater depth" what they already possess in the fullness of Christian revelation.[36] Jesus as the Christ, then, maintains his place at the center and as the final goal of all God's dealings with humankind.

He proposes that Christians have a twofold advantage to gain from dialogue with the non-Christians religious traditions.

> On the one hand, they will win an enrichment of their own faith. Through the experience and testimony of the other, they will be able to discover at greater depths certain aspects, certain dimensions, of the Divine Mystery that they have perceived less clearly and that have been communicated less clearly by Christian tradition. At the same time they will gain purification of their faith. The shock of the encounter will often raise questions, force Christians to revise gratuitous assumptions, and destroy deep-rooted prejudices or overthrow certain overly narrow conceptions or outlooks. Thus the benefits of the dialogue constitute a challenge to the Christian partner at the same time.[37]

Above and beyond these sure benefits, Dupuis insists that the dialogue and exchange of Christians with those of the other religious traditions have value in themselves. They also affect a deeper openness to God of each through the other. The dialogue tends to a more profound conversion of each to God. The same God speaks in the heart of both partners; the same Spirit is at work in all. By way of their reciprocal witness, it is this same God who calls and challenges the partners through each other. Thus they become, as it were, for each other and reciprocally, a sign leading to God. The proper end of the interreligious dialogue is, in the last analysis, the common conversion of Christians and the members of other religious traditions to the same God—the God of Jesus Christ—who calls them together by challenging the ones through the others. This reciprocal call, a sign of the call of God, is surely mutual evangelization. It builds up, between members of the various religious traditions, the universal communion that marks the advent of the reign of God.[38]

Notes

1. We are speaking here of the more extensive presentation of *DP*. The first proclamation of the inclusion of dialogue into the central mission of the church was made in the 1984 declaration of the then Vatican Secretariat for Non-Christian Religions, "The Attitude of the Church toward Followers of Other Religions."

2. *Interreligious Dialogue: The Official Teaching of the Catholic Church (1963–1995)*, ed. Francisco Gioia (Boston: Pauline, 1994), no. 587.

3. *Catechism of the Catholic Church*, rev. ed. (London: Geoffrey Chapman, 1999), no. 856.

4. James Fredericks, "The Catholic Church and the Other Religious Paths: Rejecting Nothing That Is True and Holy," *Theological Studies* 64 (2003), 248.

5. *Interreligious Dialogue*, no. 217.

6. Ibid., no. 491.

7. Fredericks, "Catholic Church and Other Religious Paths," 251.

8. Ibid., 252.

9. Richard McBrien, *Catholicism: Completely Revised and Expanded* (San Francisco: HarperCollins, 1994), 383.

10. Francis X. Clooney, "Implications for the Practice of Inter-Religious Learning," *Sic et Non: Encountering Dominus Iesus*, Stephen J. Pope and Charles Hefling, eds. (Maryknoll, NY: Orbis, 2002), 168.

11. Gavin D'Costa, ed., *Christian Uniqueness Reconsidered: The Myth of a Pluralist Theology of Religions* (Maryknoll, NY: Orbis, 1990).

12. McBrien, *Catholicism*, 383–84.

13. In the treatment of D'Costa and Dupuis I have relied on Paul F. Knitter, *Introducing Theologies of Religions* (Maryknoll, NY: Orbis, 2002), 87–93.

14. Gavin D'Costa, *The Meeting of Religions and the Trinity* (Maryknoll, NY: Orbis, 2000), ch. 4.

15. Gavin D'Costa, "Christ, the Trinity, and Religious Plurality," in *Christian Uniqueness Reconsidered*, 23. See also D'Costa, *Meeting*, 114.

16. Gavin D'Costa, "Revelation and Revelations: The Role and Value of Different Religious Traditions," *Pro Dialogo* 85–86 (1994), 161.

17. D'Costa, *Meeting*, 134.

18. D'Costa, "Christ, the Trinity, and Religious Pluralism," 23.

19. D'Costa, *Meeting*, 122. D'Costa is here quoting C. K. Barret. Elsewhere, D'Costa remarks that the activity of the Spirit in other religions "does not confer independent legitimacy upon other religions" (*Meeting*, 113).

20. Knitter, *Theologies of Religions*, 89.

21. Jacques Dupuis, *Toward a Christian Theology of Religious Pluralism* (Maryknoll, NY: Orbis, 1997), 382.

22. Ibid., 326.
23. Ibid.
24. Ibid., 383.
25. Ibid., 206.
26. Ibid., 197–99.
27. Ibid., 382.
28. Ibid., 211.
29. Ibid., 201.
30. Ibid., 191.
31. Ibid., 387.
32. Ibid., 155, 296–97.
33. Ibid., 382
34. Knitter, *Theologies of Religions,* 92.
35. Dupuis, *Christian Theology of Religious Pluralism,* 197.
36. Ibid., 382–83, 388.
37. Ibid., 382.
38. Ibid., 383.

Conclusion

THE MYSTERY OF THE
WORLD RELIGIONS

How, then, should Catholics regard non-Christian believers and the religions they practice? Surely with a sense of respect, admiration, and love. For according to the resources of Catholic faith, they are, by God's mysterious will, included in the divine plan of salvation. The God of Abraham, Isaac, and Jacob, the Father of Jesus Christ in the Holy Spirit—the one true God is present and operative in them and their religions. From within their sacred true selves, their specifically human reality, God makes it possible for non-Christian believers to be faithful to their religious practices and thereby to unite the immediate passing world with the eternal world of transcendence and salvation. God enables them freely to overcome anxiety, sin, and the fear of death and develop loving relationships with others and themselves as well as creative fulfilling connections with the world and history. Because the one true God loves the adherents of the non-Christian religions, permeates their very being, and is operative in their religious practices, they have the possibility to experience saving union with the Sacred in history and eternal life with the Sacred in the world to come. They have the possibility to transform their lives into something radically different and limitlessly better.

Catholics should also approach the non-Christian world religions with an inquisitive mind and heart, with the desire to engage in open and honest dialogue with their adherents. For while the other religions do not have the fullness and perfection of God's truth, by dialoguing with them, Catholics may learn much, not only about the non-Christian religions but also about their own religious tradition and themselves. Catholics are called to communicate significantly and respectfully with their fellow human beings of various, different religious creeds. Engaging in this dialogue has substantial meaning and value, for it helps us to become more and more human: it clarifies our self-understanding; it overcomes self-absorption and opens the way to broadening our horizons. Furthermore, as Karl Jaspers has noted, it "is the best remedy against the erroneous claim to exclusive possession of the truth by any one creed." It helps us to be appreciative of "the very fact that God has manifested Himself historically in several ways and has opened up many ways toward Himself." The various manifestations of God in history may be interpreted "as though the deity were issuing a warning, through the language of universal history against the claim to exclusiveness in the passion of truth."[1]

The time has come for Catholics, Fredericks astutely suggests, to move beyond questions concerning how Christ saves our neighbors who follow other religious paths and what role the church plays in Christ's saving work among all peoples. Now "there needs to be a genuine quest by Christians to find new and more adequate understanding of their own tradition by responding to the teachings of other religious traditions in depth."[2] By taking advantage of the opportunity religious diversity offers Christian faith, by careful study of the teachings of other religious traditions, and by working in close conversation with Hindus, Buddhists, Jews, Muslims, Daoists, Confucians, Shintoists, and others, profound similarities and differences of authentic theological interest will be uncovered. In this encounter, Christian theology will be transformed. Jacques Dupuis insists that it should not be transformed into a "universal theology" that would claim to bypass differences and contradictions for the purposes of promoting harmony between religious communities. Such religious accord will be served, he claims, "by the development in the various traditions of theologies which, taking religious pluralism seriously will assume their mutual differences and resolve to interact in dialogue and cooperation."[3]

Finally, Catholics should contemplate the diverse world religions as a sacred mysterious reality. Yes, God's love extends unconditionally to all human creatures. Yes, God makes the grace of authentic self-transcendence and salvation available to all men and women by means of their various religious traditions, and also by ways that are known to God alone. But how is it that some men and women are in religious situations identified by the church as "gravely deficient," while others are, in God's providence, given in Jesus and the Christian religious tradition access to the fullness of truth, beauty, and goodness and a self-transcendence without boundaries? This mystery calls for a response of awe and reverence from all persons of goodwill. And perhaps it also prompts our efforts to characterize the situation of those who adhere to the non-Christian religions with more nuance and precision. In the end, Catholics and all Christians should approach the mystery of the diverse religions of the world with a sense of wonderment and gratitude—and with an unwavering commitment to mission.

Notes

1. Karl Jaspers, *Origin and Goal of History*, trans. Michael Bullock (New Haven, CT: Yale University Press, 1953), 19–20.

2. James Fredericks, "The Catholic Church and the Other Religious Paths: Rejecting Nothing That Is True and Holy," *Theological Studies* 64 (2003), 254.

3. Jacques Dupuis, *Toward a Christian Theology of Religious Pluralism* (Maryknoll, NY: Orbis, 1997), 384.

SELECTED BIBLIOGRAPHY

Arberry, A. J. *Sufism*. London: George Allen & Unwin, 1979.

Armstrong, Karen. *A History of God: The 4000-Year Quest of Judaism, Christianity and Islam*. New York: Alfred A. Knopf, 1993.

————. *The Great Transformation: The Beginning of Our Religious Traditions*. New York/Toronto: Alfred A. Knopf, 2006.

Bellah, Robert N. *Beyond Belief: Essays on Religion in a Post-Traditional World*. New York and London: Harper & Row, 1970.

Bouquet, A. C. *Comparative Religion*. London: Pelican Books, 1941.

Boyce, Mary. *Zoroastrians: Their Religious Beliefs and Practices*. London, Boston, and Henley: Routledge & Kegan Paul, 1979.

Bunson, Matthew. "Pope Benedict Speaks to Muslims." *Catholic Culture*. Available at: http://www.catholicculture.org/library/view.efm?re cum=7536.

Burke, Patrick. *The Major Religions: An Introduction with Texts*. 2nd ed. Malden, MA: Blackwell, 2004.

Burkert, Walter. *Homo Necans: The Anthropology of Ancient Greek Sacrificial Ritual and Myth*. Trans. Peter Bing. Berkeley, Los Angeles, London: University of California Press, 1983.

Catechism of the Catholic Church. Revised edition. London: Geoffrey Chapman, 1999.

Clooney, Francis X. "Implications for the Practice of Inter-Religious Learning." Pope, Stephen J. and Hefling, Charles., eds. *Sic et Non: Encountering Dominus Iesus*. Maryknoll, NY: Orbis, 2002.

Cobb, John B. Jr. *The Structure of Christian Existence*. Philadelphia: Westminster Press, 1967, and London: Lutterworth Press.

Cohn, Norman. *Cosmos and the World to Come: The Ancient Roots of Apocalyptic Faith*. New Haven and London: Yale University Press, 1995.

Collins, Steven. *Selfless Persons: Imagery and Thought in Theravada Buddhism.* Cambridge, London, New York: Cambridge University Press, 1982.

Cooper, Robin. *The Evolving Mind: Buddhism, Biology and Consciousness.* Birmingham, UK: Windhorse Publications, 1996.

Cross, Frank Moore. *From Epic to Canon: History and Literature in Ancient Israel.* Baltimore and London: Johns Hopkins University Press, 1998.

Daniel, Glyn. *The First Civilizations: The Archeology of their Origins.* New York: Thomas Y. Crowell, 1968.

D'Costa, Gavin. "Christ, the Trinity, and Religious Plurality." *Christian Uniqueness Reconsidered: The Myth of a Pluralist Theology of Religions.* Ed. G. D. D'Costa. Maryknoll, NY: Orbis, 1990, 23.

———. *The Meeting of Religions and the Trinity.* Maryknoll, NY: Orbis, 2000.

———. "Revelation and Revelations: The Role and Value of Different Religions Traditions." *Pro Dialogo* 161 (1994), 85–86.

Dever, William G. *What Did the Biblical Writers Know and When Did They Know It? : What Archeology Can Tell Us about the Reality of Ancient Israel.* Grand Rapids, MI, and Cambridge, UK: Eerdmans, 2001.

Dulles, Avery. "*Dominus Iesus:* A Catholic Response." *Pro Ecclesia* 10 (Winter 2001), 5.

Dupuis, Jacques SJ. *Toward a Christian Theology of Religious Pluralism.* Maryknoll, NY: Orbis, 1997.

Egan, Harvey D. "A Rahnerian Response." Pope, Stephen J. and Hefling, Charles, eds. *Sic et Non: Encountering Dominus Iesus.* Maryknoll, NY: Orbis, 2002.

Eisenstadt, S. N., ed. *The Origins and Diversity of Axial Age Civilizations.* Albany: State University of New York Press, 1986.

Eliade, Mircea. *The Myth of the Eternal Return, or, Cosmos and History.* Trans. Willard R. Trask. London: Routledge & Kegan Paul, 1955.

———. *Myths, Dreams and Mysteries: The Encounter between Contemporary Faiths and Archaic Realities.* Trans. Philip Mairet. New York: Harper Torchbooks, 1979.

Evans, J. D. "The Neolithic Revolution and the Foundation of Cities." *The Concise Encyclopedia of World History.* John Bowle, ed. New York: Hawthorne Books, 1958, 38.

Fagan, Brian M. *Human Prehistory and the First Civilizations.* Chantilly, VA: Teaching Company, 2003, parts 1–3.

Fensham, F. Charles. "Widow, Orphan and the Poor in Ancient Near Eastern Legal and Wisdom Literature." Frederick E. Greenspahn, ed. *Essential Papers on Israel and the Ancient Near East.* New York and London: New York University Press, 1991, 176–82.

Forrest, George. "Mediterranean Culture: Cert., Mycenae, Athens." *The Concise Encyclopedia of World History.* John Bowle, ed. New York: Hawthorne Books, 1958, 48.

Fredericks, James. "The Catholic Church and the Other Religious Paths: Rejecting Nothing That Is True and Holy." *Theological Studies* 64 (2003), 225–54.

————. *Faith among Faiths: Christian Theology and Non-Christian Religions.* New York/Mahwah, NJ: Paulist Press, 1999.

Geering, Lloyd. *Christian Faith at the Crossroads: A Map of Modern Religious History.* Santa Rosa, CA: Polebridge Press, 2001.

Gioia, Francisco, ed. *Interreligious Dialogue: The Official Teaching of the Catholic Church (1963–1995).* Boston: Pauline, 1994. no. 587.

Graham, A. C. *Disputers of the Tao: Philosophical Argument in Ancient China.* LaSalle, IL: Open Court, 1989.

Griffiths, Paul. "Rehabilitating Truth." Review of *Truth and Tolerance: Christian Belief and World Religions,* by Joseph Cardinal Ratzinger. *First Things* (May 2005), 49–52.

Haight, Roger. *Jesus: Symbol of God.* Maryknoll, NY: Orbis, 1999.

Harl, Kenneth W. *Origins of the Great Ancient Civilizations.* Chantilly, VA: Teaching Company, 2005.

HarperCollins Dictionary of Religions. San Francisco: HarperCollins, 1995.

Heesterman, J. C. *The Broken World of Sacrifice: An Essay in Ancient Indian Ritual.* Chicago and London: University of Chicago Press, 1993.

Heschel, Abraham J. *The Prophets.* New York: Jewish Publication Society of America, 1962.

Hick, John. *An Interpretation of Religion: Human Responses to the Transcendent.* New Haven and London: Yale University Press, 1989.

Hopkins, Thomas J. *The Hindu Religious Tradition.* Encino, CA, and Belmont, CA: Dickenson, 1971.

"Introduction to the Prophets." *New Jerusalem Bible.* New York: Doubleday, 1985. 1157–89.

Ireland, Michael. "Pope Benedict XVI Apologizes for Speech Offending Muslims." StreamingFaith, September 19, 2006. Available at: http://www.streamingfaith.com/community/news.aspx?NewsId=420&bhep=1.

Ivanhoe, Philip J. and Van Norden, Bryan W., comp. *Readings in Classical Chinese Philosophy.* Trans. Philip J. Ivanhoe. New York: Seven Bridges Press, 2001.

"Japan's Religion and Philosophy." *AsianInfo.org.* Available at: http://www.asianinfo.org/asianfo/japan/religion.htm.

Jaspers, Karl. *The Origin and Goal of History.* Trans. Michael Bullock. New Haven: Yale University Press, 1953.

Karkkainen, Veli-Matti. *An Introduction to the Theology of Religions.* Downers Grove, IL: InterVarsity Press, 2003.

Klostermaier, Klaus. *A Survey of Hinduism.* 2nd ed. Albany: State University of New York Press, 1994.

Knitter, Paul F. *Introducing Theologies of Religions.* Maryknoll, NY: Orbis, 2002.

Landon, John C. *World History and the Eonic Effect: Civilization, Darwinism, and Theories of Evolution.* 2nd ed. New York: Eonix Books, 2005.

Lerro, Bruce. *From Earth Spirits to Sky Gods: The Sociological Origins of Monotheism, Individualism, and Hyperabstract Reasoning from the Stone Age to the Axial Iron Age.* New York: Lexington Books, 2000.

Luther's Works. Vol. 12. Trans. Wilhelm Pauck. London: S.C.M. Press, 1955.

Major Religions of the World Ranked by Number of Adherents. Available at: http://www.adherents.com/Religions_By_Adherents.html.

Martin, James. *Becoming Who You Are: Insights on the True Self From Thomas Merton and Other Saints.* Mahwah, NJ: Hidden Spring, 2006.

Marty, Martin E. "Rome and Relativism." *Commonweal* 125:18 (September 20, 2000).

Mascaro, Juan, ed. and trans. *Upanishads.* Middlesex, UK: Penguin Books, 1965.

McBrien, Richard. *Catholicism: Completely Revised and Updated.* San Francisco: HarperCollins, 1994.

———. "*Dominus Iesus:* An Ecclesiological Critique." *Bulletin/Centro Pro Unione* 59 (Spring 2001), 15–18.

Moore, G. F. *History of Religions.* New York: Charles Scribner's Sons, 1948.

Selected Bibliography

Muesse, Mark W. *Religions of the Axial Age: An Approach to the World Religions.* Parts 1–2. Chantilly, VA: Teaching Company, 2007.

Mumford, Lewis. *The Transformation of Man.* London: George Allen & Unwin, 1957.

Noss, David S. *A History of the World's Religions.* 12th ed. Upper Saddle River, NJ: Prentice Hall, 2007.

O'Collins, Gerald. "Watch Your Language." Review of *The Meeting of Religions and the Trinity,* by Gavin D'Costa. *Tablet* (November 4, 2000), 1490.

Oldenberg, Hermann. *Buddha: His Life, His Doctrine His Order.* London and Edinburgh: Williams & Norgate, 1882.

Olivelle, Patrick, ed. and trans. *Upanishads.* Oxford and New York: Oxford University Press, 1996.

Oxford Dictionary of Religions. John Bowker, ed. Oxford, UK: Oxford University Press, 1997.

Pickthall, Mohammad Marmaduke. *The Meaning of the Glorious Qur'an.* New York: New American Library of World Literature, 1953.

"Pope Benedict and Islam." Boston College: Center for Christian-Jewish Relations. Available at: http://www.bc.edu/research/cjl/eta-zxelements/texts/cjrelations/topics/Benedict_Islam.htm.

Pye, Michael. "A Tapestry of Traditions: Japanese Religions," reproduced from *Eerdman's Handbook to the World's Religions,* 1982. Available at: http://www.hope.edu/academic/religion/reader/japan.html.

Rahner, Karl. "On the Importance of the Non-Christian Religions for Salvation." *Theological Investigations.* 18:29. London: Darton, Longman, & Todd, 1984.

Ratzinger, Joseph Cardinal. "Are Non-Christians Saved?" 1964. *Beliefnet.* Available at: http://www.beliefnet.com/story/209/story_20936.html.

———. "Letter of Cardinal Ratzinger Regarding *Dominus Iesus.*" Vatican. September 14, 2000. *Catholic Culture.* Available at: http://www.catholicculture.org/library/view.cfm?recnum=7536.

———. *Truth and Tolerance: Christian Belief and World Religions.* Trans. Henry Taylor. San Francisco: Ignatius Press, 2004.

"Religion: Native Roots and Foreign Influence." *Japan Access.* Available at: http://www.sg.emb-japan.gojp/JapanAccess/religion.htm.

Schwartz, Benjamin I. "The Age of Transcendence." *Daedulus: Wisdom, Revelation, and Doubt: Perspectives on the First Millennium BC* 104:2 (Spring 1975).

"Shinto." *Wikipedia.* Available at: http://www.en.wikipeia.org/wiki/Shinto.

Smith, Wilfred Cantwell. *Faith and Belief.* Princeton, NJ: Princeton University Press, 1979.

Voglein, Eric. *Order and History.* Baton Rouge: Louisiana State University Press, 1956–58.

Wheeler, Mortimer. "The Civilization of the Subcontinent." *The Dawn of Civilization.* Stuart Piggott, ed. New York: McGraw Hill, 1961.

Wilber, Ken. *Up from Eden: A Transpersonal View of Human Evolution.* Garden City, NY: Anchor Press/Doubleday, 1981.